THE NEW AGES
AN ADVENTURE BEYOND THE
ORDINARY...

MALIK

Sterling Paperbacks

STERLING PAPERBACKS
An imprint of
Sterling Publishers (P) Ltd.
A-59, Okhla Industrial Area, Phase-II, New Delhi-110020.
Tel: 26387070, 26386209; Fax: 91-11-26383788
E-mail: mail@sterlingpublishers.com
ghai@nde.vsnl.net.in
www.sterlingpublishers.com

The New Ages
© 2010, Malik
ISBN 978 81 207 5791 2

Visit the author at www.thenewages.com
Join 'The New Ages' fan page on facebook and be part of a 75,000 strong global community of believers.
Follow us on twitter: www.twitter.com/thenewages.

All rights are reserved.
No part of this publication may be reproduced, stored in a retrieval system or transmitted, in any form or by any means, mechanical, photocopying, recording or otherwise, without prior written permission of the author.

Printed in India
Printed and Published by Sterling Publishers Pvt. Ltd., New Delhi-110 020.

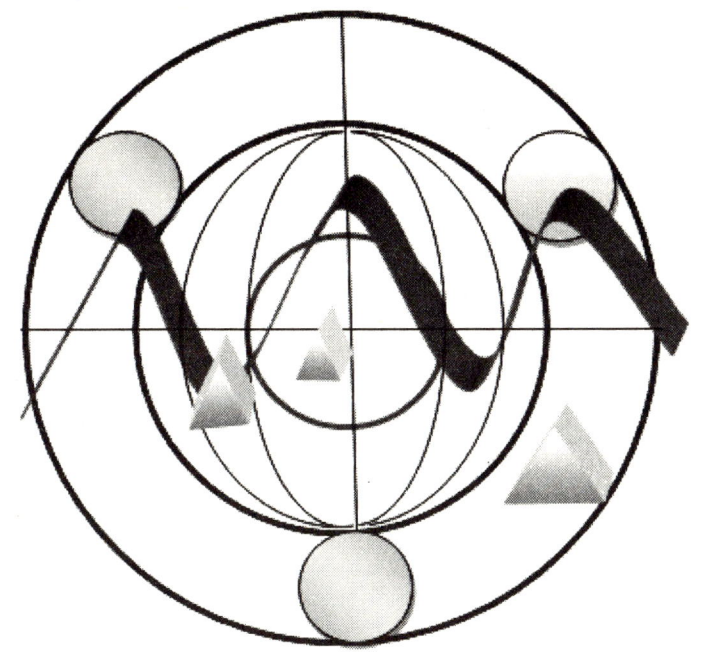

Trinity within trinity within trinity; he who truly seeks, finds…
The central and the peripheral, governed by the one that binds;
Three connected by the union of four…
The outer, the three new and the core;
The trinity of worlds, civilizations and friends…
A new order emerges while the old one ends;
And when the trinity morphs into the quartet,
A new fellowship shall be set…
As the layers are unraveled,
The Messenger would be revealed to the one who has travelled…

Author's Preface

What if you were the only person living on this planet? How would you live your life?

What if none of us had to work for money? What would be our occupations, our 'professions', our 'jobs'? What would be the avocations, the 'evolutionary pursuits' that billions would be following?

And if that were so, how would this planet, civilizations, societies & families, be different? How would so much energy, which is currently dissipated in survival, be redirected? And what would it create?

What is a better system? Capitalism or socialism?

What is more important? Wealth creation or wealth redistribution?

Is GDP a good enough measure of a nation's, a society's prosperity? Or should there also be prosperity indices? Equality metric? A gross national happiness index?

Are science & religion destined to be at odds? Is technology inherently incompatible with the spirit?

Is personal freedom the death knell for social norms? Are basic instincts & social life fundamental paradoxes?

What if women & artists ran our societies, our governments, our bureaucracies, our corporations? How qualitatively different would life be? Would wars reduce? Would defence expenditure come down significantly, and these resources deployed for health, education, sanitation, and infrastructure? Would compassion & understanding replace domination & aggression as our basic traits? Would love replace machismo & violence as the 'virtue' in our popular culture?

At a chaotic and crucial time in human history, where technological & economic growth is combined with strife, and an increasing divide between societies & communities, a normal, sensitive person like me (& millions of others out there) is forced to ask some very fundamental questions:

Is it a time to rejoice or feel despondent? Is there increasing happiness out there, or increasing disparity? What can we do differently, so that we continually have more good news than bad?

Are we ready to usher in a new world...??

Now imagine if life was not the mundane routine of survival, but a fantastic adventure way beyond the ordinary... of mysterious clues, allegorical guideposts & mystical coincidences, leading to the discovery of our higher selves... across space, time & dimensions...of our karmic relationships, resulting in the fulfillment of a higher purpose, our destiny...a memory that we, as humanity, have forgotten...

It's time to revive that unconscious memory...

John Lennon once said: *"You may say that I'm a dreamer, but I'm not the only one..."*

Here are my words:
I live in my dreams; I walk my own way,
I look at what can be, not what is today,
I dream of a world with ideals,
I dream of a world that heals,
I dream of a world, with love that flows,
I dream of a world, with warmth which glows,
I dream of society where people care,
I dream of a place where individually we dare & collectively we share,
I dream of a world where people compete but do not fight,
I dream of people who live in today, but of our collective future do not lose sight,
I dream of a world which is pure, green & clean,
And all this of a world, which can be, for it has been,
I dream of harmony between men, between nations, & between nature & man,
I know these are dreams, but if we all dream, WE CERTAINLY CAN..

So let us dream together, dear reader......let's go through this adventure...and discover our own destiny...

THE NEW AGES
AN ADVENTURE BEYOND THE ORDINARY....

PART I

1.	Life 'back home'	11
2.	The redemption and transformation	26
3.	From the heavens came the 'beings'…	31
4.	Trinity within trinity within trinity…	43
5.	Seek the 'peak'	52
6.	The royalty, the king and the monk	58
7.	The 'getaway' gateway	72
8.	Another time, another place (or is it?)	82
9.	Understanding the transcendence	98
10.	A new fellowship shall be set	112

PART II

11. The annihilation — 120

12. Transitions, sacred feminine and the new ages — 127

13. The new worlds- Zen and Kaizen — 141

14. Human being, not human doing… — 155

15. The Guardian Council — 172

16. The Clairvoyance Chamber: — 187

17. The Energy Exchange system — 196

18. Seek the heart where it all made the start… — 207

19. The Quartet and Charter of the new ages — 222

20. The New 'ism'….. — 238

21. New metric and the IIN — 250

22. Defence and offense — 262

23. The prophecy seems clear, the Messenger near… — 282

24. The dharma of karma — 305

Epilogue — 314

Dedicated to the thousands of fans, friends & fellow believers, who are part of 'The New Ages' community on Facebook, and who share their dream of a new world, with me & each other, daily…
And to all others who dream thus…

PART 1

1. Life 'Back Home'

"But Mr. President, we are close to a breakthrough. After all these months of behind the scenes diplomacy & negotiations, I finally see an agreement materializing. All we need to do is to give peace a real chance, and be flexible."

"Mr. Johnson, peace & negotiations are being construed as weakness, an inability to act. We have been discussing this issue for over six months now, but are facing the same deadlock. Moreover, the defense sub-committee has presented a compelling case for an all-out offense: a swift, sledgehammer campaign. This would be in the best interests of our national security, apart from creating a conducive environment for democracy in the region. This report has been shared with all of you in the last cabinet meeting..." said the well built man seated at the head of a cabinet.

"I have seen that report, Mr. President, including the fine print & the annexure." said the agitated leader of the opposition, raising his finger. "And I must say that it has not been able to present any conclusive evidence in support of the allegations leveled. I take the liberty of quoting Clausewitz at this juncture: *'Many intelligence reports in war are contradictory; even more are false, and most are uncertain...'*.

Most of what this so called 'intelligence report' says seems like a compilation of news reports & editorials rather than concrete, on-ground intelligence! In fact, the whole report seems to work backwards, with evidence 'created' to support interpretation, not the other way round! This is certainly not how I have seen any credible intelligence report in over thirty years of public life. And I am sure that's the view of most of us here, whether from the opposition or treasury benches.

Sir, our nation has long stood as the beacon of justice and fair play in the world- that is what gave us moral & political leadership in global affairs. Of late, a lot of that credibility has anyways been ruptured by our misadventures. If we even think of war now, based on such sketchy intelligence & a distinctly prejudiced view about the region, our allies too will not stand by us this time. The entire coalition that was so painstakingly built will lie in tatters. Not to mention the potential irreversible damage to our moral authority."

"I agree with Mr. Johnson's views." added another moderate in the cabinet. "This war will irreversibly hamper room for any future dialogue, and will rip apart the global consensus that earlier governments had so patiently built."

"So are you suggesting that we jettison our cherished ideals of democracy & rule of law? And allow despots a free run in the name of consensus & moral authority?" interjected an animated Vice President, anger visible on his face.

"It's not as simple as that, Mr. Vice President- and we all know it. We are talking about the most sensitive region in the world, which is anyways on the precipice. Any invasion will bring matters to a boil, not only in that region, but also globally-we all know that this war can have global ramifications. We certainly don't want the "War of civilizations" becoming a reality, do we?"

"No! But we also don't want to allow our national interests to be compromised because we are afraid of some hypothetical 'all-out conflagration'. I will not allow another dictator to cock a snook at us because of unfounded fears! *Rather that we be seen as strong & unpopular than weak & politically correct.* Of what use is strength if it is doesn't protect our interests?"

"Whose interests, Mr. President? By *'our interests'*, are you referring to the interests of *er, a lobby?* Our years in public life have taught us the difference between public posturing and factual reality; about how public opinion can be momentarily misled to project ultra right views as a matter of national interest- first create a hydra, then talk about how it is spreading its tentacles, and finally invoke mass paranoia & hysteria around it!"

"You are leveling a baseless allegation, Mr. Williams!" The President lost his temper. "And I refuse to take this most unfounded allegation lying down."

"And I stick by it! Every word of it, sir! I once again urge you, Mr. President- please exercise restraint. Even at the height of the cold war, leaders of both blocs had shown the requisite restraint & pragmatism to prevent an all out conflagration. The earlier wars have anyways drained our national resources and led us into recession- this one will be politically, morally & financially devastating! We will lose the last vestiges of our global leadership."

But the President refused to budge. For over a year now, he had being building a case for war, and there was no way he would back off at the last stage. *This was to be the decisive battle...*

On the other side were the liberals & realists- aware of the majority view in the senate, as well as overwhelming domestic & global public opinion, they tried their level best to stall this war- to somehow try & buy more time for diplomacy to succeed. A breakthrough was close at hand, but the neo-conservative policies of the President & his coterie of hawks were creating a vertical divide in the senate, apart from having contributed to a global rift greater than ever before. As a baffled cabinet & public opinion tried to fathom as to why the President wanted to embark on such a foolhardy mission again, *it was not as if he didn't realize what he was doing...*

In fact, all along, his pragmatism & logic as a statesman gnawed at him, telling him that this deadlock could be resolved through negotiations. He also had access to intelligence that negotiations, led by some members of his own cabinet, apart from other world leaders, were at a breakthrough stage. A show of statesmanship at this stage could help arrive at a respectable arrangement for all. But more than that, he also realized that a successful resolution of this deadlock could address a much larger global issue- *that of bridging the chasm between two civilizations,* and setting in motion a process of reconciliation- one that could heal decades, even centuries, of distrust & animosity.

Which is exactly what his indoctrination wanted him not to do...

Unknown to the outside world, the President was a high ranking member of a secret brotherhood, whose stated doctrine was *to fight the final, decisive crusade.* For decades, it had waited for the opportune moment to strike. While it always had members in influential positions, few were as high ranking or committed as this; and some of the recent developments came as a god send, presenting perfect alibis- liberation from despotic rulers, promotion of democracy et al...

What followed was a dangerous global game-a series of sledgehammer strikes, each intended & designed to further the unfulfilled agenda of centuries- *to be culminated with a final, decisive battle- the 'War of Civilizations', resulting in the cherished dream of a 'NEW WORLD ORDER'!*

This was the mandate to the President- to deliver the ultimate gift to the order; one which would make him immortal in the annals of the brotherhood...

****

Somewhere, in a different plane, a group of clairvoyants & seers were witnessing images of these cabinet deliberations with concern. *Deep concern!*

Ever since the beginning of this rightward tilt in policy making, the seers were tracking developments closely. Assembled in the central hall, they would view these discussions and project positive energies onto it, attempting to counteract the negative energies of prejudices & fear with prayers & blessings. *Hoping that reason & ethics would prevail over prejudices & dogmas...* But they failed...twice!!

On both the previous occasions, the hawks prevailed, and war was thrust upon people, with disastrous consequences for both the 'victor' and the vanquished.

However, prayers have power, and the energies of the seers worked in other ways- at individual levels...

As the years elapsed, a more enlightened populace began aggressively questioning the logic of these foolhardy conflicts- the once supportive, and then ambivalent public opinion turned decisively anti-war. *The seers were pleased at this shift in collective mood, but the clairvoyants sensed that this was not enough to stop the President on his reckless mission...*

And this time, it was going to be not just another war; as horrific as conflict always is, this one had the potential to spiral out of control; way out of control...*Leaving behind a trail of destruction which could threaten the very survival of humanity...*

Even the beings were concerned now...

****

As Dave Jones tossed & turned, the scene shifted again...this time to the gentle face of a master, beckoning:
> 'Follow the clues, be guided by the light,
> To navigate through life's days & nights,
> As one leads to another in a series of seven,
> The journey leads to the Messenger of heaven...

And finally, a vague sense of some prophecy, a bright light, followed by the scene fading out...

But before the scene could fully fade out, Dave woke up, perspiring...as always...

1999- AT THE TURN OF THE MILLENNIUM...

For the past year, Dave Jones, a senior executive with a multinational cola major, had being having this peculiar dream- about a President and his cabinet engaged in a heated discussion about some war, which would have global ramifications. In this dream, there was a group of seers & masters who projected some kind of ethereal energies onto this scene-*hoping that things could, hopefully would, change, and that disaster could be averted...*

But strangest of all, towards the end, there appeared a Master's radiant face, looking Dave straight in the eye- telling him, almost beseeching him, to follow the clues...leading to some 'Messenger of the heavens', followed by a sense of some prophecy...

Initially, Dave thought nothing more of this than just another random dream, without any apparent pattern or logic. But then the frequency & intensity increased, till it became almost a daily phenomenon, causing a sense of anxiety & discomfiture to him. While it seemed directed at him, it just didn't seem to make any sense...

Who was this hawkish President, engaged in heated deliberations with his cabinet? What was this 'war' that they were all so passionately arguing about? Who were these mystical seers witnessing this scene, and how were the two correlated? What were the clues, and who was this Messenger?

But most importantly, how the hell was he connected with any of this? He was neither a politician nor a seer, just another normal professional, having had a mixed bag in the name of life so far- some good, some bad...

A good, fast track career, a wonderful companion, a loving family, heck, even his own tree house; things were mostly good...

That was, till a couple of years back, when the balance started to tilt on the wrong side...

But first the good part...

****

Dave Jones started off as a Management Associate, and a fairly ambitious one at that, in a leading cola multinational 14 years back. A not so easy childhood gave him the much needed fire-in-the-belly and ruggedness to rough it out in the ruthless environs of corporate life, while an inherent flair for numbers endowed him with razor sharpness in detecting trends early on.

With such a cocktail of aggression & analytics, his ascent was never in doubt; and he made the best of it, having successful stints in most of his initial markets.

While his peers were busy chin wagging at the coffee machine, or discussing the latest tweet going around the office grapevine, Dave was beating the scorching sun, scouring the market for early reads, doggedly tracking it for emerging undercurrents before they became trends. This incisiveness & hunger kept him a step ahead of his counterparts, giving him an ear for the market- a virtue that saw him take several key initiatives- from increasing distributor margins, to deepening the penetration of fountains over bottles, to revamping the hub & spoke distribution model for cutting 'time to market' by 15%- all this, while his H.O. counterparts were busy poring over vacuous PPTs made for their managers, *to be presented to their managers!*

As his 'sniffing' of the market got sharper, his hunch proved increasingly correct on most occasions, marking him out in the eyes of senior management. Of course, there were times when he was pipped to the post, but his sheer determination allowed him to bounce back, for another day, another way; *guided by Gekko's words: Gimme guys who are poor, smart &*

hungry...and no feelings; you win a few, you lose a few, but you keep on playing... and if you need a friend, get a dog!'

As the years passed, Dave's scope & scale of work increased, and he kept raising the bar, pushing himself & his team ever harder. He had learnt his lessons early on, when his first boss told him bluntly: 'You know dude, there are only two things which are important in Corporate life: lick ass & kick ass; lick ass above you, and kick ass below you. Any one will do if you wanna survive, but both are needed if you wanna thrive; rest are mere details!'

At that time, the freshly graduated & sophisticated B-school alumnus had found these words rather blatant, even crass; but as time passed, he saw the truth & relevance of this statement every day, in office, and it held him in good stead. Since lick-ass was repulsive for his disposition, he was guided by the kick-ass part, leading to the tag of 'hard task master'- a medallion he proudly wore on his sleeve, as every year of sales growth added to his reputation.

His 20% + year-on-year growths, even in years of overall de-growth for the corporation, won him 3 'Star of the year' awards, making him a fast tracker by any standards.

Along with the awards came the rewards too- he moved up from Area Manager to VP-sales & distribution for the entire region, in just over a decade- a befitting reward for a stellar salesman, who fitted the bill of 'the guy who could sell a refrigerator to an Eskimo...'

Sales star he may have been, but no, he wasn't a uni-dimensional personality- if work & growth were his opium, rock n roll was his LSD. *Rock, of all types- hard, progressive, psychedelic, grunge, metal...*

Floyd & Metallica sustained & nourished him during the lows, GnR gave him kicks during the highs, while U2 and '*I still haven't found what I'm lookin' for....*' nudged him during those rare moments of inertia...

Ticking away the moments that make up a dull day,
Fritter away the hours in an offhand way...

These words of Pink Floyd were not written for a guy like him- not for him lethargy & ambivalence...

What separated him from the pack was not smarts or skills-it was attitude! *The can do spirit, the never say die approach*-leading to justifiable recognition...

And the more awards he got, the more driven he became-recognition did not satiate his appetite, but rather whipped up his hunger.
He was here to reach the very top, no less...
And he was headed in the right direction...

****

However, it was not only his professional life which was zooming. *Something else was blooming too, something beautiful blossoming in his personal life...*

Six years back, Dave happened to be at an art exhibition of a Paris based painter & musician. Not one to 'waste' time appreciating random stuff that *neither the viewer nor the artist fully understood,* he was literally compelled to attend it, his corporation being the principal sponsor (*much against his views, though- why waste good money on something that only the elite of society visit, he argued with his Marketing head, only to hear those two annoying words-brand image!*).

To him, such displays were the superficial pursuits of pseudo-intellectuals & the nouvuea riche- folks who couldn't do anything genuinely constructive in life. They were flowery folks disconnected from life's realities, the children of Woodstock, who were neither his consumers, nor supporters of his products. But once there, his regrets dimmed, if not dissolved completely- the exhibition highlighted the plight of children in war torn areas around the world, and was held to raise donations for them. Number focused he may have been, but his soul was not numbed- the haunting images of destruction & despair wrenched his soul...

However, there was hope- in the last section, there were beautiful, uplifting images of children smiling amidst the ruins, innocently perceiving the very world which was so harsh to them. They held out a hope of love in every adversity, no matter how seemingly hopeless...

After a long time, he felt moved, and a moist eyed Dave was introduced to the painter- a lovely, petite, serene looking lady by the name of Shakti. He was intrigued by her rather unusual name, but she clarified that it was a Sanskrit word representing feminine power.

As Dave got chatting with her, he realized that she was everything that he was not- intuitive, idealistic, effervescent & loving, living life on her own terms, travelling like a free spirit, holding exhibitions all over the world and working with kids. She lived life for love, for bliss & art, not for money or possession. For the first time in his adult life, he met such a person, and was instantly fascinated by her. He was also captivated by her innocent laughter, and the warmth & compassion in her eyes, not to mention her unconventional beauty. She had dark long hair, hazel eyes, petite slender frame, and lustrous skin, glowing with joie-de-vivre. Not a drop-dead bombshell, but someone whose beauty seemed to emanate from within.

"You're beautiful..." he blurted rather awkwardly, to innocent giggles from her. "I mean, *these* are beautiful." he tried to point to her paintings, again rather ill at ease. Beyond the customary pleasantries, it was proving difficult to strike up a meaningful conversation with her. It is then that he realized that he could discuss very little outside of business, markets or current affairs- arts, music, creativity, philosophy, philanthropy- all these had eluded him so far...

That evening ended with Dave sensing two things: one, that he was swept off his feet by her; and two, that the hardnosed, number crunching executive was a total contrast to the petite, soft spoken, rooted-in-eastern-philosophy Shakti! It wasn't that he hadn't had women in his life earlier- in fact, more than his fair share- ravishing, ambitious, bitchy, babes, even trophy conquests...but invariably, he was the one in control, the man in the driver's seat. The contours of the engagement (none of them deserved to be called a relationship) were clear, and when the fun & games were over, life moved on. *Friendship with benefits*...no commitments, no hang ups! Very businesslike, aptly suited to his style. But here was someone who tugged at his heartstrings in a way he never thought possible, a woman who made him feel in awe, not the other way round; alive, touched in a way he had never before been...

Now he understood that there probably was something like magic at first sight, if not love! He had heard the term *'chemistry between two people'*, but thus far, it had signified nothing more than working relationships. Now, this much clichéd term seemed to open up new vistas in his life. A humbled & visibly moved Dave noted down her email address, hoping to keep in touch, to explore this 'strange feeling' further...

The next few months were as beautiful as they were hilarious- Dave immediately dashed off an e-mail after getting back, but couldn't progress much beyond four monotonous 'how-are-you-hope-things-are-fine' lines. Each time he tried to write something beautiful, his handicap with poetry stared in the face; it then struck him how the suave official email writer was woefully lacking in serenading skills.

Man, he needed a hitch, a love guru...so desperately!

Thankfully Shakti was gracious, humble & understanding, caring more for the underlying emotions rather than their manifestations, although her replies were quite different- she wrote about her upcoming exhibitions and visits to refugee camps, about her attending a workshop on healing through mind control, about her views on various dance forms, healing techniques based on colour therapy, and how blatant exploitation of the ecosystem by 'vested corporate interests' made her blood boil!

But the conversation thread continued; perhaps the right brained utopian world of Shakti & the left brained pragmatism of Dave complemented each other; their relationship, although long distance, blossomed. Dave began to see merit in her commitment to arts and her causes, while she consciously made an attempt to understand the 'world of profit', and that all players in the domain need not be cold, calculative crooks.

As the months passed, the realization slowly seeped in that they were in love: passionate, intense, the kind that touches you from deep within- there was no doubting that!

Finally one day, Dave attempted the unthinkable, going down on his knees and proposing to her (though not in the most innovative fashion): "I think I am falling in love with you..."

Although not entirely unexpected, the woman in Shakti came to the fore, her first reaction being to cover her mouth with both hands in an *'oh-my-god-I-am-so-overwhelmed'* expression; a part of Dave expected it, while another somehow felt 'how clichéd, how feminine!' But then, she said something, in her trademark soft voice, which completely floored him:

"I think I am rising in love with you..."

With this symbolic statement, Shakti & Dave chose to rise in love, together; she moved base from Paris to share home, hearth & life with him. And most importantly, a lifetime of love...

To outsiders, their differences were 'apparent', and this relationship was just not meant to last. But they went about building their relationship on mutual acceptance and respect. Instead of allowing their varying personalities to be a source of problems, they took a leaf out of each other's positive traits, to build a union that was the best of both the worlds- so Dave actually tried his hand at the violin, while Shakti kept a home expense 'planner'! As aghast as they were initially, the outcome was pleasantly surprising...

As the months elapsed, Dave experienced a bliss he had hitherto never savored, inspite of his professional accomplishments. Here was something which felt better than numbers, sex, heck, even rock n roll! This was sheer poetry, melody...

Thus flowed life, a song in paradise...for the first 2 years...
But then, life's realities started catching up...

****

As time elapsed, the romance gradually tapered off, being replaced by adjustment, understanding & empathy as the cornerstones of the relationship. The flames of passion slowly dimmed, as routine took over. The daily grind of physical, mental & emotional pressures gnawed at the wondrous moments of life, bit by bit, even for the most passionate of relationships. As the embers of magic diffused, the differences couldn't stay buried for too long- manifesting, not as opportunities to further explore each other, but as chasms seemingly too yawning to be bridged.

As Dave rose up the ranks quicker than he anticipated, or could handle, his stresses started mounting too- exponentially. The pressure of being the youngest VP began to tell. What was once the thrill of challenge soon became a cross on his shoulders...

And then came along the pesticides controversy, which hit his company hard; in fact, the entire industry hard! A global health organization came up with tests which showed that colas contained pesticides & higher than accepted levels of not so desired chemicals, which had adverse impact on body organs, especially the intestines, over a period of time; they bolstered their case by displaying videos of human tooth dissolving entirely in a glass of carbonated drink in a matter of days, something which shook health experts.

A news hungry media, ever ravenous for that next big scoop, played out these images round the clock, for days.

The company hurriedly went into a denial mode, producing counter evidence & reports from health experts to the contrary. But by then, the damage had been done. The controversy itself lasted for just about three months, but the effects lingered on for over two years, badly impacting consumer confidence, therefore sales; no longer was it that easy to get people to guzzle gallons of carbonated drinks...

As VP- Business Development, Dave saw falling numbers for the first time- something that he was not used to, or prepared to take! Unable to handle the combination of extreme pressure & disappointment, his personality began to alter, becoming progressively cranky & reclusive. He started spending more time at office, but ironically lesser than ever before on productive solutions.

The more the goal post eluded him, the more he chased it with a vengeance; the more it called for a radically different approach, the more he pushed for the same.

The more it called for a radical surgery, the more he went about applying band-aid...

The hungry young man, once a trendsetter, now couldn't completely grasp the changing market long after it happened!

Instead of engaging with the product & marketing teams on development of new, health oriented products, he got mired further in the same rut, pushing the sales team even harder, creating nothing but more dissonance. Motivation, love & music took a backseat, as an irrational obsession engulfed his being, sapping energies all the more...

As the hum, the dissonance, got louder in office, so too its echo resonated at home. Progressively lesser time was spent in the warmth of hearth & home, and whatever was, usually in an irritable, occasionally foul mood.

A hug, which could once led to a thousand flowers blooming, now became a mechanical, perforce act. The beautiful hours spent together with the artist, coffee mug in hand, collective dreams in tow, no longer cleared his head, but seemed like distractions from the onerous task of setting things rights...

At first, Shakti was taken aback by this abrupt change, this sudden souring of things. But then, having understood Dave's world better in these past two years, she quickly reconciled & adapted to this new reality, hoping that it was a temporary phase, an ephemeral disturbance which would pass soon, a pressure that would ease with support, a strain that would heal with love, a disappointment that could be overcome with companionship.

She went out of her way to help him, relegating all her other priorities to the background; after all, she was a woman, and love took precedence over all else, howsoever profound. In this period, *her entire love was withdrawn from the outside world & shared with the one who had become her world...*

She tried hard to adapt, to talk his language, to understand his problems. But Dave refused to communicate openly, his macho self-image wary of being seen as weak and vulnerable, even in front of his love- after all, what could she understand about the pressures of office, the changing currents of the marketplace? She was still an artist, whose world lay on the canvas & the keyboard, and for whom the market merely represented unrestrained evil. *No, talking to her was pointless. She couldn't understand...*

Driven by this self inflicted barrier, the chasm started widening more & more. The paranoia of losing all the he had built over the years became so dominant that he became progressively closed, distant with everything that mattered. The more she tried, the more was his inexplicable shunning of her- a subconscious acknowledgement of the two different worlds they came from, of the fact that they could never find common meeting ground in the harsh landscape of life's rigors...

As Dave's hardness grew, so did the heaviness in gentle Shakti's heart. To a tender soul whose world view was still rooted in love, and who saw nothing wrong in feeling vulnerable or lost, this behavior was incomprehensible- *her bestest friend & love, for whom she had given up so much, had given up on her. Their differences, which once created the spark, had mutated into a flame which engulfed them...*

For a full year, Shakti struggled to reconcile to this, to come to terms, to communicate with him, but without success- beyond a point, the artist's gentle heart gave up, unable to bear the ache any longer...

At a young age of 32, Shakti died, of a massive cardiac arrest!

A shattered Dave took a long time to come to terms with this tragedy. In fact, for quite a while, he couldn't even comprehend what really happened, or how exactly his behavior contributed to any of this; driven by a combination of deep guilt & grief, he chose the path of denial. *And submerged himself more into the same morass that caused his loss in the first place...*

For a while, 'friends' supported him, but then gradually drifted away. Everyone worships the rising sun, but few care or dare to go with the twilight; in his dusk emerged the fading shadows, as they sorted convenience from conviction. As most 'buddies', including some of his most trusted confidantes, cast their lot with pragmatism over steadfastness, Dave's anguish started morphing into bitterness, even anger. He may have been a tough guy on the outside, but at heart he was a scorpio- someone who took ten steps in response to a single act of faithfulness; someone ready to walk the extra mile, simply to see that smile on the face of those he cared for...

Yet, these very confidantes conveniently jettisoned him for practical considerations; some tried to sound apologetic about how this made them feel 'conflicted', while others were blatant; some chose 'confusion' as an alibi, while others found innovative ways to avoid him. But broadly, they left him at varying points, unwilling to get mired in any mess which could distract them from their own progress.

As his resentment grew, so did the distance from those who really cared. As deep cynicism replaced his faith in love, loyalty & friendship, his heart hardened further, leading to at least half a dozen health problems- most of them 'lifestyle diseases' and 'wounds of the heart', as his doctor would call them. He popped pills for a while, but they failed to help beyond a point. He knew it and his doctor knew it- it was a deeper problem, a fundamental malaise; and the cure also lay there. For far too long have people looked up to pills as a panacea for problems- but one cannot heal the gashes of the heart simply by attacking the symptoms...

As his restlessness grew, addictions followed next. And before he realized it, alcohol, smoking, even food, became his points of succor- accompanying bitterness as his constant companions.

This volatility started impacting work too. For a while, senior management took a 'compassionate' view of things, but then it was back to business as usual- the same demands, the same pressures...

Not for Dave though; constantly nagged by his loss and hurt by betrayal, he found it difficult to focus with the same intensity & vigor- motivation was replaced with irritation, the ability to work around the system replaced by a frustration with the system, the *can do* spirit replaced by a perennial *'what-to-do'* confusion...

Both his numbers & perception suffered, and for the first time in an illustrious career, he was faced with the twin prospect of lack of faith from his management, and lack of motivation from this team. *The whole thing became a vicious cycle of negative energies...*

****

In this chronic & unstable state started the strange dreams...For no apparent reason, with no apparent trigger, except probably his distressed mind- he was not in politics, had nothing to do with strange beliefs, practices or cults, and had never met any such master ever in his life...

So was all this was merely a brain pattern going awry?

However, the more Dave tried to reason that this dream had no correlation with him, the more it kept increasing in frequency & intensity; till it became so disturbing that it compelled him to resort to sleeping pills, adding to his repertoire of addictions.

As he slipped deeper & deeper into the morass, with a lifestyle bordering on the insane, his health was bound to reach a breaking point...

And when it did, history repeated itself...

One day, Dave collapsed too; in office, of a heart attack... mild enough to not be life threatening, but strong enough to finally jolt him out of his abyss...

And significantly, at the turn of the century...the millennium!

2. REDEMPTION AND TRANSFORMATION

They say when the going gets tough, the tough get going...
But when it gets impossible, wisdom emerges from knowing...

When you hit rock bottom, there is only one way to go- up! This is equally true of individuals as of markets...

Thus began Dave's journey of exploration, of redemption from the abyss- the path of conscious cleansing, both physically & emotionally. Having wasted so much of precious life trying to seek refuge in work, pills, addictions & bitterness, he decided to finally pursue Shakti's path- the trail of inner strength, cleansing & grace; the route of meditation & yoga... the calling of the heart...

The starting point of this wisdom was knowing, accepting... that he had screwed up; that things were terribly wrong; *that it needed an inner revolution, not merely evolution*...it was not simply about healing, but deep inner transformation, of becoming a different person...

While Shakti was alive, Dave shunned her attempts to induct him into eastern mysticism- *'Don't have time for fancy fads,'* was his usual refrain. *But now he felt like paying a tribute to her memory, by trying out 'her way'*...

Over the next couple of months, he explored yoga, Ayurveda (the ancient Indian system of healing by balance) and meditation. At first, the whole concept of *'healing by balance'* seemed alien to the logical, analytical mind. But he kept his skepticism aside, practicing these patiently, diligently.

And truly, bit by bit, it worked, creating an inner transformation. Ayurveda helped him analyze his 'prakriti', his body type, and tailor-make his routine, his diet & habits accordingly; yogic asanas & breathing helped rebuild the 'prana' or life energy, while meditation helped get more centered.

The path was not easy, though- *it needed the 3 Ps*; not of *marketing*, as the marketer within would routinely rattle out, but of *'the real thing'*, as he would say, tongue-in-cheek: *practice, patience & perseverance. However, headstrong that he was, he held on...*

As he went deeper into this ocean, further on this path, the transformation became more anchored. He experienced a holistic balancing of his system, helping come to terms with his loss, enabling him to flow with life in a positive way. He realized that his withdrawal was responsible for Shakti's departure, that his past conditionings had resurfaced in tough times, creating a schism where there could have been a bridge. Yet, guilt was not the answer; love & forgiveness was! He knew Shakti, wherever she was, had already forgiven him, and wanted nothing more than for him to be truly happy again. *By being in harmony, he was paying a tribute to her memory, her way...*

****

As his inner space felt illuminated, it radiated the light outward, manifesting as balance- balance between work & 'life', inner & outer, ups & downs. With it also came realization of what was truly precious- family, 'true' friends, health, inner happiness… At work, it was not just about numbers and blind aggression anymore; gone was the irritation & bitterness, dissolved, dissipated; replaced by an appreciation of the quality of work & relationships, human capital development, and a long term vision, resulting in building of enterprise value.

The change was noticeable...

His colleagues & team members, his buddies at the club- all of them saw 'something' change within him. He was still the man with the killer instinct, but there was a human & humane touch to that. His faith was back, skepticism replaced with an ability to trust again, anger with the power to motivate again. He started viewing people as souls who needed to be nurtured, not merely as 'horses who got paid to run the fastest'- they were not simply 'resources', but living energy bundles, whose energies could be focused by care, or dissipated by negativity.

In traditional management parlance, he became the 'quintessential people's manager'...

People Management vs. task management- how he laughed at these obsolete management concepts now. *How could there ever be task management without people management? After all, he wasn't dealing with robots, but breathing human beings with emotions...*

Energies attract likewise, and transformational energies attract the wholesome & profound. As these ideas got internalized, he got drawn towards 'new age' management & leadership philosophy.

Management, he realized, was fortunately undergoing a 'paradigm shift', thanks to some wonderful thinkers, proposing new models of management, new definitions of leadership: Drucker spoke about managing in turbulent times, Peter Senge highlighted the 'Fifth Discipline'- the learning organization & shared vision, while Covey spoke about principle centered leadership, as did many others about the role of balance, spiritualism, and Zen in a world erstwhile construed as cold, detached, even indifferent to the environment it operated in. *Inspired by their 'avante garde' philosophies, Dave began building his own unique ideas, and implement them...*

Firstly, he started bi-weekly yoga classes in office- there could never a successful team unless it was healthy, vibrant, and fighting fit, both physically & emotionally. And so, *'breathe deep to penetrate deep'* became the guiding mantra of his team. While some in senior management were aghast by the sound of this war cry, Dave clarified that it was wholly innocuous, *referring merely to market penetration, nothing else!*

Then came the advice (maybe more of diktat) to his sales managers, to start their morning team huddles with a fifteen minute meditation session. This was to calm the nerves of the 'frontline soldiers', to help everybody to focus on the task at hand in a collective way.

And finally, in quite a contrast to the above, the evening meetings would end in rocking parties, with blazing music creating high energies all around- a perfect way to cap yet another *'salesful'* day, as compared to a *'stressful'* day! The 'frontline soldiers' would let their hair down, dissolving their frustrations & celebrating their achievements.

At the end of it, they would trash their negativities and carry home positive energies- office became not a source of domestic discord, but an engine of happiness which permeated at home too.

Dave would not allow another Dave & Shakti to happen again...

This was not to say that Dave Jones & team became a monastery- they were still as competitive & aggressive as earlier; if anything, even more! The performance culture was not diluted, but actually accentuated by these 'maverick' ways, as people felt a greater sense of bonding, higher energy states & clearer minds to 'go out for the kill'; being driven by motivation rather than fear. And happier families meant lower attrition...

While Dave invested more time, energy, resources & love in his people, his unit still had the same 'zero tolerance' for non-performance. So the laggards were clearly identified from the performers, & had ongoing sessions with their managers. The consistent laggards were put on a 'rejuvenation program' to bring them up the curve. Yet another of the team's idiosyncrasies, this program meant intensive coaching, counseling, even meditation! *Yes, meditation for performance!*

But if, over a 3 month period, a laggard would still not shape up, then in most cases it connoted an intent rather than capability issue; and this was something about which Dave was very clear: '*You can change behavior & effort with counseling & attention, but not attitude. To waste time on a deliberate lazy laggard is to deny the genuine guy his due. So if there is a clear intent issue, then out with it...*'

'*Shape up or ship out*' was very much still his motto, except that now he set a system which helped people shape up, in a very intense & involved way- the focus was not on the end goal, the numbers themselves, but rather the actionables, the building blocks which would lead to the numbers.

So Gantt charts replaced pie charts, project trackers substituted volume trackers, and happiness monitoring replaced simply competition monitoring- employee activities, not their resultant outcomes, became paramount! A simple and logical way to manage teams, yet quite path breaking in traditional sales thinking...

This 'avante-garde' style had a dual effect- not only did everybody in the organizational chain feel lighter, but organizational energies were focused in the right direction: in the marketplace, not in office politics or stresses...

The art of selling without selling, he called it...

As a result of these *'little experiments'*, for the first time in three years, Dave managed to bring back growth. Not the usual 20%+, but high single digit. Not that anybody minded, however...

Growth in this market was a boon, almost a miracle...

****

As the success stories of this 'maverick' unit piled up, Dave's 'offbeat' experiments became an internal case study, and were taken up seriously by the training & HR Departments for larger roll-outs. At a time when the organization was grappling with ideas to boost productivity & counter falling sales, Dave's tangential exercises were seen as not distractions or impediments, but rather as serious alternative tools to help motivation & productivity...

And the undisputed fact was that they worked!

Dave's inner transformation was now manifesting as external transformation, leading to a new, practical alternative paradigm of management & productivity- per resource productivity, output & profitability was the highest in his team, not only across the region, but even globally, besting even emerging markets...

****

As this inner & outer transformation took root, so did something else: freedom! Freedom from addictions, freedom from warped priorities, freedom from burdens of the heart.

And freedom from the dream... It was no longer needed...

Dave was ready for the next step...

3. From the heavens came the 'beings'...

Year 2000

A new millennium had set in, an epoch moment in human history, when a thousand year period had just drawn to a close. Scores of commentators, analysts, physicists, metaphysicists & thinkers had their own versions of the significance of this event- but all of them were united in the view that it was indeed a monumental time. It was no coincidence that our generation was witness to the end of a 1000 year period in human history...and probably the most tumultuous...

For Dave too, it was a momentous time, but in a different context- this was the period when the ghosts of the past had been replaced with the centricity of the present, based on a new understanding...

Six months after his redemption, mid way into the first year of a new beginning & a new millennium, a blissful & free Dave decided to spend the weekend at his *forest lodge, something he lovingly called the 'tree house'*. It is every child's fascination to have a dwelling nestled among the birds, perched on the branches of an old oak tree- and it was no different for Dave, being his dream since childhood. But unlike a child's fantasy of an imaginary house on a single plank, he built a full-fledged one at that, four years back... *He & Shakti...*

Initially, they visited this oasis of serenity at least once a month, as refuge from the city madness- an opportunity for Shakti to reconnect with the artist within her, and for Dave to clear his head. But after her untimely demise, Dave just couldn't gather the heart or muster the courage to go to a place so filled with memories...*every log, every rock would remind him of her, of what he had lost...*

But that was in the past. Now he felt free! And what better place to savor this freedom than his favourite tree house...*their favourite tree house...*

****

Set amidst the wilderness, on a ten acre plot in the outer zone of a national park, the vacation home's proximity to the core zone ensured that he always had company for morning coffee- from the variety of birds & monkeys to gazelles & spotted dears, there was always some encroacher in the estate-but this was encroachment he didn't mind; in fact, he paid a premium for it! Moreover, being located just 250 miles from the city, the forest lodge was convenient & accessible for a weekend retreat- just about a six hour drive...

The lodge itself was nothing very fancy, but had all the comforts of a modern home, combined with a rustic feel. Built around an old Oak tree, which ran through the entire height of the house, the lodge was spread out over 4 levels, with various decks at each of these levels.

The master bedroom was actually created 'around' one of the large branches of the oak, giving it a true tree house feel. The deck from this room overlooked the sprawling & comfortable sitting area & visitors lounge, with a large ornate fireplace. In fact, there was a fire place on every level, but those were more decorative than a real utility.

What kept the whole place warm & cozy at all times was simple use of technology- *large solar panels*. These solar panels collected enough heat to power the whole house, heat up 200 gallons of water even in the peak of winter, and power the 'indoor hot geyser'. This was technology combined with nature, *something he would see in a far more sophisticated form later...*

His favourite spot, however, was the deck at the top level- the UPPER DECK. Set around one of the higher branches of the oak, this deck extended all around the top of the house, giving a 360 degree view.

Since it was open, the flooring was heated up by special pipes running under it, carrying hot water at all times. This was one place where Dave actually used to light up the fireplace in the evenings, sitting with his book & coffee mug...

****

This weekend, Dave decided to try something different- things had changed between the last time and now, so even the journey would have to be different. *A new beginning called for being adventurous...*

So he set out in the night, instead of the usual early morning drive- sunrise from the top deck was a breathtaking site, just beyond the waterhole in the core zone, across the meadows. The early morning lights attracted all varieties of animals to the waterhole, since the nocturnal predators were away. *And now that he was experiencing a new dawn in his life, he wanted to catch the early morning sun. After quite a while, he was ready to savor the sunrise...*

So too were the Masters...they were hoping that this was the dawn they had been hoping and waiting for...

****

The night was cool & pleasant, with a light drizzle. This meant that he would have to drive slower, but then this was just the drive he was looking forward to- easy paced, music in tow and the wind blowing on his face. Putting on Deep Purple, and blasting away 'Highway Star', he rolled down the windows, letting the cool breeze hit him. It was heavenly- little droplets splashing on his face, ensuring that he didn't doze off.

Post 11pm though, the rain got heavier, and it seemed that a storm was brewing (more than one, he would realize later)...

Suddenly, in a matter of 15 minutes, there was torrential rain & lightning, with visibility was down to less than 10 metres. At the same time, Dave entered a remote stretch on the freeway, the next town being 10 miles away. This meant that inspite of the downpour, he had no option but to drive along. Physical fatigue, along with poor visibility, was taking its toll. *Things were becoming a little fuzzy...*

As a droopy Dave labored along, something appeared that caught his attention. **Strange lights seemed to illuminate the night sky-** *violet & amber moving at a steady pace, along with the occasional flashes of lightning...this created a strange phenomenon, a cross between the eerie, the paranormal & the eclectic...*

Dave rubbed his eyes, trying to regain composure. He even splashed cold water on his face, but the lights continued to travel with him, come in & out of focus. *At times even appearing to come close...*

This continued for about ten minutes, leaving him unsure of how to react. Suddenly, there was an amber flash, coinciding with a particularly bright bolt of lightning.

And then, **'a ball of light'** *(as he would describe later) seemed to appear on the ground, directly in his path...*

By this time, Dave was feeling too disoriented to drive, so he stopped. The *'ball of light'* however didn't- it kept rolling, coming straight towards the car...

As it came closer, he saw it more clearly. The 'thing' seemed like plasma (well, something like it), with violet amber hues emanating from a seemingly white core. And 'the ball' seemed to be getting bigger as it approached, 'gaining mass', finally coming to a halt about 5 meters from the vehicle.

Then, something strange happened- something he could feel, but couldn't narrate in words! Out of the 'ball', an image seemed to emerge: not the normal 2-D image seen on screens, but more like a laser projection...taking form in front of him...

The image was familiar, something he had so regularly seen, but which had stopped now...

Or so he thought until this point...

As Dave stood there, frozen, he wondered if he was hallucinating, seeing some sort of a mirage? But before he could put his thoughts together, the 'ball' suddenly engulfed the car.

For a brief moment, Dave was with 'the image'...*and then, it all went blank....*

The next he knew, he woke up in a nursing home!

"Holy shit!" whistled a stunned Dave, when the nurse told him he was admitted to a nursing home in an unconscious state. But that was the smaller shock- the bigger shock was to realise that he was brought here only the next morning by a good Samaritan- a good ten hours after he blacked out!

"What exactly happened?" the doctor asked him.

"I, er, don't know...I mean, I don't exactly remember." Dave replied, squeezing his eyes, trying to remember. Then he tried to piece together the events- bright lights in the dark and sultry night sky, an unidentifiable object flying in a strange rhythm along with his car, vague images of the lights and something appearing before him...a strange sensation of heat...But he couldn't make any coherent sense of it. In fact, now he wasn't even sure if this actually happened, or if it he was imagining things...

"UFO experience?" the doctor laughed heartily. "Not one more case!" Then trying to comfort him, he said. "It's Ok. Sometimes the mind conjures up images of what is subconsciously buried inside, stirring it back to life- that's all. Don't worry."

"Doc, are you suggesting that I was hallucinating?"

"Relax! What are hallucinations? Merely projections of the subconscious in special circumstances. I'm not a trained psychiatrist, but I have seen & heard of several such cases- you've obviously had some troubled past, and the heavy atmospheric conditions combined with excess fatigue caused you to see mirages from the recesses of your subconscious-images which you would normally not see in the conscious state. Have you had any traumatic experiences in the past? "

"Yes, but its behind me now."

"So you think! But these memories always remain in the deep crevices, waiting to come to the fore. The lake seems placid, but any violent storm will stir up stuff to the surface."

"So you think I *was hallucinating*? The images did have some bearing with those thoughts?"

"In all likelihood, yes. And if you don't like this word, let's just say you were imagining things." the doctor smiled.

"Since all this was probably too much for you, you had a blackout, which is not that uncommon- the body & mind's natural defence mechanism. When you were brought here, all your vital signs were normal- your BP, your heartbeat etc. It was just your body trying to adjust to a new trauma."

Dave smiled feebly. Maybe the doc was right, maybe it was simply shock or trauma. *But what exactly was it?*

"Just loosen up. Here are some tests. Get them done sometime this week. But my sense is you are a fit young man- in perfect shape! Nothing to worry at all." The doctor said chirpily, handing over the discharge slip to Dave.

Thanking the doctor, Dave headed for the bathroom to change. He was filled with mixed emotions: on one hand, still dazed and confused, but on the other also relieved. Something really strange did happen the previous night, but had no impact other than him blacking out, which was comforting, reassuring.

There was a flurry of questions, but he would get home and figure it out…

****

But no sooner did he seek comfort in this thought than something else struck him- while changing, he felt something around his neck!

A chain with a locket…rather, a *strange device…*

A small, finger nail sized device!

Dave was zapped! He wasn't delusional after all- something had indeed happened! His mind raced with questions & anxieties again…

What was this strange 'thing'? How did he get it? And what did it have to do with the episode of the previous night?

Dave stood in front of the mirror for a while, clueless. He then regained some composure, splashing cold water on his face. He removed the chain from around his neck, trying to study it. It seemed like some sort of a USB drive, similar to the pen drive he had, but much smaller & more intriguing…

And unusually shaped for any disk- like a pyramid…

Dave fiddled with it, lost in thoughts- if it was indeed some sort of drive, did it contain some data or information? 'Who' or 'what' gave it to him? Did it contain something confidential, which only he was supposed to be privy to?

It was again not making any sense…and getting spookier!

A glint from the 'devise' broke his spell. Observing it even more closely, he realized that it didn't seem to be made of any normal metal- in fact, it was not metal at all.

The disk was strangely translucent, similar to the 'ball of fire' he had seen- but more like gel than plasma...

This definitely had some connection to the night's episode!

Moments turned to minutes as Dave inanimately stood there. His initial reaction had been one of shock & confusion, but it soon morphed into disappointment- having spent six months cleansing his body & mind, he was fundamentally transformed- a more serene & balanced person, able to perceive life much more lucidly, genuinely convinced that the past was behind him. *Or so he thought...*

Till he stood in a hospital bathroom, holding a weird device from a dark night he had little memory of...the more he felt he had outgrown his past, the more it came back to haunt him, as random events...

Then a fear engulfed his being- *could it be a possible alien abduction?* Random stories of such abductions existed in the realms of science fiction, and how people had no memory of that period. When they came back, there was usually a clue, a scar, a vision...in this case, a devise?! *Good lord! Could it be true?*

A labyrinth of old emotions, neatly tucked away in a corner, resurfaced in all fury: regret, anxiety & fear...

Did he actually experience 'alien abduction' last night? Were those strange lights of a UFO? What was the 'ball of fire'? What actually happened 'there 'that he landed up in hospital? And why did 'they' leave behind the disk?

Unnerved by this mental buzz, Dave took in some deep breaths. Redemption had not been easy to come by, but it had anchored him with wisdom, sheathed him with determination- one of them being to always be the master of the mind. True, negative emotions would surface occasionally, and the unexplained could be his companion fleetingly, but the covenant with self was iron clad: the master would always be in control of this powerful beast, the mind- never allowing negative emotions to become dominant.

Reminding himself of this pledge, he inhaled several more times, allowing calmness & positive energies to fill him. The surreal & the strange were back in his life, but rather than perceiving them from the lenses of regret, he would try to view them as an adventure...

Maybe he had an alien experience, but so what? At least he was back, and in good shape. He would logically dissect this, calmly analyze its implications, and even seek psychiatric & psychic help if needed...*but he would not allow panic to set in*...

With these positive affirmations, he set for home...

****

Feeling better, he took the devise out his pocket. It was shimmering even more now, a strange combination of metallic glitter and translucence. The best starting point, he thought, was to try & plug it into his laptop- after all, it did seem like a drive, and *he had an intuition that this had some message...*

As soon as that thought crossed his mind, a bright golden light radiated from within the translucence. As it gradually acquired a shape, there was something written on it- not 'written' in the normal sense, but rather inscribed, like a carving (carving on a gel was weird enough!). And it seemed to come in & out of focus...

'Follow the clues, be guided by the light,
To navigate through life's days & nights,
As one leads to another in a series of seven,
The journey leads to the messenger of heaven...'

This certainly couldn't be!!

The surreal was unsettling enough, but to realise that it was intimately connected with his dream was severely jolting- a dream he thought was over & done with, a past with which he had made a definitive break. Words which were seemingly history were back in his life! *And how...*

In conjunction with another eerie experience...!!

For months he thought of his dream as an aberration of a disturbed mind, a thought pattern gone awry, a result of his troubled past. But now, after attaining equanimity & equilibrium, he was being confronted by it all over again...*and compelled to make sense of it, to see it as a clue...*

In fact, not merely a clue, but a series of *seven clues, probably...*

As one leads to another in a series of seven,
The journey leads to the Messenger of heaven...

Messenger of heaven? From two random, apparently disjointed events, this was turning out to be a full-fledged treasure hunt! *Seven clues as the guiding light...about some Messenger of heaven...*

While there was still no coherence between his dream, the 'event', the 'disk' and these words, Dave was confronted with a reality that this had been accompanying him in a steady way since the past eighteen months- first as a dream, then as a UFO experience, and now as words emanating from a strange disk. Amidst all the confusion & uncertainty, a part of him, a faint voice, told him that maybe something else was at work here... *Maybe there was some enigmatic quest involved...maybe it was trying to communicate something...*

As soon as he sensed this, something else 'appeared' on the disk again...*the first clue:*

'*From the heavens, came the beings,*
To help us rediscover our wings...
Leaving behind gifts to help us fly,
Scaling new peaks, to reach the sky...
To help with a new start,
Provided we look deep inside our heart...'
And just as abruptly, the clue disappeared...

Amazing! Dave took in some more deep breaths, trying to centre himself. Whether it seemed to make sense or not, *there was no turning his back on this now...*

It was no longer about some distant quest for clues-it was all happening, here & now...*the 'first clue' had actually presented itself- he had no choice but to make sense of it now...*

Closing his eyes, he mentally visualized the first line: *From the heavens came the beings...*

Indeed, something did come from the skies...it was about UFOs after all!

Eyes still closed, he strived to remember the experience: *Some blurred memories, some hazy images, the bright lights of a 'craft', but then, nothing afterwards... a vague hum, and then the hospital bed...*

Then he repeated the other lines:

To help us rediscover our wings...
Leaving behind gifts to help us fly,
Scaling new peaks, to reach the sky...
To help with a new start,
Provided we look deep inside our heart...

He pored over it for a long while- the 'clue' seemed to be alluding to a new start, a new high in life, by opening up one's heart...

A NEW START? Wasn't this something he had consciously done, steering his life in a new, healthy direction? *So why was it linked to his dream, his past? A past which primarily had only regrets for him...*

But then, another thought flashed, comforting him: it was as if someone understood his anguish, his dilemma, and was sharing the wisdom needed to comprehend it fully.

Yes, his past was painful, but it was equally true that the new man owed the transformation to the blows of the past; from the fire had emerged gold, pure & shimmering... from his painful past was crafted a new future...

The past was not something to shy away from, but rather to accept as a gift; a gift on which one could lay the foundation of a new tomorrow...

Dave's eyes lit up with this new wisdom. It now made sense: **the gift from the heavens was his past**, which contained the seeds of a better tomorrow, provided he opened his heart! With this new found wisdom, and a newly acquired 'gift', Dave tucked away the disk in a drawer in his study table...

Maybe it was not an 'alien abduction' after all...maybe something from the heavens was indeed guiding him...

True, he still had many questions, including how this wisdom was linked to UFOs, 'who' was behind all this, and what exactly was his 'experience'? But beyond those questions, at least for now, was the truth in this wisdom, this 'gift- a wisdom which could propel him further in his flight...

Little did he realize at this point that he had another gift as well, the gift actually alluded to in the clue- **the disk!** *He had opened out to and received one gift, while relegating the other to a corner of his table. Even then, he would enjoy the fruits of this, unknowingly for now...and consciously when the right time came...*

At the *same time,* in the future (whatever that means!), on another plane, there was excitement as well...*in fact, double the excitement!* One was about the gift 'reaching out' to Dave Jones, and the other about the mysterious birth of a blessed soul- coincidentally around the same time, (but separated by half a millennium!)...*Maybe not coincidentally...maybe synchronistic...*

Today, the little child was getting baptized by the masters in a secret ceremony, after the visions of the clairvoyance chamber. Master Aleus held him high in the air as he addressed the Council: *"Brothers & sisters of the Council, rejoice! The bearer of the gift of the beings is found."* handing over a disk to the little child, much like the one Dave found.

"Oh Master, the Clairvoyance Chamber has confirmed what the prophecy has alluded to- that this boy's mystical birth is not an aberration, but rather the deep will of the prophecy..." Clairvoyant Nobius added ecstatically. After all, he was one of the clairvoyants who had 'sensed' it.

Sinetha El Magdal, the wise, raised both her arms heavenwards, a deep set, heavy voice coming from within-today, she was the medium, through which the Grand master 'spoke' to the Council. *Not simply through the spoken word, but also via telepathy.*

"Blessed be this moment, this momentous occasion. The gift of the Buddhas comes in twos, like the dual polarities of everything in nature; this is truly a historic & special day..."

Turning to the cherubic little angel, the medium continued: *"Oh blessed one, may you find your dharma, your destiny. This gift has waited long for its rightful bearer..."*

"Yes, now that the gift of the Buddhas has manifest itself, it's energies shall awaken when it finds its companion. And then wisdom shall flow across the planes, across heavens & earth, as the boy shall realize his destiny as the chosen one..." lady Zenia Zenhere smiled back reassuringly.

As energy showers rained from the skies, Master Aleus could feel the weight on his shoulders. But the calming look of the endower Zenia gave him comfort. "If there is someone who can bear this sacred responsibility, it is *you,* Aleus. You are wise among the balanced, compassionate among the caring, and powerful among the strong. You are the perfect Godfather for him. Under your mentorship, he will prepare to find his calling, to fulfill the prophecy..."

"I know, but this weight feels heavy at times, even for me. *Especially since it shall not be known...*"Aleus looked at the boy tenderly.

"The Council is with you my brother. I am with you. *The Master is with you...*"

"That is where I draw my strength from in the most difficult of times." Aleus gazed at Zenia knowingly, a *look not many understood.* After all, very few even within the Council knew much about the hidden side of Zenia, or the mystery of this child's birth, although they all agreed that it was in line with the prophecy.

Amidst the smiles, the seer Zeut issued a timely reminder. "Masters, this child is destined for great things, but only at the right time. The powers of the gift shall not elevate the boy till the Messenger is found, realizes his dharma, comes back to heaven and truly connects with the chosen one. Till then, we have to be careful about holding back the secret. *After all, we hold a knowledge not meant for all...*

Atlas added to it. "And the Messenger is a long way from being found, masters..."

Zeut seconded. "Absolutely! Dave Jones isn't ready just yet."

"What happened simply means that he needs more energy." Aleus replied calmly. The others understood what was implied. "And don't forget that the gift has also found its way- that shall guide him from here on."

"Yes, but only if he goes by his intuition. Only then shall be led to the gateway. Ultimately his freewill will determine the outcome..."

For a brief moment, there was silence. Then Aleus' comforting words broke the spell. "Our prayers & energies continue to be directed, so neither grieve nor worry. The law of intention works only when there is detachment to the outcome. The Universe shall manage the details..."

"Today is a day of celebration, of joy, of baptism! Since this boy is born of the Aura, he shall bear the name of Aureon. And Aureon will be born again when the aura is seen-

**WHEN THE HEAVENS TRULY MEET THE EARTH...*"*

4. TRINITY WITHIN TRINITY WITHIN TRINITY...

A full year had now passed since Dave's transformation, and first year of the new millennium had entered its last month. In this period, Dave had not only delivered stunning growth in a de-growth market, but also developed a new paradigm in 'people management', with amazing success & visibility.

For someone who seemed down & out a year back, this was a dream comeback! Back in the game, back in business, back in the spotlight- and how! The growth was back, the momentum was back, the energy was back, and most importantly, the happiness was back!

But this time the growth 'formula' was different- it wasn't him driving & others following. This time it was a team at work, a team which shared goals, joys & energies together- a team which loved him, rather than feared him. To a Corporate structure steeped in hackneyed ways, he had conclusively demonstrated the integration of people management with task management, results with empowerment, deliveries with trust...

Coexistence of contradictions...supposed contradictions!

As these successes piled up, yet again, the buzz grew louder: Management was having a serious relook at him. In fact, grapevine had it that he was being groomed for the next regional CEO.

All this in just a year!

What a difference 365 days of focus, awareness and wisdom can make, even to the bleakest of situations! And what a difference a team can make to the lost of causes, when it is no longer merely an aggregation of individuals, but has a commonality of vision...

And, of course, what an impact the energies of a new millennium, a new perspective, can have...if we choose to...

As Dave reflected back upon the year, realization seeped in that it had been eventful in more ways than one- the dreams had stopped, his health had been regained, and freedom & balance were firmly anchored in his new found wisdom. True, there was the UFO experience & the disk, but that was six months ago. And while there were no conclusive answers, he did awaken to the 'gift' of a new beginning, relishing it more & more- the passion was more intense, the equanimity stronger, and the memories of the 'night' blurred.

He also sensed that this break was unlike any other- richly deserved, all right, but having much more to it than just unwinding; it was time to take a hard look at the overall direction of life itself, to figure out the next steps. His career was doing great once again, but fundamental questions had now crept in, resting quietly in a corner, awaiting the right time & opportunity to surface. While his demeanor or attitude never showed it, there were times when he seriously contemplated quitting and giving a completely new direction to his life.

All kinds of options, right from associating with a voluntary organization to traveling the globe to becoming a 'new age' management consultant, came to mind. But there was never the time or opportunity to get complete clarity...*to catch the bull by the horns...*

This is exactly what he hoped to get in exotic Italy: time, opportunity and a conducive, stimulating environment...

The thought of Italy brought a smile to his face and a lump in his throat. Italy- ah, that exotic blend of culture, history, romance & fashion. From Rome to Venice to Tuscany to Orvieto to Milan, not many other countries had such a mix of the ancient & the contemporary. From the religious seeker to the high fashion priest, this place had something for all...

The thought of such a place sent his adrenalin rushing- he could almost visualize pulse racing action being juxtaposed with a journey through time & tradition, across one of the greatest ancient civilizations, upon which so much of the modern world was built...

Yet, in this moment of high, somewhere inside, a subdued pain resurfaced- a vacuum, a deep emptiness, as he missed his holiday planner, the fervent googler, who figured out the best deals & most exotic places on every holiday. A detailed itinerary ready and the list of offbeat locations in tow, Shakti was the epitome of travel enthusiasm, a diehard explorer out to discover the local flavors of every new place they could visit - no tour operator could come remotely close to her in terms of an eye for detail or passion for travel. *If only she were here... if only he could...*

Getting a hold of his emotions, he realized that he would have to make do with his tour operator for now. And Italy was still some distance away, literally & metaphorically...

For one, his tour operator had to still confirm the Visa; and secondly, the tour itself was to depart after a couple of days.

So Dave decided to utilize these two days by visiting his forest lodge. What better way than the 'tree house', to kick start this break of 'introspection'.

It had been quite a while since the last, unsuccessful drive to the lodge. This time, he hoped, he wouldn't land up in hospital. With a smile, he left for the forest, making sure that he left early morning instead of being more adventurous like last time.

The drive this time was fortunately uneventful- no rain, no thunder, no strange lights and no waking up in a hospital. He reached his destination fresh & full of energy.

****

Feeling good about himself and the day, Dave decided that a cappuccino would be just great. So, he strolled across the lawn towards the rear entrance, ready to hit the pantry- nothing like lounging on the upper deck with a hot mug of coffee and a sandwich, his favourite book in tow, admiring the beauty of nature, and enjoying the company of resident trespassers...

As he walked across towards the rather rustic main door of the tree house, he saw, and admired, the level, manicured grass on the lawn- his gardener was doing a darn good job...

But wait a minute! What was that in the far corner? S*omething about the grass caught his attention...*

Something strange, like a formation on the grass...

A surprised Dave took a detour, and instead of entering the pantry, went to the far corner have a closer look. The formation itself was not very big- just about 500 square meters, but was rather intriguing, with the grass being uneven in height here…

Still trying to decipher it, Dave decided to climb up to the upper deck, to get a better view. He rushed up an old fashioned wooden staircase to reach the fourth level. Here, 50 feet above ground level was the upper deck, which ran on all four sides, offering a vantage view of the entire estate, as well as the lake flowing at its edge. On other days, he had enjoyed beautiful evenings, coffee mug in hand, savoring the sights of the birds & gazelles, and the sounds of the flowing stream.

But today, he was about to see something very different…

From the top view, the pattern seemed like a series of three concentric circles. Within each of the circles were various shapes- waveforms, little circles, pyramidal shapes, some of which seemed to extend across all the 3 circles.

Between the outer and middle circle were three circles, 120 degrees apart, forming the three vortexes of an equilateral triangle. These circles themselves were just as big as the space between the outer & middle circle, fitting in precisely. *The middle circle had lines criss crossing horizontally & vertically, as if representing something.* Moreover, the grass was cut with utmost precision across the entire pattern, at different heights...*and it seemed freshly cut...*

But how?? The gardener came only twice a week, and today was not his scheduled day. Even if he did come, this certainly was a strange way for him to express his creativity, not to mention the effort which would have gone into it. Nah, far too difficult & complex for his gardener, even the most modern lawn mower...

So who? And for that matter, why? Why would anybody create something so strange, so weird, and so alien?

So Alien...Dave repeated slowly...

In that moment, a maze of information whirred in Dave's head, his mind trying to process events & information spread across time, along with some obscure memories...

The UFO experience...the book he had read a long time back...the vague familiarity...

And then it all came together in a flash! Hell, this wasn't created by any gardener... for that matter, by any man at all!

He was staring at a crop circle pattern! A pattern supposedly created by UFOs in grass or crops...

One more UFO occurrence!!!

Dave had read about crop circle patterns in a book a long time back- one, which at that time, seemed no more than popcorn entertainment, plain speculation in the name of scholastic research...

Fascinated by the subject, however, he saw some alien movies and read a couple more books. Each had its own theory about them, but there was little consensus or clarity. From scientists rubbishing them as frauds to conspiracy theorists talking in terms of secret military projects to UFOlogists treating them as 'signs', *the pages kept churning and the flames of collective excitement burning...*

Some said that these were alien warnings, while others hypothesized that these were secret, hidden messages for mankind; for some, they were the outcome of residual magnetic field distortions caused by UFO landings, while for yet others, these were simply spacecraft navigational signs.

Between skepticism, mystery & entertainment, Dave had thought no more of these than yet another conspiracy theory genre doing the rounds. However, there was one bit that fascinated him- the astute marketing ploy, a massive collective gambit of Hollywood, the publishing world and the defense industry to further their respective interests by taking advantage of the vacuum existing in our modern consciousness.

For a society desperately obsessed with seeking meaning beyond the mundane, thanks to its loss of divine connections, there was nothing more potent than the specter of the unknown, 'heavenly' mystery. *If only cola could be marketed like this, he had sighed then. If only we could plug some gaping hole in human consciousness by positioning sugar water there- 'Alien Cola'?*

But now, as his mind altered between the dream like present and a seemingly bona fide past, old skepticisms began to be torn apart, and new realities stared in his face- this was no Hollywood movie; he had been in the midst of two UFO related encounters, and that reality was finally sinking it...

But it was nothing like what they showed in the movies- no flying saucers, no creepy aliens, no apparent alien abductions. Instead, they increasingly seemed like ***signs, clues…***

What was it about? And what was he doing in any of this?

Dave sat in silence, allowing his mind to clear- this had gone beyond anything he had imagined, but there was no looking back...

Allowing his anxieties to settle down, and visualizing his calm state, he took a sweeping view of the events. The first time around, he was able to decipher, at least partly, the clue about the 'gift' of a beautiful present germinating from the seeds of the past; but on this occasion, only a surreal, complex image presented itself- amidst the pieces, where was the big picture?

As his meditative state intensified and silence grew, words started to form around the pattern, as if elucidating the clue- he gently opened his eyes, looking at the pattern more closely.

Indeed, there seemed to be something written on the grass, next to the pattern…

Neatly etched in the grass was the second clue:
Trinity within trinity within trinity; he who truly seeks, finds...
The central and the peripheral, governed by the one that binds...
Three connected by the union of four,
The outer, the three new and the core...
The trinity of worlds, civilizations and friends,
A new order emerges while the old one ends;
And when the trinity morphs into the quartet,
A new fellowship shall be set...
As the layers are unraveled,
The Messenger would be revealed to the one who has travelled...

Messenger?! This seemed to be one recurring theme, a continuum, some sort of a treasure hunt...*a quest not for the holy grail, but for some Messenger of heaven...*

But what did the other bits mean? Trinity? Quartet? The trinity of worlds, civilizations & friends? A new order? A fellowship? And where exactly are you supposed to travel, *he smiled at himself, as the image of Indiana Jones amplified in his head!*

He had travelled indeed, all the way from Dave Jones to Indiana Jones, he smirked at the delicious irony. Man, whoever or whatever was guiding him wasn't doing a great job, what with all these *unfathomable messages...*

****

Meditating once again, his attention veered back to the pattern after a while. Some more of it seemed to become clearer: the central circle, for example- earlier, it had seemed somehow familiar- now *he understood why...*

It was like a 2-D depiction of the globe, with the vaguely familiar lines representing the continents & oceans. The other lines criss-crossing *horizontally & vertically* probably represented latitude-longitude lines. Interestingly, the various intersections stood out with raised grass, as if some points on the planet, or in the planet, were being highlighted...

The Messenger would be revealed to the one who has travelled...

Dave then decided to go down and have a closer look at these points. As an engineer, he had known that the full picture could only be known by viewing both the elevation & plan, and superimposing them. He obviously couldn't overlay these, but could at least see the elevation more carefully…

As he entered the maze, the unevenness of the grass struck him again. *But even within this jaggedness, there was an order.* The height of the grass progressively altered, from the very tall to the very short- the elevated parts were not only taller than the other grass within the pattern, but also the normal grass surrounding this pattern. On the other hand, the diminutive bits were almost completely cropped…

He went around the pattern, stopping at the central circle. He observed it from various angles & directions, but the pattern seemed to be similar- the short grass progressively becoming taller, till the tallest point was reached, and then progressively getting short again..

This pattern seemed familiar…he had seen this…
But where?

Aha, now I get it…sinusoidal pattern…waveform…

From an elevation perspective (front view), the earth circle created a waveform across its circumference, with crests & troughs, with the highest points being significantly taller than the normal grass.

Waveform, Dave wondered…

Its most common representation was electromagnetism, where the three key parameters were wavelength, amplitude & frequency. Depending upon the proportion of these variables, the wave could represent different forces- electricity, magnetism, radio waves, X-rays, gamma rays etc…

But ultimately, it meant some form of energy, a force…
What could it mean in this context?
Maybe something else, that I don't understand as yet…
And what about the height of the grass? How could they make it grow so much? In such a short span?

In the normal course, this grass would take weeks, even months, to grow to this height; but here, it had grown in a matter of days, probably hours…*maybe even instantaneously…*

Almost as if it had some special, enhanced photosynthesis mechanism, receiving far more sunlight & nutrition...

Far more energy...? Lots of energy...? Focused energy...?

As Dave, immersed in thought, began staring at the grass with all his attention, its shape began to blur, and he briefly saw a flicker of light- just for a moment, the grass seemed to 'reach out to his thoughts', 'responding to love', and grow a wee bit taller...

Focused energy...creating a special photosynthesis ability...

Everything responds to love...

Dave came out from this mini trance, rubbing his eyes- could it be remotely possible? *What if this was indeed the case? What could be its implications?*

Shrugging off this latest flash, he brought himself back to the pressing question at hand: *What did this 'clue' imply?*

The combination of meridian lines, latitudes & longitudes and a waveform on the map of the earth, all on cropped grass...the taller grass...It definitely seemed to be representing certain points...

But why these specific points? What was their significance? And why was he being shown these? What was the clue, the message here?

5. Seek the peak...

A missed call on the cellular phone from his tour operator broke his trance, forcing him into the present. He would call back in a while, once things 'settled down a bit'- for now, he had many questions to answer, a whole new riddle to solve...

Contemplating further on the whole thing, his mind flew to the disk- he recollected the previous episode, and how the disk had helped him unlock some answers... *a new wisdom...*

Tucked away neatly in his laptop bag, unattended, unused, maybe this was the time for it, again...

Dave took it out, holding it in the light, waiting for it to shimmer like last time, some 'carved message' appearing mysteriously.

Nothing...he waited for fifteen minutes-nothing...

Half hour- nothing...

About to stow it back inside, something *guided* him to connect it to his laptop- after all, it had always seemed like some sort of USB drive, so possibly some answers lay hidden electronically. *He was not wrong...*

Electronically yes, but not as anticipated...

He was partially off the mark...

As soon as he connected it to the laptop, there was a huge surge of electricity across the entire estate, like a massive voltage fluctuation. And then, after a few moments, the entire electrical system abruptly conked off!

Dave felt scared. Till now, he had never had a really spooky experience in this journey, but this was scary. Just as he was contemplating what to do next, strange formations started getting projected from the disk onto the floor, in the centre of the room...till they acquired a shape...

Soon, 3-D images illuminated the dark room- images similar to the crop circle pattern, except that the globe was far more clearly defined, like a 3-D, holographic map! A rotating, 3-D image of the earth was circling in the centre of the room, as large as Dave himself...

Dave gulped! This again seemed straight out of the movies-except that he was at the centre of it all...

Just then came another cryptic message, the third clue, as alphabets seemingly flowing from the disk to the image:

'To know, you must grow,
To grow, you must flow...
In the flow, seek the peak,
That of which the sages speak...
Highest of the high, yet deeper than the deep,
Through the gateway, make the leap...'

Seek the peak? Highest of the highest, deepest of the deep?

But he didn't have to speculate long about it. While rotating, the globe briefly paused, and specific points shone brighter than the others, mostly intersection of some of these lines. Followed by fleeting close up images of these points, some of which Dave recognized:

The pyramids...the Bermuda triangle...Stonehenge...Machu Pichu...Nazca lines...

And some which Dave didn't: *a mountain...a desert... another slow clad mountain...some points in the oceans...*

After displaying these images, the image zoomed out, akin to a satellite adjusting its focus from outer space- slowly at first, till the earth appeared as a blue marble (at which point, Dave felt a strange Déjà vu), rapidly then...

Till the earth whizzed by, then some planets, orbs, and finally the solar system...

Again, the images paused at some celestial bodies- the moon and some other objects that he couldn't identify...

Along with these, fleeting images of some great men from history- Einstein, Columbus...

Dave was confused but transfixed. The image then zoomed outside the solar system, to another celestial body, this time accompanied by a most unlikely of images- *that of the Buddha in the lotus pose!*

As he tried to make sense of these seemingly disconnected images, the whole 'projection' quickly zoomed back to focus on the earth, coming to the original frame. After a while, the rotating images finally steadied at a particular point- *similar in position to the point of the tallest grass. At this special point, all the lines intersected to create a very bright spot...*

Dave inhaled deeply...thrice...

A huge '3-D holographic projection' was emanating from the disk- not on the laptop screen, not on any screen, but in the middle of the room- a mode of display very different from even the most advanced computing systems of the day...

And talking a language similar to the crop circle pattern...

Observing carefully, Dave surmised that this corresponded to some place in the East- *between India, Tibet & Nepal...*

Wow, Dave thought! India, Tibet & Nepal- *the spiritual triangle, the mystical corridor...*

But before he could ponder more over it, the image zoomed in further to showcase the most exotic, esoteric & awed mountain ranges in the world- **the Himalayas!** *After flickering for a while, the image steadied there.*

Aha- so this was the peak- **the Himalayas!**

The highest of the high, the deepest of the deep...the mighty & the mystical...

****

Just then, his cell phone rang again- it was his tour operator. *What the hell could be so urgent that this guy was incessantly trying to reach him? And that too at such a time? What was it that just couldn't wait?*

As an irritated Dave picked up the phone, he was stunned by what he heard...

The tour operator apologetically informed him that there were some last moment glitches, and the whole tour needed to be called off! *Italy was off...*

Shit! Dave thought- *just what I needed! If only the idiot would have told me earlier, I would have made alternative arrangements. Now I lose half my leave just trying to figure out a new holiday...*

Dave could feel his temper rise. Already hassled by the spooky experiences, this was the last thing he wanted to hear. All the yoga & meditation & balanced be damned for now- this guy needed to be given a good piece of his mind!

But then the tour operator said something which completely disarmed him, even stumped him...

"I am really sorry about this, Mr. Jones. Believe me, we tried our best, but this was beyond human control- the whole tour is off! However, I have something else to suggest. I know it may not make up for Italy, but thought I'd still suggest it nonetheless."

Dave was about to say buzz off, when the operator blurted "There is a last minute cancellation on my India bound tour- *India, Nepal, Bhutan and Tibet, to be precise Twenty days in all, quite a bit around the Himalayas.* I don't know how much you know about the east, but I can bet my life that it will be a journey you will never forget."

Prophetic words...

"And here's the real sweetener- since I have let you down, *I will offer you this one at a 50% discount!* Frankly, I will lose some money here, but hey, big deal! You are an old customer, so this is the least we can do. Moreover, I'm sure we will more than cover up next year. After all, what's that statistic that you suave marketing folks quote? Ah yes, it's six times more expensive to acquire a new customer than to retain an old one." the tour operator seemed to smirk on the other side.

But Dave didn't care two hoots about this alec-smart comment- he had already lost him mid way during the conversation, at the point where he heard **India-Nepal-Bhutan-Tibet...and the Himalayas!**

The crop circle pointed to a location, with the mysterious disk showing him images of the grandest & most mystical mountain range in the world.

And now, moments later, as he was trying to decipher it all, his tour operator called, offering to fly him there! Last minute cancellation! 50% discount! Only one seat remaining...

All this was beyond coincidences now!

"Mr. Jones, you there?" the tour operator said after a long silence at the other end, now worried that his cheeky comment had further offended his client.

"Uh, yes."

"Great! So what do you say to this offer?"

"Uh, what offer?"

"The discount, Mr. Jones. The India tour? Himalayas?"

"Oh that, yeah, sounds fine." Dave was still lost in thoughts. "But you know what, I am kinda a little lost right now, so call me tomorrow, and we can freeze it."

"Actually I can't, sir." The tour operator tried to be as polite as he could. He knew this was going to be tricky, even make or break. "This tour leaves in twelve hours, sir, so you kinda need to decide now. And get ready if you coming…"

"We can, of course, arrange to send you a luxury pick up. With our best compliments." He added as an afterthought..

It was not needed.

Twelve hours later, Dave was flying first class, in a plane bound for India…

In another plane, something else was flying too- time! And it was flying much faster... RELATIVE TIME...!!

It was now 18 years to the momentous day, when the child was baptized & christened as 'the one with the Aura'- Aureon! After that secret ceremony, things went back to normal, and the child sent to the Zen Holiversity, in accordance with his godfather's wishes...

At the varsity, he spent his formative years getting a holistic upbringing, gathering knowledge & wisdom, being prepared to find his unique talent, the calling of his Dharma.

Unknown to his own self, he went about honing his skills, as Master Aleus facilitated right 'knowledge'. And before he knew it, his eventful stay at the Holiversity came to an end- today was the 'convocation' day, the day on which the apprentices would leave the hallowed hallways & warm confines of the varsity to 'face' the 'outside world'- armed not with degrees but holistic understanding of the systems; not with certificates but character; not with fragmented learnings but a holistic understand of the seamless thread connecting all streams of knowledge...

But it was no 'big, bad world' t they were preparing to step into, ready to hold fort against a multitude of cunning & deceit; instead, they were eager & excited to apply their 'holistic' understanding for the betterment, for further advancement of their world and its systems. Ready to follow their 'dharma'...

Each apprentice at the Holiversity had chosen a dharmic vocation as per her avocation, to actively engage with the 'system', to 'do' what she enjoyed most deeply...

What her inner calling was...and what would contribute to the overall evolution of society...

All this was happening under the vigilant gaze of Master Aleus, as the beings watched both these journeys closely...

The future of the earth & the heavens depended upon them...

6. THE ROYALTY, THE KING AND THE MONK

To Dave's pleasant surprise, the tour itinerary was comprehensive yet easy paced. None of the military style 'assemble in the lobby at seven am sharp' stuff. Working to a regimen was something he did every day for a living- on a holiday, he wanted a relaxed pace- lounging around, allowing his fatigued body much needed rest, as also calm to clear his head. Not merely about the direction of his professional life, but about life itself...and this mysterious quest...
Including WHY HE WAS HERE in the first place...
In India...

****

India, the land of a hundred religions, a thousand languages, a million cuisines & a billion contradictions...

An emerging economic superpower, with the second fastest growing economy & a burgeoning middle class, yet with the largest population of hungry souls in the world; glitzy malls in world class urban centers, yet a majority of the rural population untouched by any shred of this 'India shining'; a fast growing services economy supporting the back offices of most developed economies, yet a pathetic, almost criminal neglect, of agriculture in its own backyard...

One of the most thriving democracies in the world, yet having possibly the sharpest divide of haves & have-nots anywhere, leading to a social unrest of massive proportions; an entire generation of teenagers hooked onto facebook and associated exhibitionism, yet an equally large young population whose faith in home & family stood unshaken; and an upwardly mobile middle class, increasingly placing its burning ambitions over traditional values in a blind aping of the west, while the west itself increasingly looked eastward for answers and anchors...

And yet, India was a land like no other- among the five oldest civilizations in the world, it boasted of a history as old & rich as the Chinese, Egyptian, Persian & Sumerian civilizations, being the cradle of many a landmark event, empires & philosophies of the world.

At various points in its 5000 year old history, it had been at the pinnacle of its power- economically, culturally, even militarily- during the pre-Christian era, much before the glory of Rome & Greece; during the reigns of Ashoka, Vikramaditya, Raja Rajah Chola; and more recently, during the Mughal Empire. In fact, as late as the 18th century, India & China accounted for over 40% of the global trade; before the rise of America & the spread of the British & French empires...

However, India's biggest impact on the global stage was neither its military might nor its emerging economic superpower status; rather, its most enduring gift to the world was the bequeathing of its rich cultural & spiritual heritage.

The birthplace of the Vedas & Upanishads, likely the oldest spiritual texts, predating the works of Confucius or Lao Tzu; home to the Mahabharata, one of the greatest epics ever written, about the triumph of good over evil; and the land of Bhagvad Gita- the essence of the yoga of Krishna, the multifaceted epitome of the fountainhead of divinity, to Arjuna the warrior, in his moment of deepest reluctance & questions- highlighting the ephemeral nature of life & relationships, and the true nature of divinity & karma- *timeless concepts, as relevant in the modern world as back then...*

Born as the Indus valley civilization, the terms India & Hindu emerged from it etymologically. But India was never a homogenous entity; rather, it was an emerging spirit, a perpetual aggregation & seamless assimilation of diverse cultural & spiritual traditions over the millennia.

While the land itself was the cradle of many a world religion like Hinduism, Buddhism, Jainism & Sikhism, beyond all these 'isms' of organized religion, the common thread was an underlying quest to explore the nature of the Universe, with each master bestowing his own unique gift as incremental, not substitutive to the beliefs of this land.

Therefore, till date, India's real strength, its inherent character, lay in its diversity, an all encompassing spirit- which saw its disposition morph as each 'outsider' came to this land, to become one with it...

Of course, xenophobes & dinosaurs were, and had been, stuck with their own parochial version of history, suiting their blinkered, exclusivist, even paranoid agendas; but the truth was that India was all these influences put together...

A melting pot whose aroma & flavor arose from its diverse ingredients, not from its exclusivist ideology...

So while Hinduism, rather the vedic religion, was the original pillar of this land, Siddharth Gautam, the Buddha, was born here 2500 years back, forever altering our understanding of the nature of the mind, suffering & freedom from it. Masters like Mahavir, and 2000 years later, Nanak & Kabir, embellished its spiritual treasure in their unique ways, while the Muslims, who came from lands as far as Arabia, Turkey & Persia, made this their home, bringing with them the gift of Sufism.

This eclectic fusion was reflected in its current demographics- home to the largest population of a single religion in any nation of the world, yet secular by constitution; abode of the third largest Muslim population in the world, yet a minority; and housing a miniscule Christian minority, yet boasting of one of the oldest surviving lineages in the Christian world- born in the 1st century AD, when St. Thomas set foot on the shores of East India, founding Christianity in the East, much before there was any trace of it in the West. In fact, unknown to most, India housed one of the only three Basilicas built upon the tombs of the *original apostles*- the other two being the Cathedral of Santiago de Compostela, built over the tomb of St. James, in Spain; and of course, the St Peter's Basilica, the seat of the Vatican!

It was not coincidental that Dave's mysterious journey led him to such an eclectic land...

****

The first part of the tour was largely centered around North India- not much of a Himalayan experience, but exotic nonetheless- India had a lot of beauty & richness to offer.

And much more...

The tour kicked off with a visit to Agra, home to the beautiful Taj Mahal. In spite of having heard & seen so much of the Taj on the net & on television, seeing one of the seven wonders of the new world in person was a different experience altogether. Indescribable in words...

Love immortalized in marble...a work of ultimate craftsmanship, chiseled in pure, hard marble...

An overwhelmed Dave couldn't help but feel a lump in his throat on seeing the tomb of Shahjahan's beloved wife, Mumtaz, in whose memory the emperor built this mausoleum-The ultimate, timeless tribute to love...

Love revisited through the centuries & cultures...

The evening ended on a high note, as the group enjoyed a special fusion concert with a moonlit Taj in the backdrop. The whole thing was as close to divine as humanly possible- *ethereal ambience, elevating fusion of Indian Classical & deep bass, marble glittering in the soft light, various hues of love...*

Oh love- *the most powerful & profound emotion in the Universe...and also the most painful...*

Professed by all, but understood by few...not from the outer to inner, from overflowing from within...

Neither about the object nor subject, but a surrender, absolute & abject...

On this glorious evening, Dave felt deeply euphoric, ecstatic as well as anguished- the air reverberated of love through the centuries...

Of Shahjahan & Mumtaz...of Dave & Shakti...

How badly he wanted to meet her once, to tell her about his true feelings...to show her how he was a transformed man...and how he had finally found solace & wisdom in her path...

But alas, they were separated by space & time...life & death...

****

From Agra, the tour proceeded to Rajasthan, the land of the Maharajas. An arid belt in the northwest of India, this was home to several princely states in pre-independence era, and some of the bravest warrior clans, most notably the Rajputs. It is said that the soil of this land had the fragrance of blood & valour of the fiercely self respecting Rajputs, for whom nothing mattered more than honor. For over a millennium, the history of India was rendered rich with tales of Rajput valor, loyalty & color.

Post the independence of India in 1947, all these princely domains were merged with the newly established republic. For a while, the maharajas got privy purses from the federal government, but in the 1970s, this too was abolished. Faced with the prospect of either forfeiting their palaces & estates, or making them self sustaining, several maharajas turned enterprising, thereby spawning probably the largest & most lavish assortment of palace resorts anywhere in the world.

Dave felt fortunate to experience this awesome blend of history & tradition- heritage retrofitted with modern comforts to make guests literally feel like royalty- the vicarious thrill of sleeping on the same bed that a Maharaja once lounged on, dining in the same hall that once hosted imperial feasts, and strolling across the same courtyard where the Maharaja once held his 'durbar'- across Jaipur, Udaipur, Jodhpur.

But his highpoint was the stay in a 16th century fort, converted into a luxury, heritage 'UNHOTEL'. Like a victorious knight returning from battle, seeking refuge, yet readying for another epic battle, this fort provided the perfect context to Dave's visit: reminding him that beyond the lounge by the pool, the warrior had to step out of the ramparts in search of his 'special treasure', one that had proved elusive so far. But for the valiant, adventurous & faithful, the treasure was eventually bound to be uncovered...

This 'unhotel' also gave him another perspective, a professional one- the place was class & simplicity combined with authenticity, attracting several offbeat travelers, both westerners & Indians, who preferred to shun 5-star luxuries in favor of a heritage, rustic & eco-sensitive experience.

The marketer in Dave instantly perked up at this opportunity- set up a chain of rustic, eco-friendly, heritage 'Unhotels'? A growing market, a nascent industry at the early stage of the S-curve...

After the knight, it was time for the 'king', literally. From Royal India, the tour proceeded to 'wild India'- an Indian safari in Ranthambhore National park, one of the many national parks created by the Indian Government as part of a conservation drive: project tiger. Rendered famous by National Geographic documentaries, this national park offered the thrill of yet another treasure hunt- the search of the elusive king, who chose to appear only as he pleased, wandering around his territory with gay abandon, stamping his authority when he left- the pugmark serving as a reminder of his clout.

Dave was lucky to see a tiger in both his safaris. The lord of all that he surveyed, the tiger was truly a majestic sight to behold, a beast who stood neither in awe, nor fear of humans, or their jeeps & canters- this was tiger territory, and whether he chose to cross the tracks, or simply wander off higher into the mountains, was purely his own regal choice...

****

So far, the going was good- fun, relaxation & nature- just what he needed. But no sign of anything related to the 'clues'...

Dave, however, was alert, ready to feed his mind & soul with new information. Thankfully, all that he was fed so far were the spicy Indian delicacies of biryani, kebabs & tandoori chicken! *Food for the mind & soul would have to wait...*

****

After ten days came the last leg of the north India tour- a visit to 'paradise on earth', the northernmost state of Jammu & Kashmir. The group was scheduled to travel by road to the capital- Delhi, a five hour drive from Jaipur, and from there, fly to Srinagar, the picturesque capital of the Kashmir valley.

The covey set out, along with the local guide, in a luxury coach, ready to take in the sights of both urban & rural India along the national highway connecting Jaipur to Delhi. However, barely had they proceeded for fifteen minutes, when the bus suddenly came to a screeching halt- a flat tyre! Not quite expected from a brand new looking Volvo!

Dave and his fellow passengers disembarked grudgingly, some worried about missing their flight, others simply grumpy at having been rudely woken up from a nascent afternoon siesta.

Sensing the mood, the guide tried to lift their sagging spirits by excitedly announcing that it was quite a coincidence for the bus to stop at this exact spot- *they were just a 100 meters away from one of Jaipur's most famous landmarks: Jantar Mantar- or literally, the calculation instruments...*

While they could not make it to this fascinating location during the course of their regular itinerary, this was a fortuitous event that allowed them yet another opportunity to get a glimpse into the India of yore- a great blend of science & spirit-the harmonious coexistence of Aryabhatta & Patanjali...

Not exactly enthused by the pronouncements of the guide, the group entered the complex rather drearily. However, what they saw instantly captivated them. A huge complex of astronomical structures of all shapes & sizes, it was like a peek into the gizmos of earlier times, their sheer scale & diversity enough to astound even the most skeptical & hardened of tourists. As the suddenly awake & alert group followed the guide like mice marching to the beat of pied piper, Dave was enchanted by the striking combination of diverse geometric forms, their grandeur and precision engineering, and the undercurrent of symmetry that pervaded this place.

The guide explained that there were five Jantar Mantars built in India, of which this was the most famous & significant. Built between 1727 & 1734 by Maharaja Jai Singh II, both out of his love for astronomy, as much as a dedication to the Mughal rulers of Delhi, the observatory consisted of fourteen major geometric devices for measuring time, predicting eclipses, tracking stars in their orbits, ascertaining the declinations of planets, and determining the celestial altitudes and related ephemerides.

But the piece-de-resistance was the *'Samrat Yantra'*, or the king of instruments- a 90 feet high sundial, the largest in the world! It's massive scale was configured to offer a 1mm per second movement of the shadow cast upon it, allowing for an accurate determination of time.

As Dave stood there, watching the shadow move roughly a hand's breath every minute, he sensed that it was trying to tell something...

Indicate something...something which he was unable to fathom just yet!

On their flight from Delhi to Srinagar, Dave read about their heavenly destination. Literally the 'crown' of India, the beautiful valley of Kashmir was once the favorite summer holiday destination for the maharajas, and later the British officers of undivided India. But for the past 60 years, this 'Switzerland of the east' became the bloody playground of a territorial dispute between the carved out nations of India & Pakistan, the most bitter legacy of the sub-continent's partition.

Roiled in sixty years of bloodshed & strife, this conflict spared no one- India, Pakistan, or the local population. While the local Muslim populace lost their lives & livelihood to the brutalities & excesses of the armed forces, the ethnic Hindu pundit community was forced to flee from their homes & neighbors, targets of a vicious ethnic cleansing campaign at the hands of fundamentalist militants. Centuries of amity, fostered by a liberal & tolerant Sufi tradition, lay torn to shreds.

Once a beacon for communal harmony, Kashmir was now a sore spot, a classic case of misguided, dogmatic viewpoints fighting for a piece of land, but caring nothing about those who inhabited this land, or its culture.

Why do humans still fight? Why can't we respect diversity? After all these centuries, why can't we talk to resolve issues?

Dave was always angered by conflicts, especially the ones that he thought were foisted by politicians & vested interests on the gullible masses. Here, he was witnessing another case, a paradise turned into hell. Silently he prayed that peace & amity would return to the valley, that rapture would be restored…

His prayer & actions would help…

Dave's anger, however, completely dissolved as soon as he checked into a luxurious hotel overlooking the Dal lake, with great views of lush pine & apple trees from his balcony. And his emotions turned to pure exhilaration when came the ultimate Kashmiri fare- a night in a beautiful boat house, the Shikara- the placid waters shimmering under a moonlit sky connecting him with the beauty of creation. Feeling like he was floating in the clouds, Dave slept deeply, and woke up refreshed the next day morning. *Later than usual, but it didn't matter*…At 7 am, he could still catch the sunrise from the deck of his boat, sipping hot Kashmiri *'kahwa*. After all, it mid December-17th to be precise, so it was only natural that the nights were getting longer;

They were approaching the winter solstice in the northern hemisphere...
At that time, this meant nothing except the opportunity to catch a late sunrise. But it would mean a lot pretty soon...

****

Kashmir was followed by yet another Himalayan fare- one of the most exotic, yet unexplored parts of the subcontinent- North eastern India, along with the surrounding nations of Tibet, Bhutan & Nepal- pristine lands with deep spiritual & mystical tradition; the lands of mountains & monasteries, exotic flora & fauna, and *paradoxically, home to the 'happiest' nation, as well as some of the bloodiest conflicts & repression in the world.* Yet, they were bound by a common sacred thread- *the majestic Himalayas-* the holy mountains…the bulwark…

Two out of the three highest Himalayan peaks lay in this region- Mount Everest & Kanchenzhonga. *This was where he was being guided, he sensed. For what, he hoped to know soon…Dave was alert as he was ecstatic…*

****

The first day's stay in Gangtok was relaxed & easy paced, allowing the tourists to explore this small, but modern capital of the North Eastern state of Sikkim. Little hotels & guest houses dotted the landscape, prayers flags in a multitude of colors fluttered in the gentle breeze, and roadside stalls offered Tibetan tea, steamed momos & 'Alu dum' to the weary travelers.

Situated at an altitude of about 6000 feet, the town had an old world charm, yet modern stores were sprinkled in the main market. Selling everything from Tibetan thangkas to Nike & Reebok, these stores embodied the juxtaposing of the modern & the traditional, the branded & the heritage. On either side of the town, the mighty Himalayan ranges guarded the valley like sentinels, while the pristine Teesta river flowed at the bottom, a constant companion to gargantuan sentries, as both complemented each other in the circle of life-*the mountain snow feeding the river, and the river nourishing life in the towns & valleys…*

Yin & Yang…origination & sustenance….

The state itself was tiny, but stunningly beautiful, and blessed with a large variety of flora & fauna. The eastern part was where the majority of the population resided, while the north & west beckoned the more adventurous traveler, being richer in natural beauty, but more remote & inhospitable.

The state's population was a blend of the ethnic tribes, primarily Bhutias, along with the Nepalese & Tibetan races, seamlessly integrated with each other- caste identities juxtaposed effortlessly with a common 'hill' identity to create a shared sense of culture & history.

After all, the Himalayas towered, literally & figuratively, over any petty differences...

As Dave thought about the contrasts between this part of the Himalayas and Kashmir, he couldn't help but feel a deep sense of irony- in one case, diversity contributed to tearing apart centuries of amity, while in the other, diverse groups came together to form a common, new identity.

Why should similar circumstances lead to two such different situations? Wisdom would bless him with answers along the journey...

A short drive away from the capital Gangtok was the popular Changu, or Tsomgo lake, a famous tourist attraction, especially in winter, when the lake froze. Another hour or so away, at an altitude of 14,000 feet was the Nathu-la pass, the Indo-Tibet border. *The entire stretch was the historical silk route, offering the tourist a glimpse into millennia of history of two of the oldest civilizations..*

Dave & the group were put up in a comfortable, 100 year old heritage hotel, which once served as a guest house- first for the Namgyal dynasty- the Chogyals of Sikkim, and then for British officers. Exotic paintings & murals adorned the walls & ceilings, narrating stories of the Buddha, Guru Rimpoche-the patron saint of this part, and the Chogyals themselves. However, the big draw was the panoramic view of the Kanchendzonga from every room, just across a soccer ground, where the budding Peles & Maradonas of India trained.

While Everest dominated the 20th century traveler's & adventurer's consciousness, Mt. Kanchendzonga, the third highest peak in the world, was the most revered in these parts, practically a guardian deity...

The guardian deity was blessing him...

20ᵀᴴ DEC 2000

It was biting cold on the morning of 20th, when the entourage left for a visit to the Rumtek monastery, at the outskirts of Gangtok. Even in the land of Monasteries, this one occupied a special place...

The tour guide explained that apart from its beauty & wealth, Rumtek monastery had a rich history- it was the seat of the Karmapa, a much revered figure in Tibetan Buddhism, and the head of the karma kagyu sect. Derived from a Sanskrit expression meaning 'the one who functions as a manifestation of Buddha-activity', the karma pa was appointed by senior Lamas, notably Shamar Rimpoche, and anointed by the Dalai Lama himself, occupying central place in the spiritual life of the local populace, all the way down to the 16th Karmapa.

However, the monastery was currently roiled in a succession dispute, with three rival 'Karmapas' staking their claim- One blessed by the Dalai Lama, one recognized by the Shamar Rimpoche, and one supported by another ethnic group. Marred by intermitted conflicts between the supporters of these three, the monastery was taken over by the Indian government, and secured by the Indo-Tibetan police force.

As Dave entered the monastery, he was impressed by its beauty & design- it was a huge complex housing the actual pagoda, the prayer halls & stupa, the sanctum sanctorum, dormitories and the Nalanda University- an accredited university for advanced studies in Buddhism.

Bright reds & yellows encrusted the brick & woodwork of the entire complex, while exotic frescos & thangkas adorned almost every wall, column & ceiling. A rich tapestry of statues, be they of the historical Buddha, Guru Rimpoche or Maitreya Buddha, blessed the resident faithful & the curious visitor alike. In essence, the complex was resplendent with colors, chants & soothing energies.

Initially the group was together, savoring the grandeur of the pagoda, and later the sanctum sanctorum- the inner sanctum housing various relics of the Karmapas through the ages, including the legendary 'black hat or crown' of the Karmapa, used to anoint him. The guide explained that whoever would see the Karmapa wearing his black crown, even in an image or photograph, would be blessed.

After a while though, they scattered, with some interacting with the monks, others spending time in the sanctum, while yet others setting off to gain 'good karmas' by rotating the prayer wheels. Dave, meanwhile, meandered to the rear, where the Nalanda university stood- a pet project of the 16th Karmapa, for creating a centre of learning for Buddhist traditions.

As Dave was admiring this structure, a monk walked up to him, apparently from nowhere.

Nothing unusual about that, since the dormitory of the resident monks was nearby, except that Dave didn't notice him coming. What was unusual, however, was that he was not dressed in the typical red & yellow robes of the monastic order, but had a flowing white robe.

Moreover, he didn't have any woolens on, even in near freezing temperature. And was walking barefoot on the cold, jagged ground, without the slightest hint of any discomfiture.

Dave also noticed that this monk did not have a shaved head like the other monks, but had lustrous black hair.

But before he could react, or even offer his salutations, the monk abruptly handed over what seemed like a small player, much like an i-pod, along with a headset...

Dave was taken aback by this, but before he could realise what was happening, the monk started conversing in broken, accented English-a typical oriental accent. "You have come till here, guided by dream & gift. Now you find peak to make the leap..."

"The dream? gift? You know about the gift?!!" Dave blurted out. *He thought the monk was alluding to his past, but was equally surprised that he actually mentioned the peak.*

The monk ignored the question."Tomorrow, visit Monastery of disappearing Lama, *via the pass*. Over there, you find big pagoda in the centre- *on either side of pagoda, there be 36 prayer wheel of different height, in straight line from west to east*. This is 600 year old configuration, made by founding Lama, with utmost precision. Man of science & spirituality in equal part, founding Lama understand astronomy much before Galileo discover telescope. *Special knowledge...*"

Wait a minute- did he just mention Galileo? Astronomy? And something about 'special knowledge'...

The monk continued, unmindful of Dave's surprised expressions. "Every day, for past 600 years, with sun rise, tip of pagoda cast shadow on successive prayer wheels, one at a time- from west to east. In first half of day, when sun rising, this shadow move from 1st to 36th wheel till noon. At noon, sun directly overhead pagoda, so no shadow. And then, shadow move to other side, from 37th to 72nd wheel, till sundown."

"You follow?" the monk asked rhetorically. Dave stared blankly, as if immobilized, dazed & confused...

The monk continued, nonetheless. "This happen every day, and monks pray at the wheel on which shadow fall, moving with the shadow. Each shadow last for 10 minutes, so this give monks discipline to chant & meditate. At same time, it also tell them position of sun; very useful as sundial & astronomical tool, before modern clock invented."

A pagoda & prayer wheels as an ancient sundial? And a sundial yet again, after their 'accidental' stopover at Jantar Mantar? This was no coincidence- and was becoming more & more intriguing...

"As I say before, this happen every day- *except once in 12 years*." the monk suddenly became more circumspect. "On this special day, strange celestial phenomenon happen..."

Dave was virtually on the edge now. *Yes, he was expecting some more clues, maybe some hint of the Messenger- but here he was, being told about a strange solar phenomenon by a mystery monk appearing out of nowhere.*

The questions came back to besiege Dave at frenetic pace- *was **He** the Messenger that his quest was leading to? If so, what was the leap he referred to? And why did he give him another 'object'?*

What was the message in this strange astronomical story?

Some of the answers would come in the monk's subsequent words.

"When you reach monastery, open your heart and move with prayer wheels, praying with all your faith. Keep moving. Do not wonder or worry- simply be at wheel, praying, *feeling the Buddha inside you. The gift is with you... within you...*"

Dave smiled as he remembered his wisdom about the gift.

There was a brief silence, after which the monk looked at Dave straight in the eye, and raised his pitch, although lowering his voice, as if telling him a secret. "You have come here at *right time...*" emphasizing the last two words.

"*Tomorrow is day of this special configuration*...once in 12 years!! That's why you need to go there tomorrow."

Dave was taken aback! The circumstance leading to the India trip was repeating itself, thrusting him in the midst of something he had to participate in immediately. Nonetheless, he maintained his calm by breathing in the mountain air deeply.

"If you missed this, the next cycle come only after 12 years! *Good you follow the clues...and be aware of meaningful coincidences...*"

Dave soaked in these words- *meaningful coincidences...*
There were so many which connected his strange dreams to a special day...once in 12 years...which was tomorrow! *Last seat on an India bound tour, as a replacement for an Italy tour that got cancelled at the last moment...coinciding with the Himalayan images & the clues of the disk...*

And then, as if revealing a long lost secret, the Lama finally whispered. "Tomorrow is 49th time this special day come after monastery was established- last cycle before 50th time- a sacred day. 300 years back, the flying lama- head lama at that time- went to forest on this very day...the 25th special day...

It is exactly 24 cycle after that incident tomorrow...second last cycle before *the day...it is as if Flying Lama bless you...*"

The monk winked at the last statement, a mischievous twinkle in his eyes, and without another word, walked off. Before Dave could assimilate all of it, or ask him any further questions, the monk had already disappeared...

Seemingly into the same nothingness that he came from...

7. THE GETAWAY 'GATEWAY'

On reaching back at the hotel, a dazed but composed Dave sat in the lobby for a while, watching the huge stone fireplace crackle, casting a golden light on the library nearby. He reflected upon this latest incident, and all the incongruous pieces- a monk who was different from the others in the monastery, a 600 year old secret revealed to him, a strange celestial configuration, and him in the middle of it all...

Just when he was expecting clarity in his quest for the Messenger, yet another mystery presented itself...

After a brief contemplation, he gathered that there was nothing better than getting a local perspective- so he took his guide aside and casually asked him about the monastery of the disappearing lama, taking care not to appear overtly suspicious or excited.

"Oh that?!" The guide seemed surprised. Not many enquired about a remote monastery, which was hardly a tourist draw. "It's a beautiful but small, 600 year old monastery, about 150 miles off Lhasa, near Xigaze. Built at an altitude of 14,000 feet, it is quite remote to be a popular tourist spot."

"Did you say Lhasa? You mean, *Tibet*?!" Dave seemed slightly taken aback. "I thought this was somewhere close by."

"Well, sir, actually it is not that far away from here- about 150 miles, through the ancient silk route; via the Tsomgo lake, and then into Tibet via the historic Nathula pass; just about a five hour drive."

"Nathula *Pass*..."Dave played out in his head.

Via the pass? Hmn...and I do have a valid visa...

Well, it seems we are back in business!

"So tell me more about the monastery." Dave queried further, realizing that his visit actually seemed feasible, as implausible as the context. He wanted to understand what was so special about this place.

"Nothing much to see except an ornately maintained pagoda & 72 intricately designed prayer wheels, strangely, of varying heights. Some say it is related to a celestial configuration, though most believe it to be nothing more than yet another intriguing tale. The story also has it that the founding Lama was quite an astronomical scholar, hence he built this complex on some principles of astronomy."

"What celestial configuration?"

"Forget it, sir. Different monks have different versions, so it's most likely just another yarn spun- you see, in a mystical land, you will find many such mythical stories." He smiled.

"However, since the monastery is not that far away from Tsomgo lake and Nathu La pass, some curious tourists do venture there, fascinated by the legend. En route, with a slight detour, they also get to see another mystical lake, Khecheopalri- a body of water that supposedly doesn't have any leaves floating on it, even though it is in the middle of a forest.

For the adventurous types, serves well- multiple mystical sites in a single trip- viable from time & cost perspective."

"What legend?" Dave pushed further, still trying to appearing to casual. but with increasing difficulty.

"I see you are bitten by the bug." the guide smiled. "The legend is the kind of stuff that tourists find equally fascinating and incomprehensible- it says that about 300 years ago, a new grand lama was appointed on a special day. This Lama supposedly developed special powers, including the ability to levitate, thanks to years of meditation, Yoga & mastery in tantric sciences. That's why he is also called the flying Lama."

"Flying Lama?"

"Yes sir, the ability to raise one's kundalini to counteract gravity- supposed to come only to the evolved..."

"Kundalini?"

"Simply put, the latent energy present in human beings, residing at the base of the spine."

"And...?"

"Then, on another special day, 12 years after he was appointed, the flying lama went to the forest surrounding the monastery, & disappeared- supposedly at mid day."

"Disappeared as in?"

"Disappeared...vanished!! That's why the monastery is also called the monastery of the disappearing Lama. The other Lamas & monks searched long & hard, but in vain. The matter was then brought to the attention of the Chogyal king of Sikkim, who had the whole forest searched by the royal guards, for over a week- 200 guards searched every & corner of the forest, but not a trace was found- no body, not bones, not even shreds of cloth.

Finally, just as it was assumed that the Lama was dead- either killed by a wild animal, or having fallen off one of the steep cliffs- he supposedly appeared to his favorite disciple; just another ordinary monk, not very high up in the hierarchy of the monastery."

"Appeared?"

"This is in the realms of myths & legends, Mr. Jones- so no one really knows what this 'appearance' means- some interpret it as an apparition, some as a ghost, some as spirit, and some as just a hoax. However, as per the legend, the Grand Lama supposedly told this disciple a secret- *a promise to appear around the chosen day, to guide those with a pure heart:*

'When long & dark is the night,
Fleeting is the light,
The pure one shall experience higher guidance
In the eye of the storm, guided by providence...'

"Jeez!" Dave muttered under his breath, now understanding who it was who appeared to him.

The 'flying lama' had appeared around the chosen day, to guide the one with a pure heart. His dream & journey had now placed him at the centre of a 300 year old legend-and not as an observer, but a participant!

"What?" a surprised guide asked.

"No, nothing. The whole thing sounds so surreal, that's all." Dave labored to not look shocked.

"Ah yes, to the western mind, all this sounds, well, illogical, unscientific…irrational…Yes, that's the word- irrational.

But there are many mysteries in our world, which cannot be explained, Mr. Jones." He smiled, his eastern grounding coming to the fore.

Tell me about unexplained phenomena, Dave bit his lips...

The guide continued the story. "Most of the other lamas & monks at that time were skeptical about this claim, and they actually expelled this disciple for spreading rumors & canards-they felt that if the Grand Lama had to communicate about his reincarnation, he would have given signals to the higher ranking monks, not some lowly initiate in the hierarchy. However, a select few did believe in this story, and secretly concurred with the initiate- they felt it was the Lama's prerogative to appear to whoever he felt was of 'pure heart'. To this day, a select group of lamas consider this day holy, & revere it. They also believe that a special soul of 'pure heart' is destined to come here, and that the flying lama would manifest himself to this soul…"

Special soul of pure heart? Dave wondered if he indeed fitted the bill...

"Has anybody seen this lama after that?"

"Many locals & tourists have attempted to see the lama, but without success. After all, the legend has it that the lama appears to only those with whom he wants to share something... you cannot seek the lama-he seeks the ones of 'pure heart…'"

After some more polite conversation, Dave thanked the guide and wished him good night. But instead of retiring to his room, he sat in the stepped lawns of the resort. On one side was sheer darkness, with the moonlight scarcely revealing the silhouettes of the grand mountains, while on the other were the lights of the town- shimmering like stars in an unblemished sky. Darkness & shadows one side, twinkling light on the other, and Dave in between…*metaphorically and literally…*

In a few hours from now, these very silhouettes would be awash in the hues of orange & golden, revealing their full glory. Similarly, maybe some glorious secrets lay just beyond the silhouettes in his life too…

Year 2000: December 21ST Winter Solstice
(when long & dark is the night, fleeting is the light...)

Dave reached the monastery by about 10 am, well in time for the mid-day phenomenon. *And the path to here had been predictably mysterious...*

Deep into the previous night, Dave finally woke up from his fitful sleep in the lawn, and groggily walked across to the duty manager, requesting him to inform the guide that he would skip the next day's tour.

"Actually sir, *today's* tour." The manager corrected him, politely glancing at his watch. It was 3 am.

"Whatever..." Dave ignored his warped sense of time. "And please arrange a car for me at 5 am *today*, to drive me to the Monastery of the flying Lama, near Xigaze."

The duty manager tried to ignore the sarcasm. "But sir, it is very late to contact the travel desk now, and all available cars have already been booked. I can only contact them at 6 am at the earliest- which means that, at best, a vehicle can reach you by 8 am. And you are talking about Xigaze, which is beyond Nathu La pass; so I would need to arrange a vehicle with due border permit."

"Don't worry." Dave winked. "There will be a cancellation, and a car will be available before 5 am! Just make sure to wake me up at 4:30. Not that I'll get much sleep anyways..." He said, turning back before the bewildered manager could protest.

And sure enough, there was a vehicle at 5 am!

What, where, how, didn't matter now- all that mattered was to reach the monastery...

****

The five hour long drive was beautiful, taking him through some of the most pristine & scenic parts of the Himalaya in Sikkim, and beyond it, to the mystical land of Tibet, via the oldest trade route between India & China- the silk route...

Along the way, he got an opportunity to witness the 'miracle' of lake Khecheopalri- situated in a dense forest, it was part of the 'Demazong'- a valley of rice often referred to as the land of hidden treasures. Surrounded by a dense tree cover & foliage on all sides, its very presence exuded divinity...

Holy water, Dave thought, as he recollected various legends & traditions- *the Ganges, the holy spring in Mecca, Nile, Amazon...* holy water which nourished life, healed, blessed...

Water, which was so central to human life & soul...

Then he noticed why the Lake was considered holy- *inspite of trees all around it, there was apparently not a trace of a leaf floating on its blessed waters.* Blessings of the vanishing Lama, some said...

Today, it seemed, the lake was blessing him....

After coming back on the trail, he crossed the frozen Tsomgo lake at an altitude of 12,500 feet- a sight to behold, with Yaks gliding on the lake as if they were on terra firma.

A short drive away, through the full glory of the Himalayas, he arrived at the Indo-China border- the Nathu La pass, at an altitude of 14,000 feet. The weather was freezing cold, but fortunately, the rising sun cast its rays on the mountain trail, allowing the early morning travelers a free passage. Dave was at the border post prior to 7 am, and before the weather turned inclement, his vehicle was cruising inside Tibet, driving northwards towards Xigaze.

Xigaze, or Shigatse, was the second largest city in the Tibetan Autonomous region, the administrative centre of Xigaze county. It's landmark was the Shigatse or Samdrubtse Dzong, a miniature version of the Potala palace in Lhasa, the seat of the Dalai Lama before the Chinese invasion. If Lhasa, the capital, was the Dalai Lama's domain, Xigaze was the traditional seat of the Panchem Lama- the second highest ranking Lama in Gelugpa Buddhism.

Dave's quest, however, was for neither the glorious Potala Palace, nor the historical Samdrubtse Dzong, but the nondescript monastery of the flying Lama. After referring to the map a couple of times, his car clambered onto the *rocky path* to the Monastery.

Rocky path, he smiled at the play of words- literally yes, it was a rocky road to his destination...figuratively though, time would tell...

With the weather not playing truant, he was at the monastery by 11 am, well in time before the *supposed noon phenomenon...*

Dave noticed that the monastery itself was as simple & modest as could be- no signs of grandeur, no intricate architecture or exotic artwork; nothing to suggest anything out of the ordinary- *except the central pagoda & the 72 prayer wheels, precisely arranged along the East-West axis.*

To the untrained eye, there was nothing special about the pagoda & prayer wheels too- all monasteries had it, several more elaborate & grander. But what set it apart was its configuration & the resultant astronomical significance- *an ancient, closely guarded secret..*

The pagoda was of moderate height, but the 36 prayer wheels on either side varied in height, from twice as tall as the pagoda at the farthest ends, to very short, just next to the pagoda… almost as if the whole thing was graded…

An ancient sundial, and a precise one at that, Dave smiled; not to mention the secret of the shadows, which happened only once in 12 years… **Today was that day!**

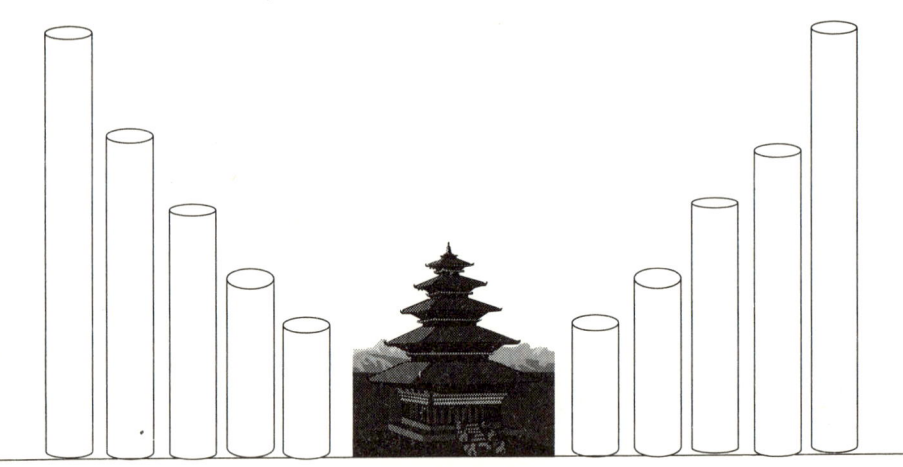

Representative illustration, depicting 36 prayer wheels on either side, of graded height

Dave spent some time casually browsing around, not to appear overly suspicious or strange. But there was a heightened sense of anticipation; till now, one clue had led to another, each propelling him further into the realms of the unknown, the surreal. *Is this where it would all culminate? Would he finally find the Messenger here?*

After a while, he finally did as instructed, going along with the prayer wheels, rotating them, praying. Even then, nobody seemed to notice much. After all, he was just another of those curious foreign tourists.

Initially, the shadow moved normally from one prayer wheel to another in a sequence, at regular intervals- at each wheel, the shadow lasted for roughly ten minutes, as the monks prayed accordingly. From sunrise, it moved from 1st to 35th wheel till almost noon- and just before sun came overhead in sky, the shadow reached 36th wheel, which was normal...

But instead of disappearing at noon, and then reappearing at 37th wheel on the other side of pagoda, the shadow remained static at 36th wheel, not moving forward, even though the sun crossed over to the other side. This was the strange celestial phenomenon referred to by the mysterious monk, not fully understood even by the resident monks!

Amazed at what he was witnessing, the image of the monk flashed in his head, as if guiding him further: *'Even though shadow not move at all, you keep praying...know that 36th wheel is special, but only to those with pure heart...this wheel blessed by Lama himself, so that on this one day, sun send special energies. And 36th wheel retain special solar energy within, amplifying it- therefore, shadow not move forward...'*

For what seemed like a long time, the shadow was standstill. And then, after an hour, the shadow moved northwards, instead of eastwards. *Into a forest at the edge of the complex...*

Again, the vision of the monk appeared: "After exactly an hour, shadow finally move. Not towards the next prayer wheel, *but towards north*...to forest north of monastery. Follow shadow as it guide you into forest. Allow higher energy to guide you, keeping negative emotions away- no skepticism & anxiety. Inside forest too, shadow move as it guide you, till it stop at a point. Once you reach this point, *connect your disk* to this player. After that, you will be guided...*and find gateway*..."

Keeping bouts of incredulity at bay and continuing to mutter his prayer, Dave followed the shadow into the forest. Just a few hundred meters before the edge where the forest sloped steeply into a valley, the shadow disappeared suddenly, abruptly...

As Dave vaguely wondered about what exactly was happening, a special celestial phenomenon was playing itself out at this very moment- the shadow had a special significance, being the shadow of the sun on a day when it was up for the shortest period in the year- THE WINTER SOLSTICE!

And here today, on this special day, the shadow followed a rather strange path...

****

Once in the forest, it was time to connect the disk to the player. *As soon as he did that, he began to hear, or rather feel, 'spatial sounds'...*

First came the deep chants of 'Aum', vibrations so powerful that it shook at his very core. **Aaa...Uuuu...mmmmmmm**... *the amplitude rising with each chant...*

As Dave began 'vibrating', literally shaking, he felt another high energy- that of 'Allahu Allahu'. As the tempo & pitch increased, he started whirling spontaneously, arms outstretched, much like a Sufi in a trance...a whirling dervish...

For a while, it was all **La ilaha Illallah...**

Along came the mystical Gregorian chants- sounds from afar, sounds of the universe... in his whirling state, Dave could feel himself reaching 'out'...expanding...

As if the whirling was 'throwing' him out from within'...

As the trance intensified, Dave started 'sensing' swirling images of stars & galaxies along with these spatial sounds. The whole experience seemed like a 4-dimensional (or maybe more) rendition of the Universe...*a merging of senses... synaethesia...*

Along with these visions, the colors & images, both within & outside, became more radiant, surrounded by white-amber hues...the sounds became more expanded...it was almost as if there were an energy storm all around him, with him in *the eye of the storm...*

Witnessing the storm....

Then, he felt a strange sensation at the base of his spine, as if heat was moving up it- starting as warmth, intensifying, literally becoming hot on reaching the base of the skull. His breathing became lighter, and his eyes rolled up, focusing on the 'brightness' in the 'gap between the eyes'...

As the 'strange sensation' (as he would call it later, in the absence of a more suitable adjective) reached the top of the crown, the light between his eyes became exponentially brighter. All this while, he continued to whirl, arms spread outwards- the trance intensifying, the vibrations of the sounds merging with his energy centers.

And then, as if completing the 'circuit', the heat radiated outwards from his hands & crown in all directions...

The Universe & Dave were now in a divine communion, *an exchange that he would understand later...*

For a few minutes, this energy flow continued, leaving him in utter bliss & a feeling of expansion...and then, it got too much for him...

In a flash, Dave passed out!

8. Another time, another place (Or is it?)

"Ow, my head hurts", Dave groaned as he tried to get up. His head was hurting at the crown, and felt warm at the top. As he lifted his head, he could see a stranger across the room- a tall, beautiful, radiant lady, smiling at him! She had a lovely face, thick, lustrous, straight black hair, a well proportioned physique, and dressed in a black skirt along with a lycra top. Dave just looked at her blankly, and then looked down. H*e felt that he was floating in mid air, on a bed which itself seemed to be suspended without any support...*

What happened? I was expanding, and there was light & heat, the energy surge...yes, it was a surge towards the end, seemingly too much to handle; then, something happened, and I blacked out...

But he sensed that this was different from the passing out on the night of the UFO experience- not only did he get a sense of the UFO night's events, he also felt the most 'amazing, indescribable sense of calm- eternal calm, and a connection with the whole', if just for a brief while...

And he did remember all the 'sensations' just before the 'black out' with clarity...

So just where & what was this? Not another hospital, he hoped. *Definitely not a normal hospital, if one...*

The place seemed like an apartment high up somewhere (this was something he could make out from the views beyond the transparent walls; and, as he was to realize later, the walls were transparent inside out, but not so outside in).

He was in a huge circular room with supposedly transparent walls and ceiling. The room itself was rather minimalistic, but had a futuristic design- a large semi-circular couch was placed at the far wall, while one wall seemed to alternate between transparent glass and a plasma screen, displaying various images.

There was not much else in terms of furniture, apart from the 'floating bed'. However, there appeared to be some consoles at different points, which seemed like switchboards. The walls seemed to be made of full height glass, offering a panoramic view of the surroundings, while the expansive ceiling gave an atrium like feeling, with skylight pouring in...

The view beyond these 'walls' was absolutely captivating, unlike anything he had seen before! Or even imagined...

On one side were mammoth towers, seemingly 'floating' above the ground. However, unlike other skyscrapers, these mega structures seemed to rise up far above & beyond the horizon, and were arranged in some sort of a network, to form a mini-city; yet, they seemed to be made of a very different, almost gel like material, which seemed to give them a plastic like look along with rubber like flexibility- evident from the way they seemed to sway and change contours...*like giant trees swaying in the breeze...*

Beyond these mega structures, he could see hundreds of small aircrafts, floating & zipping across the sky with amazing precision & harmony. Several of these mini crafts seemed to be entering in & out of these structures, and *in & out of view*...in a rhythm which could put any philharmonic orchestra to shame...

All around, there were amazing lights & displays, like high tech, 3-D laser images- hundreds of illuminated, floating towers, billboards, flying crafts- scenes which seemed straight out of a futuristic, science fiction movie...but unlike the movies, everything here seemed in so much in harmony...

That, though, was only one part of the story- as Dave turned his head the other way, he saw beautiful mountains & streams in the background, in what seemed like a twilight sky.

Ahead of this backdrop, all the way in front till the eye could see, he observed the most beautiful meadows. Strangely, he couldn't recognize the vegetation & flowers- hues of blues, purples, whites, lavenders, pinks, greens- in all kinds shapes & heights, some as tall as midsized trees...this was the most enchanting & radiant display of nature he had witnessed in a long time!

Dave sat there, motionless, soaking in the contrasting beauty from all sides, taking in a deep breath...

Then it hit him that all this was even more abnormal than his experience at the monastery; he was led there in rather mysterious circumstances, and remembered something about the gateway...*but where and what was this?*

"Don't worry, & calm down. The head does feel heavy after such an experience." the lady smiled. Dave smiled back feebly, unsure of any of this...

"I am Ikona, and **you are on the moon,** at one of our urban communes." She spoke in a soft, mellifluous voice.

"What?" Dave blurted, half unsure of what he heard- **the moon...??**

"I was at the monastery, in the forest to the north, experiencing something, er, uplifting...*and then something happened...*" he held his hand to his head, grimacing in pain.

"Yes, that something was that you landed up here, **on the moon**..." she smiled, her lips rose pink.

*There was no mistaking what she said this time...***THE MOON!**

Dave just sat there blankly- *this time he was definitely hallucinating...*

"No, you are not hallucinating my dear. This is as real as the monastery back there on earth...or back then..."

"*Real? Back then*? And how do you know about the monastery?" Dave was still trying to rub his crown.

Ikona moved next to Dave and placed her gentle hands on his head. He instantly felt better...*as if some healing energy entered his crown...*

"Back then means that you are not only in a different place, but also a different **time...** you are on a **different plane**.."

"*Different plane?!!"* he stared blankly at her beautiful face.

*"Different coordinates in space & time. On your very own satellite, the moon, in a different age- **the 25th century**, as per your calendar..."*

What was all this? 25th century..!! Moon! 'Your calendar'! He wanted to just run away...but was feeling too frail to even get up, let alone go anywhere...

She stroked her hands gently on his head, with a warmth he had not felt in a quite a while. "I know it is difficult & complex for you to assimilate what I just said, so just calm down & rest for some time. I shall come later.."

A tired, weak & dazed Dave immediately crashed out.

****

Come back later she did- in an hour or so; or at least that's what Dave felt... guessed... his expensive Swiss watch had also conked off at just the right time. *(whatever time it was!).*

However, this time Ikona wasn't alone. The radiant lady was with an equally bright young man, of brown origin-probably Asian- casually dressed in jeans and a tee, that had an image of Kurt Cobain in the front, and an image of 'Om' on the back. That he was good looking was an understatement- tall (close to 7 feet), broad shouldered with sharp, chiseled features, he could win any male supermodel contest...

But it was not his looks alone. The guy had some radiance...

"Hi, I'm Plutus. Welcome to the future, my man." he said with smile that was both genuinely warm & sheepish."Rather, your future...*welcome to the NEW AGES, human...*"

Ikona immediately chided him for his last remark, and handed Dave a drink in a pure white, oddly shaped chalet. "Ignore his cheeky remarks- we aren't exactly some aliens from the future." she smiled. "And here, have this drink- it will build up your energies."

"Even if you *were* aliens, I wouldn't be shocked. By now I am kinda used to that variety." Dave joked, taking his first sip, surprised at his humor in an 'alien situation'!

"OK, so where am I?" he queried, getting serious again. "Who are you? How did I get here? *I remember you mentioning something about the moon and the 23rd century...*"

"25th ." Ikona corrected him. "By your calendar. For us, it is 3rd century NA."

"What do you mean, *my calendar*? So what do you guys follow- *NA*? Tell me honestly, who are you guys?" he asked, taking another sip. "And how the hell is this bed floating? Where really am I?"

"Honestly bro, *you are on the moon, in the 25th century.* A few hours back, you just 'projected' here, immediately zonked off, and have been sleeping ever since." Plutus summarized in his smooth voice.

"Ikona came and checked upon you a few times, but you were still recovering from the 'leap' I guess.."

"Is this supposed to be a joke? And now that I remember, how do you know about the monastery? Who exactly are you guys? Some secret intelligence fellas tracking UFO stuff or something? Is this some special facility?" Dave said falteringly, suddenly feeling anxious. That was the last thing he wanted…

"You've been watching too many of those movies, I bet!" Plutus smiled. "We are no secret intelligence guys, so just relax. Didn't you have an 'uplifting' experience, in your own words? "

"Yeah, but that was supposed to lead me to some, er, Messenger…where and how am I here? This seems, er, *strange…*"

"So, you've not had any strange experiences before this?" Ikona asked softly.

"Yeah, but this *moon thing can't be real!* And this 25th century bit? *This is supposed to be the stuff of science fiction?* Time travel & all that…"

"Science fiction? *What is fiction in one plane can be fact on another…"* Plutus replied rather matter-of-factly.

"I know there were many strange, mysterious, mystical incidents-all of that I understand. But for all my adventures, this one is seems quite out of whack- I mean, this is pure fiction! "

"Ok. Forget fact & fiction for a while- tell us more about your experience just before coming here."

"I was in the monastery, the forest to the north, having an experience which was filling me up…an, er, expansive experience…"

"And?"

"And I felt an energy surge, as if I was getting 'uplifted'.. and then, at some point, I blacked out...don't remember anything after that."

"That expansive experience got you uplifted, teleported, transcended to another plane!" Plutus looked at Dave in the eye. "In other words, you have done a journey across space-time, a transition through a gateway into a higher plane."

Dave continued to look at them, expressionless...

Gateway? The monk had mentioned something about a gateway...but he didn't say anything about space-time travel...

"Now, wait wait wait!" Dave crossed his hands in a time out gesture. "So, I was at the monastery, and I came to the moon in the future, through a gateway? What exactly is this gateway now?"

"Dave, you were at a very high energy spot back in your plane. *That* was the gateway..."

The forest...the monastery of the flying lama...the special day & configuration...that was the high energy gateway?

Some of it was making hazy sense...

"You experienced the surge, but towards the end, it was too much for you to handle, especially since it was probably your first time. That's why you blacked out..."

"Hey, you blacked out during *your first time*?" Plutus winked at him. "What kinda guy are you?"

"Plutus, enough! No more corny stuff." Ikona said in a firm voice. "Dave may not find all this exactly funny, not in his current state."

"No, no, it's OK." Dave said in a staccato voice. Something about their demeanor, their energies, told him that they were friendly- he could sense it...

"Though you blacked out, the energy lift was enough for you to make the transition through the gateway..." She continued. "And after the transition, you landed straight here, at this house."

"Your house?"

"No, actually Plutus' house."

"And I feel happy & fortunate about that. I mean, *not too many people get teleported, transcended, from your plane to ours;* and never heard of a fascinating journey like yours. So, glad to be your host, Dave Jones!" Plutus flashed a warm smile.

There was silence for a while, as Dave looked straight out in the distance, pondering over this new information. This was giving a whole new dimension to the India trip...

When he was guided to India, to the Himalayas, he somewhere believed that this is where his quest would end- with some holy person, some yogi, some wise man- who had special abilities, powers or wisdom...and this Messenger would either come with him, or share some new age wisdom...

But space-time travel!! This is not where he had wildly imagined his quest was leading him, he mumbled incoherently...

"Call it space-time travel, astral travel, quantum jumping or energy transcendence, whatever suits you- the terminology aint important; what's important is the fact is that you are among the rare people on earth who have experienced a psycho-somatic transition..."

"Psycho-somatic transition?" yet another unknown jargon, Dave grimaced.

"Yes, a transition across planes, dimensions. Not merely in the spirit, but the body as well..."

"And mind you, transcending across planes is not a very common phenomenon." Ikona said softly, almost in a whisper. "So *there certainly is a very strong element of synchronicity at work here*...you have very high energies... "

"I know. Have had a sense of being led somewhere, onto something- something beyond ordinary realities...some answers came, some questions remained...all that was OK; but how come I am *here?*"

"*Whatever, wherever* 'this' is.." he added as an afterthought.

"Or *whenever!*" chuckled Plutus.

Dave smiled back. "Yes- wherever, whenever, whatever... and *WHY?*. The big question still remains..."

"*Special questions need special people...*" came an electronic sounding voice from near the entrance. And, out of the blue, appeared another smiling young man- not as tall as Plutus or Ikona, but nearly the same age...

He was bizarrely dressed in a smart silk shirt, a loosened tie, revealing two open buttons, a metallic wraparound on top of lycra pants, and metallic boots. Long, unkempt hair, peculiar glares, and devises on his ears & arms added to the freakish...

As he entered, he removed the outlandish looking glares & arm band, placing it on the table. The arm band beeped softly. After that, he headed straight towards Dave. "Hi, I'm Lyon. Welcome to our world."

"Hey, you came pretty fast! Which means your travel module detected this surge? Good improvisation, I must say." Ikona half jokingly complimented him.

"Of course, my dear." Lyon spoke in what seemed like a pompous, flirty tone. "*What else* do you expect from a network genius?"

Ikona frowned, half in jest. She knew what was coming...

"Accept my proposal, lady, and you shall be the partner of an important Network Administrator, maybe even a future Quartion."

"Modesty, thy name is Lyon!" Ikona waved him away.

"Hey, modesty is just another name for mediocrity."

"Right, future Quartion, sir...any other pearls of wisdom?"

"C'mon Ikona, it's better to be with a future Quartion than with some ordinary energy scientist." came Lyon's wide grin, looking at Plutus from the corner of his eye.

"See, even in the New Ages, simple guys like me lose out to the more successful ones." Plutus joined in the banter. "Some things don't change, irrespective of time or place, do they Dave? Good guys always finish last..."

"Well, not always true." Dave smiled. "Good guys do get their rewards." he said rather instinctively. He also sensed that Lyon was their good friend.

"Rightttto said" Lyon replied grandly. "See, he is already feeling the energies and wisdom of the New Ages..."

"Stop it guys. Dave is still trying to terms with his big leap, so please stop fooling around." Ikona gave a half reprimanding, half smiling look.

"No, it's Ok. It happens between friends." Dave smiled. Their banter seemed to lighten up an otherwise heavy atmosphere. Heavy, at least for Dave...

"Not just friends-best friends! Childhood buddies..."

"Hmn, nice...so what do you guys do? *Just whom am I interacting with on the moon, in the 25th century?* "Dave replied in a tone which smacked of sarcasm, but was more a manifestation of his continued bewilderment.

"Lyon is a brilliant network administrator, and now handles the entire travel sub module. He has just developed a new program which also tracks teleportation. And I must say the program was successful, going by how soon he landed here." Ikona gestured towards Lyon.

"See, she knows how good I am." Lyon gave another sly grin. "My prospects with the lady just went up!"

"Keep fancying your chances... but for now, shut up & let me explain to Dave." Then, looking at Plutus she remarked. "Plutus is an energy scientist with the Central Energy Repository, and has worked on some interesting energy projects."

"And our lady here is an endower at the Zen Holiversity." Plutus smiled, his eyes twinkling while looking at Ikona.

"Actually it owes a lot to lady Zenia. She was a big influence in me choosing this as my dharmic vocation."

Dave was lost in this, er, jargon...*Endower? Zen Holiversity? Central Energy Repository? Travel module?* And which network were they talking about?

"Sorry, we should not be throwing around 'jargons' like this. So, in simpler terms, endower is the equivalent of a teacher in your world. But since she endows wisdom instead of merely teaching, we call her an endower. She who endows knowledge & wisdom is as special as the one who endows life."

"Interesting..."

"As for the Zen Holiversity, it is roughly the equivalent of a University in your plane."

"And the best one at that- say an Oxford or Harvard." Ikona added. "But nothing like your Universities. As the name suggests, it is a 'holistic University'. So, the Zen Holiversity is a place of holistic learning, which awakens the Zen within."

"This sounds more like a theological school or an institute of philosophy, rather than an advanced University."

"Don't be mistaken- it has the most advanced curriculum across streams; but the wisdom imparted here is holistic, not fragmented like yours. That is one of the pillars of the NEW AGES."

"Who says we have fragmented learning?"

"Don't you? But let's keep that for some other discussion." Plutus smiled. "For now, let's just say that we have the advantage of a view from another plane, a higher plane..."

"Network administrator & energy physicist you would broadly understand, I guess..."

"Yes, less 'alien' than the other things & jargons here." Dave smiled.

"But still radically different from what it connotes in your plane. As for the Network & Central Energy Repository, they are important pillars of our new systems. The details will take some explaining, so let's park it for now."

"So one works with the Network, & the other with er, Energy Repository?"

"Yes. And both are brilliant at their work."

Both Lyon & Plutus gave Dave thumbs up.

"In fact, Lyon just recently upgraded the travel module of the Network- this allows him to track any significant energy spikes in the teleportation sub module." Plutus complimented his friend.

"Thank you, sirs. Just for the group's info, Dave's teleportation was the first pilot of this upgrade. So imagine my pleasant surprise to know that the first energy blip could be traced back to my buddy's place..."

"And that's how he zoomed in here, by detecting the energy surge." Plutus added, explaining to Dave.

"That was rather fast, though. I just reached a couple of hours back, and your friend is already here!" Dave remarked. "Is he coming from somewhere close by? And by the way, how come I didn't see him coming?"

"Was that fast?" Lyon seemed genuinely surprised.

"From his frame of reference it is, Lyon." Plutus replied.

And then turning to Dave, he clarified. "Actually, he comes from a reasonable distance- his lab is in a remote corner of the moon, approximately 10,000 kms from here. But we have some advanced travel devices & solutions. In fact, his actual travel time would have been much lesser had he left immediately after he noticed the blip."

"Yeah, gotta spend some time analyzing my first reads, you see." Lyon quipped.

"Serious? 10,000 kms in an hour? Did he come by some rocket?" Dave asked, fascinated.

First the moon, then the 25th century, and now super fast travel...

Maybe someone would pinch him real hard, and he would be jolted from this rather fascinating dream...

"You can say so. You see, our PATs (personal aerial transporters) travel at very high speeds, using technology that is way ahead of your time. *At these speeds, your eyes & senses are not trained to see these things coming & going*...that's probably why you couldn't see him coming."

Dave's mind flew back to the UFO...appearing & disappearing in a way human eyes couldn't fathom...not yet...

"And the special energy sensors of this place allowed me direct access-somewhat like your biometric access." Lyon added. "The privileges of being a cyborg, you see..." he winked.

'What *Borg*?'

"*Cyborg*, dude...never heard of 'em?" Lyon retorted, seeming genuinely surprised. "Thought you earthlings had some sense of this concept."

"Are you referring to *cyborg, as in part man, part machine*?" Dave asked, shocked yet again! *Fascinating, hypnagogic, even mind numbing revelations were tumbling at an exponential rate...*

"Yeah, the kind they show in your sci-fi movies...*the terminator is here, earthling!*" Lyon raised his hands in a mock fashion, clawing his fingers to appear scary...

"Dave, just ignore him. He is more talk than walk! "Ikona waved Lyon off with her hand. "And no, it's not like what you see in the movies; no terminators here!"

"I knew he was kidding." Dave tried to join in the banter.

"Well, actually, er, *he wasn't completely*- about the terminator bit, yes; but cyborg he indeed is..." Plutus clarified tentatively, unsure of how his guest would respond to this.

"What do you mean?"

"Broadly speaking, cyborgs are an evolved, hybrid race, best described as having meaningful synthetic increments to the organic...not like your popular perceptions of robotic humans, or destructive machines, but rather like a human using technology as additive, rather than substitutive, to the organic human qualities. Cyborgs are very much like humans, probably just better & more integrated users of technology. Does that make any sense to you?" Plutus tried his best to explain simply.

Dave shook his head.

"See, you wear these spectacles dude? What's this, if not technological enhancement to your organic nature?" Lyon pointed out. "Compare these with my shades? Mine are just more high tech, that's all

"Rather high tech! Allows him to 'see' beyond merely the visible spectrum. In fact, *these are holographic network sensors, allowing Lyon to 'see' dual locations at one time...* " Plutus smiled in a knowing way at his friend.

"Holographic network sensors? Dual locations at once?"

"Yeah, my vision & the network vision; integrated…that's how I can 'see' dual locations without actually being there."

"I still don't follow…"

"Imagine being able to see two places, two scenes at the same time? One, with your normal eyes, the other like a view from a video broadcast. Well, Lyon's shades do something similar, being connected to the network- they allow him a wider view without the need to be in the other place…"

"But that's not the core point Dave." Plutus continued. "The point is, synthetic addition to our organic nature is the logical, progressive way in which humans have evolved. Honestly, we believe humans & technology are indivisible, that there is no inherent conflict between the synthetic & organic, between technology & man. Just think of how many lives pacemakers have saved, or how many have been rendered able by artificial limbs, knee replacements, implants etc?"

"Interesting perspective…" Dave smiled. "So we are all cyborgs in a way. And I definitely am one, since I wear glasses! Wow…"

"It's all about points of view. Lyon, of course, has many such integrated enhancements like 'stereophonic sound'- a simple enhancement to the larynx- allows him to pursue & manifest his passion for the electronic & metal."

"Electronic? Metal? As in musical sounds?"

"Yeah buddy…" came a deeply electronic, almost crudely robotic kind of sound.

"So you fond of metal too? Let's give it to our space traveler…" And with that, he broke out into an impromptu rendition of *'Spaceman'*- an old pop-rock song having electronic sounds.

'Spaceman, I always wanted you to go into space, man...'

"Hey cool, this used to be one of my favs back during my graduation days. Think we will hit it off quite well..." Dave was beginning to feel comfortable in the company of these three 'characters', although he had no real idea of who they were...

"Even we can..." Plutus smiled. "I may not be a 'happening' cyborg like this dude, but have some interesting elements up my sleeve as well...". And with it, he gently touched the Kurt Cobain image on his tee, as the words rang out:

'I am not what I seem
I am nothing but a dream..'

And then, a gentle tap at the back, and the humming of 'Aum' resonated throughout, combining with the metallic sounds... Aa...uu... mmmm...

For a while, this seemed familiar, and then he felt a certain elevation up his spine...

Sensing this, Plutus added. "Take it easy now. We know you have many questions, and lots will come up as you see more of this plane. The best way is to take it as it comes, and give yourself time to absorb this knowledge."

"After all, considering the circumstances of your 'visit', I don't think you are likely to go back in a hurry!" smiled Ikona.

The last statement struck Dave! In this frenzy of questions, the most important one eluded him: *How would he get back, and when would that be?*

"So what does this mean? I am stuck here? How do I get back?" A wave of anxiety swept through Dave.

Never in his journey was he so far out of the comfort zone. This was as testing as could be...

"Relax pal." Lyon spoke, his voice less electronic & high pitched than before."What you have experienced is the cutting edge of human consciousness in your plane. If synchronicity has guided you across space & time, I am sure it has a purpose & design for you."

"You know what, I had a thought- let's inform Master Aleus about his journey. I am sure he will be able to throw more light." Ikona suggested.

"Good idea- maybe even meet the Council. After all, I'm sure the seers would have seen it. And maybe the Clairvoyants can sense the direction..." Plutus added.

Seers? Clairvoyants? Council? Ignoring the new set of jargons, Dave asked "Yeah, but what do I do now? I mean, where do I stay? How do I manage? I don't know the ways of this place, *if at all I know for sure about this place itself...*" realization once again seeping in that this was not some holiday spot on earth, but supposedly the moon...

And his only image of man on the moon was very, very different!

"Don't worry. You are our guest, our friend here. It's not a random coincidence that you have manifest on this plane at our house. All your needs would be taken care of, at the right time. You will not lack anything..."

"And as for doing, there is no need for doing here. *You can finally be a human 'being', not a human 'doing'...*" Ikona made a telling statement.

****

Dave spent some time on his floating bed, just trying to absorb it all in...*cutting edge of human consciousness, they said; Was he indeed at the cusp?* Strange clues, mysterious coincidences, bizarre & the unexplained led him to the monastery, where he had an 'expansive experience', in the eye of the storm...*but why him?*

And how did space-time travel fit into any of this? There wasn't even the sci-fi thing of a time machine here- he just 'popped' into the future, into an unknown world, at some strangers' house. But instead of treating him as an unknown intruder, three different entities were unified in treating him as a welcome guest...

He didn't really know which world he was in, what were the ways of this place, when & how he could get back, and how did this translate into the ever enigmatic quest for the Messenger...

But there was a strange sense of calm...less anxiety than he would have imagined...

As 'evening' approached, he walked across to the transparent walls, observing this new world. He wanted to step out onto what seemed like a deck, but there seemed to be no door or window. Strange, he thought, and gently touched the glass-it expanded outwards, like a flexible rubber sheet.

Dave immediately recoiled his hands.

Then, like a little child experimenting with a newly acquired toy, he did that a few more times with increasing force, and each time it expanded outwards further…till his arms actually penetrated through the 'glass'…

A fascinated Dave was about to step out through this penetrable 'glass', when an electronic voice announced: 'verifying access codes; please hold on.'

After a couple of seconds, it said: 'You may step out now.'

Intrigued by the message, the 'glass walls', and this place itself, Dave 'walked out' through the glass, standing on a deck which seemed to extend on all sides.

And then he saw something spellbinding…

A beautiful blue diamond gradually rose over the horizon, casting hues of azure over the evening sky…

It was the earth rising! Yet another rare celestial phenomenon for a human…

Dave had spent many evenings on his deck back home, observing the moon. *But here he was, a man of the earth, watching it as an observer from the moon…*

He just stared at it, his anxieties & questions gradually replaced by pure love…As he took in his customary deep breaths, his energy & love began to grow, and seemed to overflow from him onto this resplendent blue diamond. From this vantage point, things seemed so clear- just one glittering blue planet; no geographical boundaries, no artificial divisions, no partitions! It needed a higher perspective to see the 'oneness' of earth…

And suddenly, all conflicts based on boundaries seemed so illogical, so unnatural…

Minutes seemed to turn into hours as he just sat there, spellbound by the sheer beauty & amazement of what he saw...

As evening set in, thousands of glittering, fluorescent lights lit up the whole place, reminding him of Las Vegas by night. All around him, thousands of small aircrafts (did they call them PATs or something?) hovered at different altitudes, floating in a beautiful rhythm. And yet, there was no sign of pollution or smoke or noise…

The crafts seemed to come in & out of focus, appearing & 'vanishing' in an instant…

On top, he could see stars by the thousands, filtering from the beautiful 'night' sky (or was it day sky? He was feeling partly disoriented about the loss of the 'time framework'.

After all, if he could be in the 25th century, night sky could be day sky...).

He was reminded about his childhood days, when he used to go to the terrace with this handmade telescope, observing the stars & the magnified moon, fantasizing that he were there.

Dave closed his eyes, taking in some more deep breaths...he remembered the night in the lawn of the hotel in Gangtok, where he felt that the boundary between the real & surreal dissolved...well, here it truly was...

But he was not feeling anxious- disoriented, lost, strange, yes; but also calm, peaceful, in harmony...

Whatever this whole journey was, it was out of the ordinary-at the turn of the millennium, incorporating mankind's great fascination- space time travel...

And he was chosen for it....

So he would surrender himself further to this adventure, to synchronicity, & allow destiny to flow through him...

That night Dave slept in complete peace, like a baby sure of its mother's love & warmth...

Blessed by both the earth & heavens...

9. Understanding the Transcendence

The next morning, Dave woke up fresh & light. The earth, its deep blue now hues of pale blue, was near the horizon, about to set. The sun was just rising up, but was unlike anything he had seen from the earth. It seemed larger & closer...

In what seemed like a large mid air lawn, in a corner of this huge house, he could see the silhouetted figures of Plutus, Lyon & Ikona through the filtering light, apparently doing some exercises. These seemed like Yogic asanas & breathing, but the movements were slow, rhythmic & graceful...almost like a combination of Tai-chi & yoga...

As he lazily woke up, the three entered inside. Ikona flashed Dave a lovely, sunshine smile, her milky white teeth evident in all their glory. She was looking beautiful & shapely in her tracks & T-shirt, her silky straight hair tied in a cute pony tail. Plutus was looking muscular & fit, while Lyon seemed to glow brighter than he saw yesterday.

After a while, all four of them sat for breakfast, on a huge dining table at the other end of house. Dave was initially aghast at the thought of eating without brushing or flossing, but was assured that they had many interesting alternatives. Plutus gave him a small spray, which was an anti oxidant & cleanser, while Ikona suggested something simpler-having a glass of water...

"The water here has all the nutrients & anti bacterial properties your body needs…"

As they sat on the table, 4 trays popped out from some sort of a shaft underneath the table- sitting right in front of them. "Since you are still getting accustomed to the place, thought I would *'set'*, rather than *get* the breakfast today." Ikona smiled.

"Set, rather than get?"

"Oh, it's like ordering food from outside vs. making it in-house, except that home delivery here is automatic…and on the table! Just a little more high tech…" smiled Plutus.

"And super quick! As much as technologies & races progress, there is no joy greater than that of the palate-especially after a morning of exercises…" remarked Lyon, slurping his tongue in a baby like way. It was hard to miss his innocence here…

As Dave took his first bite, it didn't exactly seem like a joy to the palate. And his first sip, though not exactly repelling, hardly seemed to give him the joy that his cappuccino used to…

"Oh, you will feel something different the first few times." Ikona smiled, reading Dave's expressions. "After all, our cereals & concoctions are made from a rather different combination. The grains for the cereals are from the farms of Columbus, while the concoction is brewed from special herbs of the healing gardens, right here on moon itself. The best quality stuff, as you would say."

"*Farms of Columbus? Now who is that? And healing gardens?*" Dave asked surprised.

"Never mind. Let's just say these are special farms…and mind you, these are considered delicacies here. Your palate may not agree to it as of now, but in time, you will develop a taste for these things, maybe even love it. Your palate & digestive system are used to your half dead, pesticide-ridden foods, extremely low on nutrition, and you find them tasty! Our foods, on the other hand, are not only much, much richer in fiber & nutrition, but also 'modified' to be higher in energy content."

"How's that?"

"Well, genetic modification of foods had already begun in your time. But unlike your myopic genetic mutation for patenting, our genetic modification was for enhancement of nutrients, for the free consumption of all. Add to that energy enhancement using energy focusing techniques at these farms, and you have live foods that are a great source of both energy & balance, for our mind-body systems."

"And in agreement with the palate…" Smirked Lyon.

Dave took in some more bites, trying to consciously feel the energies of these nutrition rich foods. He continued to look around, observing the house and the views outside in the 'daylight'. The place looked similar like the previous evening, buzzing with activities & flying vehicles, but whiter & brighter. He then looked at the table & chairs, and noticed that they seemed to be made not of wood, but some other material.

The fancy looking trays & cups caught his attention next- *avante garde design*, he smiled to himself, and felt like pocketing one... at least it would serve as some kind of proof to skeptics who would not believe his 'Alice in wonderland story'... *maybe even to himself when he 'woke up'*...

"Oh, these cups and trays?" Plutus spoke, sensing Dave's curiosity. "They are made of special materials, very high in malleability-advanced compounds having a special coating which doesn't need washing at all-the ultimate recycling! You see, we take special care here to not pollute the environment in any way."

"All this greenery & natural beauty-I don't think this environment can ever be polluted." Dave smiled as he absorbed it...

"That's how the earth was too, for millennia; till human 'progress' polluted it, stripped it, ripped it apart..." Plutus' face turned somber. Silence for a while...

Then Lyon pitched in, this time the electronic voice echoing shades of a baby voice. "Hey, let's talk about more pleasant things, in line with this beautiful morning. Like this beautiful tea cup that our friend is apparently fascinated by, and wants to keep as a memento..."

Dave was caught off guard- how did he sense this....?

"OK- so *this cup*... is all yours." Plutus said with a flourish, handing over the same to Dave. "Here's the holy grail of your quest, buddy! Keep it so that you may forever reminisce this wondrous journey. And just so that you may know, the material also has a extremely low friction & coalescing property, ensuring that very little residual waste or particles are left behind. Each dish lasts upto a million meals, and can be easily cleaned by vacuum suction."

"Not to forget the energy retention qualities. It has the highest fidelity in terms of retaining the nutritional qualities of the dish served in it- yet another of our inventions at ensuring that what we consume is one of the highest forms of nourishment & energy for us." Lyon clarified.

Apparently, the term 'energy' was repeatedly thrown around, and in many contexts, Dave mentally noted.

"As for the design, all these cups have been designed by me." Ikona beamed. "Its ultra malleable nature means that one can design the mould in various aesthetic shapes-so the dishes can be 'designed' to suit the occasion."

"Wow. You are a beautiful designer, an artist..." Dave quipped instinctively. However, no sooner that he made this statement, *he was reminded of another beautiful artist...with a similar sunshine smile...how he wished she could be here in this fascinating place with him...*

"Eat my friend, and build your energies." Plutus smiled. "You will need lots of it in the evening.. After all, a special evening awaits us..."

A special evening it indeed was...

Unknown to Dave, the Guardian Council's representative had contacted Ikona, in response to her reporting Dave's transcendence. And the surprise was that Master Aleus, a leading member of the Council, and Ikona's mentor, was himself coming...

This, as they would later explain to him, was not a common occurrence, & meant that something special was at play here...

To the uninitiated, Aleus was simply a leading light of this sacred institution; but to those who understood, he was *the* leading light, the wisest, most benevolent of all masters of the Council, second only to the Grand Master in stature...

Enlightened, yet firmly rooted in life's day-to-day realities, the Master was a classic epitome of all that the New Age represented- arms soaring skyward, touching the stars, yet feet firmly entrenched in the ground, discharging one's obligations on this plane.

He was an inspiration, a balancing force in the Council, someone even the Masters turned to in their hour of doubt or moment of despair. A poet by disposition, he had the habit of occasionally breaking into poetry during his conversations. With such rich past and exalted present, it was an honor for any apprentice to be ordained for tutelage under his wings…

However, there was another sacred responsibility, an enigmatic secret that the Master carried, even protected, in some ways- to the ones in knowledge, he was the Godfather of the *chosen One-* the 'one born with the Aura'…*anointed by the wisest of the Council, and blessed by none other than the Grand Master himself…*

****

"Young man, welcome to the New Ages." Aleus warmly greeted Dave as they met.

"Thank you sir." said Dave, almost instantly captivated by this magnetic personality. Tall, muscular, with an erect posture that would put most twenty year olds to shame, the Master exuded an energy that was almost infectious. Though he had flowing white hair & an equally flowing beard, he hardly looked more than 60, being smartly dressed in glossy tuxedos, bow & chic boots. Strangely, for this stylish attire, he was wearing lots of beads of different materials- from crystals to quartz to what seemed like rosary beads. Nonetheless, all in all, Aleus looked more like a graceful, middle aged Hollywood celebrity, than a Master! *There was something about him…*

"So, how old is this Master exactly?" Dave had asked his friends earlier, when told about Aleus' impending visit.

"How young is more like it! He is actually 120, but not a day more than 50 in his demeanor. Bet you wouldn't have made out his age had we not told you." Plutus had smiled. *Now Dave understood why...*

As they all sat around comfortably in the lounge area, Dave seemed to be the only one not completely at ease, inspite of the luxurious upholstery & elevating ambience created by his three friends, especially for this evening…

Soft lights cast eclectic shadows of all shapes across the 'walls', rosemary & mint aromas wafted across the room from scented candles, adding to the mystique, while soft instrumental music played in the background, completing the tranquil feel.

Ikona had prepared a special herbal brew, which would further soothe the nerves & calm the mind, but Dave was feeling edgy nonetheless- the yet to seep in fact that he was in a distant future, that he had made a 'teleportation' across space & time, and that a highly respected master of this world was meeting him, all contributed to this...

And, of course, Master Aleus' towering personality added to the awe!

"So how was your teleportation experience, Dave? Heard you blacked out?" Aleus asked, coming to the point.

"Oh, that? Yes, I did pass out. I have been explained that the sudden energy surge was too much for me to handle." Dave replied a bit tentatively, glancing sideways at Plutus & Ikona. They nodded in approval.

"Rightly so. I see that my student & apprentice have explained well, so no need upon this to dwell." As the impromptu rhymes flowed, it was the Master's turn, this time, to look at his protégés with pride.

"Hmn, a brief understanding about how you got here you have- about your way, and the energy dynamics at play...good." He said, raising his cup, about to sip his special herbal brew.

"Not exactly, er sir." Dave replied, wondering how best to address such an exalted yet dashing personality. "I am still quite confused about this thing...in fact, about many things..."

"I understand; questions many burden you, confusions numerous torment as answers are few...but agonize not, and eliminate all negative thoughts..." his continued to speak in rhyme, feeling more poetic by the minute.

"Each time you were confused, answers emerged, sometimes in the most unexpected of ways. So too they will here." He took a long, deep inhalation of the aroma before sipping his brew. And then, as if suddenly energized by it, he added in a deep, baritone voice. "Dave, life is an adventure, a song...and it is so precisely because of the unknown...what seems like mystery, indeed may be its great poetry! So doubts just let go, and enjoy its lyrical flow...open your heart, live this mystery...*that is true synchronicity...*"

Dave gently bowed his head in concurrence. "I understand & agree sir. I did feel a '*connection*' at so many points along this journey...and I know it is some sort of synchronicity which has brought me, er here...

But where & what is this '*here*'? I am told that I am on the moon, in the 25th century, and that I have undergone a space-time teleportation;

But I am still unable to fathom it, to reconcile to it... *and shouldn't I?* I mean, *how is that possible?*" asked Dave, his incredulity pouring out.

"It is as possible as your other adventures!" The Master's baritone voice became deeper. "At that time, did they seem plausible, much less possible? Possible & impossible are simply limitations of our mind...*apparent duality creating a false bind...*" this last remark elucidating a powerful concept.

"But to put things in perspective, yes- *you are on the moon, 500 years ahead of your time...in the New Ages;* harbor no doubts, bear no skepticism..." He allowed the words to sink in.

After a momentary silence, Dave regained his composure after a sip from his own brew. It seemed to possess a strange energy to uplift. "And what's this about the NEW AGES, sir? *This certainly wasn't or isn't my idea of the NEW AGES.* I mean, I would think of it metaphorically, not literally- a new vision, simply a new way of looking at things. I thought that I would meet some wise man in the Himalayas, some Messenger, who would share a new vision...and that was the genesis, the purpose of this journey. *But space travel? The future? What does any of it have to do with this vision? The whole thing seems more of science fiction than philosophy...*"

"Indeed, the NEW AGES is an allegory for what a new world ought to be, *a vision for the future; but it is right here...* the future *itself*...a real place, a real world, built upon higher consciousness & energies, and based on higher dimensional reality...it is a world, an AGE where people live this new vision, both individually & communally. *It is a higher world based on a higher world view...*" Aleus spoke emphatically.

Dave shook his head, apparently confused. "A real place, yet based on a higher world view, a superior consciousness?"

"I couldn't have said it better! But simplify let me further..." Master Aleus smiled as he ran a hand through his silky, snow white hair. "You see, everything in the ordinary plane of reference, your world, is based on 4 dimensions- the 3 dimensions of space & one of time, right?"

"Right. There are the 3 dimensions of space and the arrow of time."

"But it wasn't always so. In fact, for most of human history, 'reality' was always about the 3 dimensions of space; time was never a variable in this equation at all.

All your classical physics, based on Newtonian principles, saw space as a distinct, 3-D entity, and objects as solid, discrete, having a distinct compartment between matter and energy..."

"It was only in the 20th century that a pioneer named Einstein brought the 3 dimensions of space & time together in a 4-Dimensional continuum. Born thus was the theory of General relativity, in physics emerged a new poetry; and along with it came the understanding of relative time, as opposed to absolute time. You with me?"

Dave nodded in assent.

"So, did reality actually change? Did space & time really merge? Did time really change from absolute to relative? No, what simply changed was our understanding of it. Our higher consciousness lifted 'reality' from a 3 dimensional to a 4 dimensional plane...from an absolute, solid construct to fluid, evolving, based on certain uncertainties...

Thus was born a world based on a 4-D space-time continuum, instead of the 3 axes of space...and of a new understanding, this formed the base...

You see, truth is absolute. The only thing that changes, or rather evolves, is human consciousness, and hence our understanding & application of it. Thus, my friend, is born, a higher world. And the higher our consciousness evolves, the more doors to the mysteries of the Universe it opens..."

Dave acquiesced, trying to absorb it.

"Where you are right now is one of those higher planes, *higher worlds*...you transcended your ordinary space-time reality, to arrive here; to 'teleport' into the future..."

Each time he heard the word future, a strange knot appeared in Dave's stomach- *the folks here spoke about future travel so normally, even casually, that he finding it rather hard to assimilate...*

"Remember, this is just not a future from your current frame of reference- it is a future where the collective consciousness has evolved to the next levels...and in conjunction, or probably as a result of, so have our technology, our systems, our institutions.

In summation, we have created a NEW WORLD- the NEW AGES..."

"So, is this a utopian place? Some fantasy? What exactly is the New Ages?"

"From your plane, yes. In fact, to you all this may seem like a cross between science fiction, fairyland & utopia. But let's just say that the NEW AGES is a place & time where utopian realities *do exist*.

A heaven of sorts, if you may say so..."

"After all, what is heaven except an experience of higher reality." smiled Ikona, a glint in her eyes. Dave looked at her eyes & felt a strange tingling, a sense that what she said was sagacious- *indeed, aren't heaven & hell just an experience of higher or baser realities...*

"So how does one reach out to the heavens? That's what our entire race wants to do." Dave said wistfully, his mind playing out the significance of his journey. Apart from mankind's fascination with space-time travel, it's greatest quest, deepest void was the creation of heaven on earth.

"Absolutely! What else is the goal of mankind but to strive for heaven on earth..." the Master said, lifting his arms in a symbolic gesture, apparently reading Dave's thoughts. As if on cue, a rendition of *'This could be heaven for everyone'*, a powerful song by the band Queen, started to play.

Mood control music, Lyon gestured...

"The problem, though, is that they don't know how to... they are not evolved enough yet...reaching out to the heavens, or creating heaven needs us to raise our energies, to lift our consciousness...deliberately, consciously..."

"Is that what happened to me at the monastery? After all, what I did experience at the monastery can be defined as paranormal... " Dave said slowly.

"Why only the monastery Dave?" Master Aleus spoke forcefully. "Recollect your journey over the past one year, and you shall see how your entire life changed...you consciously elevated your energies, raised your consciousness, became open to synchronistic coincidences. These prepared & nurtured you for a higher journey."

"You know about my journey! The past one year?"

"Of course we know!"

"But how? I was, by your explanation, in another world, another plane..."

"That's why we guided you. Not just you, we send energies to all of mankind...and sometimes, special souls we find..." he winked.

"So *you* were guiding me all along?" Dave asked, stunned.

It was as if a big mystery was solved in a simple sentence! So much in the last one year revolved around who was behind all this, who was guiding him...at last, he got some answers...

"Aw c'mon...it wasn't just me." The master's tone suddenly turned casual. "Don't gimme any more credit or blame than what is due. It was the entire Guardian Council. After all, that's their role."

"The Guardian Council?"

"Oh, they are the conscience keeper of the NEW AGES." Plutus clarified.

"But who or what are they?"

"Save some questions for later, son. You should hopefully learn about the Council in due course, in a significant way." The Master's eyes shone.

"OK. But I still have other questions..."

"Go right ahead! Shoot." it was hard to visualize a Master who was poetic minutes back was now talking colloquial...

"Coming back to the monastery, what exactly was its role? And the Himalayas? Why was I guided there? I was told that it was the gateway."

"You answered it. So where's the question?" Aleus winked.

"But what exactly is a gateway?"

"Exactly what the name suggests!" Aleus convivially joked. *"You see, a gateway, or a portal, is a conduit to higher planes, thanks to its inherently high energies.* Across the universe, there are several gateways, including in your plane- the Himalayas are one such very high energy channel. And of course, the monastery of the disappearing Lama is a blessed gateway; moreover, it helps that it is a nondescript monastery, so keeps it away from unnecessary public gaze.

While you will get a more comprehensive understanding of energy dynamics during your stay here, for now just understand that because of their inherently high energies, these gateways facilitate teleportation of matter & spirit to higher dimensional planes. Of course, the gateway only facilitates, opening up a window; ultimately, the 'lift' has to be achieved by the individual himself."

"Lift?"

"Yes, lift; After all, higher dimensional travel is the flight of the soul, along with its accompanying matter. So, the analogy of flight would be apt.

Let's see, how about the example of an airplane? You understand how an airplane flies, right?"

"Somewhat- the thrust produced by the engine gives it lift, due to which it can fly against gravity."

"Good. You know your science well. Using this analogy, the gateway is like a very powerful engine, which produces the energy, or thrust, required to create the lift. But till the wing, or the individual consciousness, is in the desired aerofoil shape, even this great thrust will not create adequate lift. So while the gateway has inherent energies, the 'wing shape' or consciousness, is something that only an individual can craft.

This is what happened in your case- your 'redemption', your meditation and your wisdom over the past year crafted in you into the right 'aerofoil design'. And at the gateway, you experienced an energy surge- all set to take off. However, your consciousness was not a fully designed aerofoil, hence you blacked out during take-off. *Of course, had it not been for the gift, you couldn't have even made it to either the gateway or through the transcendence.*"

"I know- the gift of the past, which resulted in this new present of mine." Dave remembered how the clue was cracked.

"Yes, but also the gift of the 'beings'- ***the disk itself***!" Master Aleus smiled. "You miss that out…"

"The *disk was the gift?!!* And all this while I thought the gift was my understanding of the relationship between our present based on the seeds of the past. It was as if my past was the gift."

"Everything in life can be a gift, son- the past, the present, the pleasure, the pitfalls- everything can teach us; *but in this case, the gift referred to was indeed the disk!*"

"Wow. So what was the role of the disk? It seemed to give me some vital answers, some vital clues at just the right time."

"Exactly! *The disk is a very powerful gift*, having multiple roles in your case- in acted as a guide, a magnet and an amplifier, all put into one! Unknown to your conscious self, it facilitated the raising, the amplification of your energies, thereby enhancing the 'right aerofoil design'. At the same time, it acted as a magnet by furthering the coincidences, which ultimately led you to the gateway.

Remember how it showed you the Himalayas when you couldn't clearly fathom the crop circle?"

"Yes I remember-vividly. As also how spooked out I was then!" He smiled. "But why something so shocking?"

"Because each time you were rising up, you also had a counter force dragging you back- into complacency, into disbelief, into skepticism...something shocking was needed to jolt you."

"So what about the crop circle clue itself? What was it all about?"

"It shall reveal itself, layer by layer..."

"And what about the strange monk at the monastery? What was the 'object' he gave me?"

"Many players and forces helped you with this journey, so individuals don't matter beyond a point."

Dave seemed disappointed. He was convinced that the flying Lama himself had appeared to him.

"As for the object..." Master Aleus continued. "It was a special player containing spatial sounds & vibrations. Not like your conventional music players, but a player from a higher plane, containing higher vibrations of those sounds. This helped you immensely in the final energy lift."

Dave smiled as he recollected the 'experience'- it was a high, a bliss that was indescribable.

"However, you still couldn't handle the surge towards the end, and blacked out again. But not before you got teleported here." Aleus put the pieces together. "That, my friend, is the long & short of your journey till now."

Dave tried to soak it in, trying to absorb all this new information. He was genuinely overwhelmed, even though he got many answers. "So, bit by bit, I was drawn to the gateway. And there, ala Star Trek, I got, er, beamed to the future in my entirety, to the NEW AGES?"

"Aye Scotty. You may say that you have been beamed up & ahead!" Said Lyon, in a mock tone.

"Dave." Aleus added in a profound tone. "Your entire journey in this period was a continuum-preparing you, nurturing you, guiding you, clue after clue, tool by tool. And your wise choices, in opting for the path of self discovery over self destruction, helped. In fact, it was primarily your choice, your freewill, which helped you accept the clues, the gifts, sometimes in the face or extreme despair, anxiety or skepticism. We only facilitated, ultimately it was you..."

Dave smiled. "I am definitely clearer about how I got here, and happy about it; though I guess, it will take some time to absorb the *where*..."

"Take your time."

"But sir, why me? *The clues seemed to suggest a quest to find a Messenger. I thought I would find him in the Himalayas. No sign of him there, and here I am now- in the future*...but still no sign of him! So, why the NEW AGES? And why me?"

"You *still* don't understand?" Master Aleus asked, as compassionate as bemused. "Didn't all those events, those supposed random clues tell you anything? Now that they form a coherent pattern, don't you see it?"

"See *what,* sir?"

"That it is your *dharma,* your life purpose which brings you here. Your destiny has been guiding you, and by your freewill, you have made the right decision to align with synchronicity."

"My *dharma?"* Dave asked, astonished. "My life purpose brought me here? This far? Into the future?"

"Yes, your dharma, your life purpose."

Doesn't make sense, Dave thought... *I was living a mixed life back on earth, quite like a normal guy- had my own joys & challenges, but nothing out of the ordinary; at least not before these events began. Even with these, I simply had a sense of something eventful happening in my life...but 'life purpose'?*

"Master." Dave said thoughtfully, finally ready to address Aleus as such. "I did experience a deep personal trauma, and developed some fundamental questions about the direction of my life. Yes, this gave me a new, spiritual outlook to life. But I guess a lot of guys at my age & stage go through this. So why me? And what did my evolution have to do with a Messenger or the future? How does any of this tie in with my life purpose?"

"The karmic cycle spans more than what you can see. What seems like life's mystery may be its fundamental quest, its dharma...

What is mysterious today may be obvious tomorrow; remember, many forces were, and are, at work here- the Masters & beings bless you..." the Master answered enigmatically.

And then, with a comforting tone, he added. "Don't think too much, son. As I said, life's mystery is its poetry, so enjoy it, observe & absorb it. You will keep getting clarity, at just the right moment. Just as you now understand how your clues led you here. Go with the flow and remain centered; synchronicity is as work here, and your job is to be aware & consciously meditative. The more conscious you are, the higher in energy you shall be; and yes, keep making the right choices." he concluded, as wisely & mysteriously as he had all evening.

Dave smiled back. The Master's words & demeanors, though somewhat enigmatic, were definitely laced with wisdom & comfort. They had given much clarity about how he came here, but also left him with newer bits of information, raising fresh questions- almost as if he were being given more clues...

"I bless that you find your calling to the Council...*be guided* to it..." Aleus said, somewhat as an afterthought. "And the *clairvoyance chamber* hopefully facilitates your being able to 'see', rather 'sense', your journey, and gain clarity of purpose. The clairvoyants should be able to throw more light after that..."

Clairvoyance chamber? Yet another clue, yet another enigma. How & why would he 'sense' his journey in this chamber...

"So Plutus, take good care of our friend here." the Master instructed as he got up, readying to leave. "Take him around, show him our world. The more questions he has, the more he will learn..."

Turning to Dave, he said. "Since you have made a transition to this plane, there is obviously lots to see, to learn here. This world & its systems are far more, if I may say, **evolved**...be aware & open..."

"Dear ones, I must be going now- have to reach in time for the evening bliss meditations."

With that, Master Aleus bid them farewell- a warm hug & blessings to all, and was gone in a swanky mini jet...

10. A NEW FELLOWSHIP SHALL BE SET...

For a while, Dave simply kept staring in that direction, wondering about the evening- momentous it had been, but equally astounding...then he quietly trudged along, entering his room. When he didn't emerge for quite some time, Ikona went inside, finding Dave lying on his 'floating'' bed.

"Are you alright?" Ikona enquired in her kind tone, her voice soft as snow.

Dave simply nodded. "Guess so."

Just then, the other two entered. "So, how was the evening, buddy?" Plutus asked enthusiastically. But sensing the dreary silence, he figured out that all wasn't chirpy & effervescent.

"He seems overwhelmed." Ikona assessed. "I guess it's been an overdose for a single evening.."

"We understand." Plutus replied empathically.

"Do you?" Dave replied, a sudden tinge of sarcasm laced with irritation, in his voice.

"*I have just had more surreal information in an hour than most people in a lifetime.* I was explained the mysterious circumstances behind my journey, and how each clue led to another. As if that thing itself is not tangential enough came about some sci-fi stuff about traveling across planes and emerging in the future, and an explanation about heavens & earth...and about how the NEW AGES, which I thought all along to be an idea, a vision, is the place, the heaven, the future, where I literally am in..."

"Dave, don't you see it? *You are* special..." Plutus said genuinely. "You have made a leap into the NEW AGES, something folks from earth rarely do. Aren't you happy about it? Ordinary people don't make extraordinary leaps...and aren't you glad you got so many answers in the last one hour?"

"Yes, I am relieved about the answers I got, about how I emerged here, who was guiding me et al; but each time I think I get some answers, more questions emerge...first it was about who was sending me messages, then about what my quest was about, and who the Messenger was? Then, as the Himalayas turned out to be merely a gateway into another world, the question of how & where in this *'future'* do I find the Messenger gnawed at me... and now I am told that my dharma that brought me here! *What Dharma? What karma?"*

Ikona flashed a million dollar smile. "Remember what Master Aleus said, Dave? Allow the answers to flow to you...your role is to just observe. Go with the flow, as you have done so far."

Dave beamed back, feeling better already. Something about her energies touched him in a very special way. Was it a deep connection, or just the fascination of a single man in a new world, who had lost his love mid way? He couldn't fathom, nor did he really bother at this juncture.

"I am trying. I have gone with the flow; I mean, no ordinary person would have come so far & landed on the moon, in the future. But now that you say so, I will try more...consciously..."

"Ahem..." Lyon coughed mocking. "*Just what do you say to that? Buddy Dave will try consciously 'cause our lady here says so...and I* thought ol' master Aleus said so..."

Dave felt awkward at this insinuation. Plutus immediately changed the topic."So what's the plan now, guys?"

"Let's go out for a ride. Dave will hopefully be spellbound by this place in the evening." Ikona suggested, a spark on her face. She just loved outings, and was the primary driver of the trinity when it came to social activities.

"What do you say pal?" Plutus asked Dave. "Upto it?"

"No, you guys go ahead. I feel a bit under the weather."

"Precisely why you should come! For a joyride, or a thrill ride, whatever you choose."

Dave arched his eyebrows. "Thrill ride?" Ikona nodded vigorously, multiple times, like a child trying to coax it's caretakers to take it out in the open.

Dave had to respond. "Ok, let's try; if it's in one of those swanky jets, like Master Aleus', then why not…"

"You call that swanky?" Plutus seemed surprise at this.

"It was a fairly average PAT, dude. Master Aleus is a man of simplicity & functionality. If you want to see something really hip, see what our friend here has. And, not one but two of them." Plutus smiled as he pointed towards Lyon.

"Really? Didn't know Lyon was, er, that rich? But guess he must be…" Dave raised both his arms in an I dunno gesture, realizing he still had a lot to learn about his hosts.

"My friend, rich & poor have a very different connotation in this plane. Yes, Lyon is rich to the extent his energies allow. For that matter, Master Aleus is richer, and has half a dozen PATs. All functional, of course…"

Dave threw back a puzzled look- *now what is 'wealthy in accordance with energies…'?*

"Your confusion, buddy, is simply a result of your world's paradigm. We don't live in a fragmented world, where wealth & spirit are inversely proportional. In our world, they have a direct correlation. As you will hopefully realise later, the metric of wealth is energy itself-so, the higher your energy, the more 'wealthy' you are!"

Whatever, Dave shrugged. He didn't follow it…

"But what exactly is a PAT? Wanted to ask since yesterday…" He added as an afterthought.

"Simply put, an advanced, flying version of your car. A *Personal Aerial Transporter…*"

"A flying car!" Dave exclaimed, an sudden thrill in his eyes. "That's so cool! I always fancied one when I was stuck in all those horrible jams."

"Great, so you can have one now…" Smiled Lyon.

"Hey, I was just joking."

"But I am not."

"No seriously. I just said it by the way…don't need it, & don't know what to do with it!"

"Do what? Just fly!"

"And how? I aint no pilot."

"Pilot?" Lyon repeated. "If you can play a video game, you can fly this....all I need to do is reset the access code."

"It's that simple?"

"Yes, my friend- simple & sophisticated! Basically the whole thing is automated, and connected to the network-all PATs & CATs. That means that you practically have to just set the coordinates…"

"And before you ask, CAT is a Common Aerial Transporter. Equivalent to your mass transport system. A bit like your bus, train or aircraft service, depending upon the nature & distance of travel. In fact, the high end CATs are used for interplanetary travel."

"Did you just say interplanetary travel?" Dave bordered on mild hysteria now.

"Yeah. But forget all that; let's go for a ride; let's paint the town red!"

"Yup, I'm game." Dave responded, keen to check out which *'town' they wanted to paint red!*

That evening, Dave got his first real glimpse of this fascinating world, glitzy & magical by night, as they drove around, rather, 'flew around'. He felt very comfortable inside the PAT, not realizing the phenomenal speed at which was zipping by, as they went to the most 'happening' district- the night market district.

A 'night market' carnival was in full flow, as people seemed to be converging in and out- lots of little, but high tech looking, tents had interesting wares on display- different varieties of clothing (most of material that he hadn't seen, others simply little packed boxes), artifacts, several items he couldn't make out, special cartons of what seemed like tools. Lots of people were 'taking' these, but strangely, no one was paying anything! The most unusual purchase format, Dave observed- each time anybody picked up an item, there was a 'beep'; in other cases, there wasn't even that-

People simply picked up their stuff and walked off!

Then there were his favorites- food joints. Simple, open air cafes, serving 'local' delicacies. Each table had an electronic touch screen 'tablet' serving as the menu. Dave found most of the names rather incomprehensible- 'crater grass soup', 'healing garden avocado pudding', 'lasagna Columbus' etc. Finally, there was something that he decided to try-'charter stew'.

As soon as he pressed it on the tablet, a brief description of it appeared- the recipe, the calorific value, the 'energy' content, as well as a brief history of the dish. Since most of the other things seemed like a 'Greek and Latin', rather 'lunar' to him, Dave read the history- apparently this was the same stew served to members of the 'Council' and the 'Quartet' when the 'Charter' was signed. *'Fit for a king of the old world'*, it read.

Interesting, Dave smiled, and punched his order. The dish 'popped' out in a while, through the same mechanism he had seen back home. Even while 'relishing' this 'new age delicacy', he was constantly looking around, like a child fascinated by a carnival. After a leisurely meal, his friends got up & simply walked off without paying, intriguing Dave further.

"On the house?"

"Not exactly! Energy credit, energy debits!" Plutus smiled cryptically. Dave bothered not to ask further, as they walked around in the market, with the lady browsing the 'stores'.

Women will always love shopping, no matter where or when…

Unmindful of Dave's smirk, Ikona continued to browse at leisure, picking up something like an accessory, followed by a perfume. Dave was expecting a rather strong, fresh fragrance, but it was nearly odorless...

"Enhances the *feminine appeal…*" Lyon winked at him in a hushed tone. Dave gave an *I-understand-you* look, smiling sheepishly at the code language of guys! In the meanwhile, Ikona simply took her stuff without paying, yet again, and the group walked back to the *hangar* where all PATs were parked.

On the way back, they chatted & chatted- Dave about his life, highs & lows, work, and about Shakti & her untimely, shattering loss…he wondered how he felt so comfortable sharing his deepest feelings, opening his heart out, to three 'strangers' just about a day after meeting them…

But then he had sensed that there was something special at play here, some special bonding.

So he poured his heart out even more, reminiscing about his subsequent loneliness, jolting experiences with 'friends', and finally his redemption, which placed him on a new path. He then narrated the adventures that followed, bit by bit, clue by clue, leading him here…

"So that's it about me; that's how I landed here- an ordinary man with a seemingly extraordinary journey…" he said with mixed feelings.

Part of him felt wrenched as the old wounds got scarred again, part anxious as the magnitude of the adventure seeped in further, and part exhilarated at being in a 'special place', meeting special people…

In turn, the trinity was fascinated by his tale- it had all the elements of a thriller; but they were neither cynical nor dramatic about it; to them, this roller coaster ride, from the abyss to the peak, was special by itself, and reason enough why he should have been part of such a mystical adventure.

For them, it wasn't spicy, juicy tale, with twists & turns- *it was an uplifting journey of the soul…an adventure primarily inwards…*

****

When they finally reached home late in the evening, Dave was feeling elevated and high. This was his first real sense of the world here- high tech, teeming with energy and yet having an underlying of serenity. Gone was his anxiety, replaced by joie-de-vivre. For the first time since 'coming' had he smiled & laughed- in fact, after a long time had he laughed so heartily, as he responded to some of Lyon's jokes with his own…

A day back, he had been a stranger in an unknown world, one which he initially refused to believe he had actually transcended in- but now, he had experienced some of it, marveled at its wondrous & slightly incongruous ways, had a tete-a-tete with a venerated master, and best of all, bonded with three newfound friends- kindred souls with whom he felt closer in a day than with most so-called pals in years…

"Guys, I wanna thank you.." he said in a slightly trembling voice.

"For what?"

"For this evening…for all your affection & warmth…for your unconditional love & acceptance…" Dave said, choking..

"Hey, hey..." Plutus went up to him. "Synchronicity has put you on a special path, and brought you in contact with us. So we consider it our sacred duty, our privilege to assist you in this, to be your companions in this journey; we are there with you, always, in everything!"

"These are precisely the words that make me feel so fortunate, so blessed- to be gifted with friends like you! I have seen life & 'friends' at close quarters, and understand the value of virtues like loyalty, faithfulness & unconditional giving. I have felt closer to you guys in a day, in an alien world, than with 'friends' over years, back in my comfort zone." and with this, Dave broke out into tears as old wounds resurfaced. All three gave him a bear hug.

"We understand your pain Dave, but remember what you experienced was primarily self seeking acquaintance masquerading as friendship...with weak, shallow people in a low energy & evolutionary state, you cannot expect intensity- they weren't ready for a special friendship, busy as they were choosing the picks from life's spoils; no wonder they felt 'conflicted' when they had to stand by you!

An intense energy like yours cannot find true friendship among low energy folks, whose understanding of friendship is merely contextual companionship! For them, it's just a word, an association mean to last only through pleasure but never through life's tribulations. This is probably the first time you are experiencing real friendship, of a higher nature..."

Then they put their hands on each other's in a show of solidarity: "This is to our true, deep, lasting friendship; our fellowship...I can feel it...we have special connections..." Dave said, a deep look in his eyes.

"Yeah, true friendship; relationships not of convenience but conviction; not circumstantial, contextual companionship, but timeless bonding which can withstand the sands of time & change..."

"Yes, from this moment onwards, three becomes four!"

At that moment, the words flashed in front of Dave's eyes:

Three worlds, three civilizations, three friends...
A new order emerges while the old one ends...
When the trinity morphs into the quartet,
A new fellowship shall be set...

Three friends had been found, and their trinity had morphed into a quartet of four; a new fellowship ...*One layer was unraveled...*

PART 2

11. The Annihilation

After the initial surprise, anxiety and euphoria, Dave began settling into this new world- the place, the food, the ways of living, all of it...while his previous questions remained, especially about him & the Messenger, he spent time trying to satiate his curiosity about a new set of questions:

What exactly were the NEW AGES? Why was it called so? And more importantly, how did this 'future' relate to his world? Our world? Did the Messenger have something to do with this?

Over the next few days, Dave tried to piece together various parts of the puzzle, aided by his friends. He spent long evenings together with both Plutus & Lyon, accessing the archives on the *'Intelligent Interplanetary Network' (the IIN)*. Ikona was busy travelling in this period in her role as the endower, with a group of 'seekers'. The time spent with them brought him closer to his friends, allowing him to decipher their personality traits...

Plutus was relatively the silent, deliberate, profound and introspective kind of guy- the type for whom they would say 'Still waters run deep'. Lyon, on the other hand, was garrulous, spontaneous, vivacious but slightly full of himself. Yet, both were warm in equal measure- intense, committed, loyal, passionate...

Dave did have a nagging curiosity about Lyon's 'cyborg' origins, but didn't get an appropriate opportunity to talk about it. Nor was there anything particularly strange in his demeanor that warranted any urgent discussion around this.

As Dave went about accessing the archives, he figured out that along with voice recognition, *'thought recognition' was well established here, thanks to brain wave frequency mapping.* However, voice input was most widely used- so all search commands fed into Lyon's high tech computer were oral. The computer itself, though, was the little arm band Lyon wore- compact but having super processing capability. *Moore's law, Dave smiled...*

Interestingly, the search results were not merely text or images, but a complete anthology, *much like an impromptu feature film pieced together by the network;* powered by the next next next next generation crawlers, these search spiders didn't merely scour the network basis keywords & Meta tags and index billions of pages & files, but actually had the intelligence to collate & alter display format, real time- akin to a new collage being made every time from pieces of scrap- function not merely of the scraps available, but the creativity of the one who put it all together...

It wasn't without reason that the network was called the *Intelligent Network...*

And as he had experienced earlier, the search result film was not 2-D, but 3-D; akin to the holographic images he had seen earlier, being projected in the centre of the room.

But this time Dave was shocked, scarred, and horrified by what he saw....

Scene 1

Circa- planet earth in the late 21st century. The world was bursting at its seams, in all respects. The population had reached a nightmarish 10 billion, proliferating to unmanageable levels. From the inception of human history till the late 20th century, the population had grown to 5 billion. And now, in a space of a century, it had ballooned to double of that.

Add to this the climatic changes on account of global warming, along with uncontrolled industrialization, and the result was a severe shortage of natural resources.

Although there was a 4 fold GDP growth of the world in the 21st century, mindless, greedy capitalism was causing increasing disparity between haves & have-nots; be it between the poorer continents of Afro-Asia & the richer ones, or within continents, countries & societies themselves. Moreover, the emergence of a middle class, bred on the mantra of consumption, use & dispose, only exacerbated the problem, as fewer resources were available for a large portion of the world's poorest. And the global economic collapse of the early 21st century didn't help matters either, as capitalism lost a large part of its sheen…

Along with these, & partly due to these, the world was also getting ideologically polarized. Extreme left was emerging as a bloody counter to the extreme right, and neo-conservative policies of the West were causing its increasingly alienation from the East, especially the Middle east. The values of freedom, democracy & fair play, which symbolized the west's moral leadership earlier, were now replaced by a widespread perception of unilateralism, interference, even control.

This lead to reactionary forces in large parts of the world, who saw their aspirations as legitimate, in some cases even necessary, to counter the west. Due to these schisms, the easing of tensions between blocs, which began after the end of the cold war, seemed to have reversed completely- caused by economic disparity, regional aspirations and ideological polarization.

The developed world, which should have taken the lead in ironing out these disparities, instead took a rightward shift in policy. The increasing ascendancy of blind faith in market forces, along with a neo-conservative polity, led to twin vicious counters- the emergence of radical left on one hand, and religious extremism on the other. Their ideological plank, however, was common- rallying forces against perceived authoritarianism & imperialism of certain developed sections. The appeal of these twin forces spread across disgruntled nations & elements across continents, from Latin America to Far East. Very soon, it became large enough to ignore, and the more the powers tried to control it, the more it spread.

Extremism, many a times manifest as terrorism (either religious or ethnic) was becoming the tool of the frustrated masses against establishments. This took on the shape of increasing acts of violence against the developed world- acts perpetrated against their citizens on their very own soil. However, they resulted in a backlash & further jingoism, thereby accentuating the circle of violence. In this, sane and moderate voices were increasingly marginalized...

Even at the individual & society level, things were going downhill. The family was becoming dysfunctional, not only in the individualistic west, but even the aping east. The collapse of such an important support system left individuals feeling insecure, lonely & frustrated. Drug abuse increased, there were more frequent instances of insane & random shootings in colleges & universities, and society became more accustomed to networking in the virtual world than in the real.

Anthropologists were increasingly concerned that what started as an expression of individual rights soon degenerated into an anchorless, rudderless society; what was supposed to be rebellion against suffocating, obsolete social norms became a deep vacuum; a vacuum that individuals tried to fill with everything from drugs to sex to new age therapies. But the hole in the heart only increased...

Then there was the long neglected problem of climatic imbalance, leading to increasing natural disasters & resource scarcity. But instead to countering it with life & death urgency, nations dragged their feet, preferring to pass the buck in the notion of 'self interest'. What was supposed to be common problem degenerated into a blame game between nations, blocks & lobbies, while the myth of 'economic growth' allowed these lobbies to keep spewing more & more poison onto the planet's atmosphere. Mother earth was literally choking up!

So here was the world in the late 21st century- polluted, insecure, anxious, full of disparity & heavily polarized...

However, everything wasn't so gloomy. Technology was evolving at an accelerated pace, offering hope & solutions to many of the problems; with the explosion in communications technology, experts started calling the world 'flat', or a 'global village'. But with the evolution of human consciousness not keeping pace with the growth of technology, application of this technology became confused.

So, instead of bringing people closer, communications technology actually disrupted social engagements & units. Similar things happened with energy, manufacturing, computing, travel etc. What could have been a potent tool for making sense of a fast changing world became a tool for escaping from its problems, for withdrawing from the grim realities...

Technology spawned the ostrich, not the majestic soaring eagle or the hardworking, collective ant...

And of course, there was the criminal waste of technology & resources getting diverted into furthering the stockpile of destruction, in the name of national security, rather than utilizing these for a greener, more equitable, more sustainable world...

All in all, instead of accelerating human development, technology seemed to become a tool for furthering the misguided ambitions of vested groups...

Given these forces, *the "clash of civilizations" now seemed like an imminent reality, instead of the time tested & exalted values of reconciliation, dialogue & joint reconstruction.*

The scene paused here for a long time, as if allowing the viewer to see things in perspective; about how the choices made at this juncture could make or mar the future of the world...

Humanity was standing at the crossroads like never before...

Scene 2: deja vu

After the long pause, the 'picture' continued, with some kind of play with numbers: 0,1,2...along with an uncoiling snake, and a mermaid jumping out of the water, floating in the air...

What...??

However, Dave didn't have much opportunity to contemplate it- what came next was as remarkable as shocking!

The scene shifted to a President & his war cabinet! **It was the same PRESIDENT, the same WAR CABINET, the same heated discussions...**

Dave was stunned!

His entire journey started with this dream, a strange dream he couldn't identify or recognize. For a long while, he had thought of it as a mental disturbance, an aberration in his normal thought pattern, rather than a clue. But now he was seeing it in the NEW AGES, fathoming that this was indeed a vision- *about the future of the world...*

A future in jeopardy!

The scene of the dream played for a while, and then the scenes shifted. However, what came later was rather fuzzy...it was as if he was perceiving something surreal, rather than actually seeing it in the movie- something only he could probably perceive...

A forceful President overruled the moderates in his cabinet, and declared a WAR!

The majority was steamrolled yet again, as a cowboy in the quest of a supposedly maniacal mission rode roughshod over popular sentiment, unleashing yet another conflict on an already emaciated earth. What supposedly started off as a 'war of ideology', of 'liberty', soon degenerated into a war of 'civilizations', engulfing the entire planet into rival camps; And thus came true the biggest fear of mankind- the 3rd world war!

The Allies & Axis of this conflagration included players not only from America & Europe, but from all over the world. Each participant plunged in, keen only to protect its 'self interest', and pledged loyalties accordingly. The establishment's 'self interest' was to protect its place in the 'pecking order', while the 'axis- a nuclear armed, rag tag coalition of emerging nations & groups- saw its interest only in destroying the 'heart of the establishment', acutely aware of its inability to win a conventional war. Ideology & humanity took a complete back seat, as realpolitik & insanity became the only guiding forces...

The few remaining voices of sanity tried to impress upon all that no self interest was possible outside of collective interest, but they were completely drowned out in this cacophony of madness..

The 'annihilation', as it came to be called later, was not only the most widespread war ever in terms of its reach, but also the most devastating.

The brutal war lasted about a decade, and by the time it got over, there wasn't much left to destroy. Entire cities, even countries, were wiped out...

Both sides suffered massively, resulting in no winners, only victims. Every element of modern society was torn to shreds, every institution either destroyed or destabilized, every symbol of humanity in ruins...Over a quarter of the world's population perished (mostly men) in a mad rage of nuclear attacks & counter attacks. But the problems didn't end there. For the residual population, there was the looming danger of radiation-induced diseases, & an even greater shortage of resources.

The world, it seemed, was on the brink of a collapse, and that all of humanity would perish!! Life, as known to man, would collapse as a result of his own greed, hatred & folly...

Dave was quavering as he saw this, his soul numbed. *He was stating at the future of his own world going up in smoke...mother earth in the ultimate distress...in less than a century...*

He desperately hoped & wished that he could do something to stop it...anything...but he felt helpless...after all, what could a single, normal individual do in a world about to be blown to smithereens by own its mad rulers? *Just what could an individual do?*

But then he did the one thing an individual could do- he prayed, deeply, as deeply as an individual could, blessing mother earth; hoping that this was a nightmare which would never turn real...

As he prayed from his deepest self, Dave felt a strange calm engulf his entire being in that moment of utter despair...

As if he knew something...

Something, that told him that it need not be like this...

Though Dave didn't comprehend it, the soul knew it!

12. TRANSITIONS, SACRED FEMININE AND THE NEW AGES

"Today I shall shed light on an important aspect of our history, our evolution...something not so commonly known..." lady Zenia told Dave at the museum.

It was not without reason that a senior member of the Guardian Council, a leading Endower by the name of Zenia, was the curator of the Holographic history museum. A New Age landmark, it contained some priceless & timeless relics, apart from some critical information. Located on the highest peak of the moon, the museum was quite remote, and deliberately kept low profile, to maintain the confidentiality of these artifacts.. in fact, some believed that it housed mystical objects related to the birth of the New Ages, but no one really knew... except those entrusted to know...

The museum was a huge complex, shaped a bit like a castle of yore. Spread over 15 levels, it had an array of intricate alleys, passageways, turrets & spires, with multiple approaches to each section. The approaches varied each time a new visitor entered the complex, setting off a unique combination of stairs, passages & alleys. Much like a combination lock, this ensured that access was allowed only to authorized visitors, with the access code being controlled only by the security module. The pass code to this, of course, was available only to the curator, & advanced biometrics ensured no compromise.

****

As Dave and friends went around the museum, before meeting Zenia in her chamber, he noticed that each section dealt with different periods of history- and these followed a new calendar, and not the traditional BC & AD Christian calendar: *BD (before destruction/dawn), TR (the transitions) and the actual NA (New ages), starting with unveiling of the charter...*

BD referred to the history of the world until the late 21st century, just before the annihilation, and was varyingly referred to as '*before destruction'*, or '*before dawn'*- when Dave enquired as to why there were 2 descriptions, he got a cryptic reply- 'depends *upon one's perspective...*'

Ignoring the strange explanation, he proceeded in this section, noticing that it had several holographic images of preserved relics, books and artifacts from both the BC & CE periods-remains of an earth that he could identify with. To his pleasant surprise, there was also the Mona Lisa in the Arts section-apparently, this masterpiece had somehow survived the destruction...

"The museum was built quite some time back, and there wasn't too much emphasis on the BD period. So you may not see much of it. But I hear that a team of leading engineers, designers, architects, historians & archeologists has just been commissioned to submit plans for the GRAND DOME-that would be truly awesome." the museum guide clarified.

"I think *this* place too is awesome-even in its current form..."

Similarly the sections on the transitions had some holographic images of the relics & important scenes from that period, *but a lot of it was rather fuzzy...*

The most detailed & exciting section was the one on the NEW AGES itself, which housed several important & historical relics. Most of the stuff on display was actually holographic manifestation, rather than the actual relics themselves, which were safely housed deep inside the museum.

However, some original items were displayed too, like *the actual biometric scanner, through which leading members 'signed' on the CHARTER OF THE NEW AGES...*

With a sense of wonderment, the four of them headed for the curator's chamber. *It was no ordinary chamber, though...*

Made of a special material, it gave the appearance of a wall from the outside, but was actually transparent glass from within. There were three such 'walls', or access levels, which could be activated only by 3 unique, randomly generated voice pass codes, thereby ensuring the strictest security and minimal probability of unauthorized entry- in this case, the precise question directed at a specific individual.

Next to the chamber was the command & control centre (CCC), from where all the activities of the museum were monitored & controlled...

****

'What brings you here? The quest for knowledge, or fear?' came the first pass code question.

"When true knowledge comes, fear goes." replied Ikona.

'Those who know, further they may go...'

And the wall seemingly dissolved for a brief moment (the work of nano-bots, instructed by the security system), allowing them to pass. As they came inside, the 'wall' supposedly reassembled in a matter of moments, but all they could see was the view outside the chamber, as if looking across clear glass...

Then came the second questions, this time directed at Plutus.

'Knowledge those who seek,
Are they strong or meek?'

"The only real strength is that of character." Plutus replied.

'True strength those who show, further may go...'

Wow, what a security system...made for poets & philosophers! It would seem that we are here in the quest for the philosopher's stone...

Then came the last one, addressed to Dave, clearly intended to test both his understanding & perspective.

'He who has transcended,
Has his quest begun or ended?'

Trick question, Dave smiled. Then, after a moment, words came out of his mouth smoothly, as if flowing from a higher realm, a deeper self.

"Happiness is my quest; it is a journey, not a destination..."

'He who has been with the flow, further may go...'

Having been granted access, the four entered the chamber, and saw Zenia sitting at her desk. She was petite, slender, with unblemished skin & pepper grey hair. Strange looking rimmed glasses sat on her nose, adding to her charm & grace, apart from giving her a sense of authority. She was dressed in long flowing white gown, a cross between a monk's robe & a kimono. Dave assessed that she looked not a year older than 40, but having seen Master Aleus, realized that she was probably older… *Maybe 100*, he smiled to himself!

As soon as they entered, Zenia smiled warmly at them, giving Plutus a warm, long hug. After that she kissed Ikona on the forehead. For Ikona, lady Zenia was had been a major influence, as close to a role model as someone could be. Sensing the mischievous *'you-forgot-me'* expression on the face of Lyon, she called him over. "Oh, this is my favorite child. Come here my baby." She said in an equally mischievous way, giving him the tightest hug. Then, she looked at Dave, & said "Oh, so this is the young man who came here, and is full of questions?"

"Yes, ma'am. Pleasure to meet you!" He reached out his hand. Instead, she gave him a hug too, and gestured them to sit them on a large couch in the corner of her chamber. Dave noticed that the chamber was filled with high-tech looking gadgets, artifacts and digital books, which either contained content, or could simply 'pull relevant' content from the network, both text & audio visual.

As they settled down, Plutus told her about their research on the NEW AGES, the movie & images that Dave saw, and finally about how he chose to stop viewing it mid way, just after the war...

"You mean to say that you actually *witnessed* the war?" Zenia's words were deliberate, tinged with a certain surprise. The emphasis, though, clearly was on *witnessing*...

"Yes, but in a fuzzy sort of way…" Dave said, trying to figure out why she seemed so surprised.

"Uh, huh." She nodded.

"Then I just left it at that."

"You know pal, I was quite confused about why you left your research at that stage, just after the most gruesome part? After having actually seen the war?" Plutus asked Dave.

"I don't know. It's as if I sensed something...a strange sense of bliss & calm. And I must say, it seemed rather incongruous to feel bliss after witnessing the bloodiest war in history. But something came over me at that point..." Dave trailed off, trying to narrate the morphing of his emotions, from horror to a strange peace. But he couldn't exactly place it...

Zenia smiled beatifically...

this was something very important, even though Dave didn't understand it just yet...

"So what happened after that?" Zenia asked excitedly

"Just then, some words from the crop circle clue came flashed in my mind- especially the *Trinity*, as it played repeatedly. Like all other clues, at that time, it felt completely out of place; after a while, though, my mind went back to it- processing the various references to the trinity in history, religion and culture- in Christianity, as the father, son & the holy spirit; then in Hinduism- as Brahma, Vishnu & Mahesh; the creator, preserver & destroyer; and in some esoteric Shia traditions as Allah, Muhammad & Ali- God, his messenger and the esoteric master...

It seemed every tradition had its version, its own interpretation of the trinity, each profound in its own way...but none which seemed to really fit in here...leaving me flummoxed about which one it referred to..."

Zenia smiled in anticipation.

"For some reason, then, the thought of my friends as the trinity struck me. After all, that was my first brush with the concept of trinity here." He looked at them with a by now familiar warmth. "But what about them? Since the time I barged in, it had become the Quartet, in our words!"

Plutus flashed him a thumbs up sign.

"Unable to go any further, I left it at that. A couple of days later, I felt ready to move forward. So we spent more time trying to access the archives. But surprisingly, there were large gaps in it. The archives spoke about some 'transitions' and 'beings', but rather vaguely. Then they moved fast forward, straight to the point where a highly evolved society was established, and the historic 'CHARTER OF THE NEW AGES' was signed & adopted by all races in the 25th century. After that, there were enough details about the NEW AGES, but I was confused about why the archives of such an advanced society would be so, so..."

"Incomplete. Inconsistent..."

"Yes. Inconsistent..." Dave smiled at Lyon. "It's as if a large part of your initial history has been blacked out...and this bothered me. But I was still kind of groping in the dark; then one day, Ikona & Lyon were discussing a research paper that she is working on, when the image of trinity reappeared in my head, but in *rather unexpected ways....*"

Ikona & Lyon looked at him, surprised. They had no inkling of this until now.

"Unexpected?"Zenia spoke slowly, with the emphasis on *un*...

"Yes. Unlike the common notions of trinity, I saw three women...three goddesses, from different traditions- Durga, the mother, Saraswati, the goddess of knowledge, and Laxmi, the goddess of abundance, from the Hindu traditions; and Gaea, goddess of mother earth, Athena- goddess of wisdom, and Aphrodite- the goddess of love, or more commonly, lust, from the Greek traditions..."

"So why was it *un*expected?" Zenia pressed on.

"Because, in no tradition have goddesses been referred to as the holy trinity- it seemed like my mind was conjuring up something... and it seemed strange to find the goddess of lust in a holy trinity..."

Zenia bit her lips, her facial muscles tightening. But she said nothing.

"Then, another incongruous image crossed my mind- the mention of trinity as a character from a *famous science fiction movie* of our time... as a woman in whose love the chosen one almost allows the destruction of his people, choosing his love for her over his people..."

"*You referring to the Matrix? Trinity from the Matrix??!*" Lyon perked up, his electronic voice replicating its haunting soundtrack. "Clues from Hollywood movies? Man, you are something..."

Zenia was still stone-faced.

"While I was trying to process this new bit of information, Ikona mentioned your name as a possible reference source. I instantly had an intuition to see you, even though I didn't know you. Why, I'm not sure, but I sensed that you would share something important, something significant with me..."

Zenia was silent. For a good two minutes...

Sensing the awkward silence, and not sure of how his words were received, Dave attempted to continue the conversation. "I felt that maybe you'd throw some light on all of this..That's why I am here, ma'am-Following my *inner guide...*"

Zenia eased into her chair, and broke into a gentle smile. "Hmn...good that you continue to follow your intuition...though, of course, you have many incorrect notions that need to be dispelled...not your fault though..."

She got up from her desk and walked across to a book rack, picking up a digital book. "So, you want some answers? *Answers about the missing pieces of our history...*" she said deliberately, raising her glasses on her head, as she pressed the touch screen of the digital tablet. "But why? After all, isn't a large part of even *your* history, probably a majority of it, shrouded in mystery & darkness?"

"*Our* history?"

"Yes. Like tales of ancient civilizations which were at the peak of their power & prosperity, only to suddenly vanish from the annals of history, without a trace. Or ancient mythologies across cultures, which talk about strange technologies, beings & races, lots of which don't seem to add up. Or for that matter, the fact that large parts of human history have no recordings- Absolutely blank! Do you know why it is so, Dave?"

"Because history got distorted during recordings, and erased due to war & natural disasters."

"That's only part of the story. The full picture is that different civilizations are ready only for certain things... limited things...according to their ability to comprehend...

Beyond that, things are kept hidden till the right time...*need to be kept hidden...*"

"Are you suggesting that *large parts of human history have been deliberately blacked out?*" Dave asked, somewhat cynical and confused. "If so, by whom & how? And what about the missing pieces of history around the evolution of the NEW AGES? Is that deliberately blacked out too?"

"Held back is more like it- let's just say that *we all know what we need to know...what we ought to know...*higher knowledge comes only to those who are either ready to digest it, or chosen to be revealed to. *That's why history's mysterious are known only to a select few...*"

"Well, I think I am ready to assimilate it, ma'am." Dave sounded a bit peeved. *What was she trying to drive at by being so mysterious*? He came here hoping to get some answers on a new world, not more mystical stuff. However, he instantly realized that his edgy tone may not have gone down well with his host, and drew in a deep breath.

"My apologies, ma'am. I didn't mean to sound rude- just that I have digested enough new information here..."

"I know- you have seen a lot, including some that only *you* are chosen to see, even though you don't understand it yet..."Zenia smiled, replying as enigmatically.

Dave looked at her expectantly. "I had a sense that you will share some important information..."

'And I had the sense that you would...' Zenia smiled at this thought. *'Which you did...'* Then, looking at Dave's earnest eyes, she said. "Sensed correctly you have, Dave. Your intuition has served you well so far. So today I shall shed light on an important aspect of our history, our evolution- something not commonly known...*and something important for you & your world to know...*"

"Just what is that, endower?" Dave perked up.

"The role of Women in the evolution of the NEW AGES, and their connect with the being Hopefully, this will also end up dispelling some of your myths, & clarifying other questions."

Dave seemed confused. "What does the evolution of your civilization have to do with women?"

"More than you understand..." smiled Zenia. "Let's start off from where you left. What you *saw* was the destruction of your world, by its own mad inhabitants. Obviously the beings were not pleased with this development."

"Heard this before. So who, or what are the beings?"

"Souls who care..."

"I don't quite follow..."

"You don't?" Zenia looked at her in a knowing way. *"From the heavens came the beings, to help rediscover our wings...?"*

"The first clue! Don't tell me!" Dave gaped. "The same forces which facilitated my journey helped women of the transitions?"

Surprises would never cease to occur here...

"That's for you to decipher. But for now, let's continue. The war destroyed almost everything that the old world was built on- nation, religion, society, race- virtually every institution that your society was built upon was erased, exterminated...

But there was the proverbial silver lining- one inadvertent, and lucky, fallout of the catastrophe was that a majority of the residual population was women. And women, having lost their families & lives, started interacting with each other to share their sorrows & experiences. Determined to help each other out, irrespective of the artificial divisions which lead to the catastrophe, 'self help' groups were formed, which morphed into 'evolution' groups, first via the internet, and then on-ground.

Soon, these groups multiplied, and 'feminine evolution groups' became the largest post war social movement. Women, who are inherently gentler & open to receiving love & energy, came together to create a *'new age'*. This was the first time this term emerged."

"So the New Age was actually a fallout of a catastrophe?" Dave asked, not sure if he was with her.

"Life & death, creation & destruction are the circle of life, Dave- every outcome is eventually the result of our own action..." She replied enigmatically. "So, when we deeply seek with a pure heart, evolutionary forces aid us in the strangest of ways. Legend, therefore, says that *'the beings'* played a critical role in helping women in this mission..."

"Legend?" Dave raised his eyebrow. Now, which new legend was this, as if the flying Lama legend wasn't enough.

"Remember, *we all know what we need to know? No more & no less...*" Zenia smiled back. "So, to summarize, the getting together of women in such a coherent manner was a key catalyst to creating a new world, aided by the beings. They helped women to emerge in an important period of history, called the *transitions*."

"What was so important about the transitions?"

"As the name suggests, this period was a transition between the old, dying world & the formation of NEW AGES. And there were two key defining developments of the 'TRANSITIONS'- *the first was that women assumed leadership roles in the emerging governing institutions*. Legend again says that the beings had a key role to play in this."

"Women actually ran governance?"

"Yes, after a long time in human history, women got their due-women, not men, were in charge!" Zenia said profoundly.

"Not true. Since time immemorial, *women have been in charge. Men have always followed them, both before and after marriage*!" Lyon smirked.

Marriage & women jokes…boys will be boys…*Zenia gave him a stern look. Lyon hung his head down, sheepishly grinning, like a naughty student being berated in a classroom.*

"It was the first time, after a long period of distortions, that women, as a group, were driving the destiny of our planet."

"Distortions, ma'am?"

"Yes, Dave. For a large part of history, the ancients considered women sacred, life giving, even close to the divine. No wonder, the life giving planet you stay on is called mother earth, not father earth; and one's land is called the motherland, not fatherland…

But subsequent distortions erased the goddess, and as you pointed out, the holy trinity became a male turf- the goddess of love, of an activity that is so fundamental to the flow of life, even divine, became labeled the goddess of lust. Procreation- the germ of life, the base energy of the human system, became the great sin of Adam…*all thanks to Eve, of course*, and the temptations she induced!" The scathing indictment was unmistakable.

"Look at how everything related to Aphrodite or aphrodisiac has come to be regarded- the Goddess of love & procreation has been reduced to association with everything that is vile & sleazy.

And to think this is the defilement of a goddess-I am not even dwelling into the endless falsification, even defilements, that other women, normal women, had to endure in emerging history, religion & culture! My job is made easy by a string of *your bestsellers* that have harped upon that!"

There was a certain twinkle in her eyes at this last statement, but Dave failed to pinpoint whether it was humor or a continued disgust at our world's propensity to thrive in a herd mentality, albeit helpful for dispelling false notions at times…

"But the fact is, women progressively lost their spiritual role in the world, being slotted as objects of desire, something the chaste ought to shun…" Zenia continued.

Then, looking Dave straight in the eye, she continued. "For confirmation, look no further-just look at how you referred to the female character of trinity-*as someone who led the chosen one astray, not as a key character in the redemption of humans!* Doesn't this seem to echo the same stereotyping, the same labeling that has now become synonymous with most women of power and influence in history. And you probably said this rather nonchalantly, even innocuously..."

Dave lowered his eyes, now aware of why the endower was stone faced at his loose, even reckless pronouncements.

'It's Ok, Dave. It's not your fault. As a matriarchic society gave way to a male dominated structure, women got either branded as impure or relegated to the margins-and given this social backdrop, it's only natural for someone to be surprised at the depiction of women as the holy trinity. But I guess it took precisely such a vision for you to understand that your next answer was to come from a woman." She smiled broadly now, allowing Dave to relax somewhat.

"So, coming back to destruction, fortuitously, women came to handle key institutions again- and that itself would lead to a big, big change. A lot of the negativities would be undone. Whenever men have been the dominant race, masculine energies have only brought forth conflict & destruction, including this final catastrophe. The time was ripe for feminine energies to come to the fore. Only feminine energies could give wounded humanity the healing, care & a new direction that was needed. Only women could truly usher in a 'NEW AGE'!" Zenia settled back into her chair, allowing the words to settle in too...

Beyond the prima facie logic of what Zenia had just narrated, and his own faux pas, Dave seemed to agree-women could run things differently from men, and in most cases, better! In his own small world, be it in office or community service, he had experienced it.

Women seemed to bring about a new perspective, a different energy, and were more open to receiving and giving love & energy-where men tended to take the path of confrontation, women took the path of conciliation & compassion, gently achieving the desired outcome with minimum friction & conflict; while it seemed slow & weak to the male mind, it mostly led to a more lasting, acceptable outcome.

"A simple piece of advice for your world- *replace all your politicians, bureaucrats & business leaders with women & creative people, & see the flowering of heaven in your own plane...*" Zenia smiled, reading Dave's mind.

Dave smiled back. "Now that I think about it, I sure hope so. *And what was the second development?*"

"Related to the first development and the scars of annihilation- *the conscious lifting of collective energies, thanks again to the centricity of feminine ideals.* Aided by the beings, human consciousness evolved to the next level, and thus began the transitions, which were as magical as mysterious; it would suffice to know that they lasted for 200 years, in which the world healed, stabilized & progressed yet again, but this time with a different purpose and in a different direction."

"Let's just say the transitions were the new age equivalent of the Renaissance, when a distinct break from the past was achieved. There was the development of advanced technologies, along with the evolution of new, more evolved systems & institutions- based on universal ideals of love, peace, creativity, & true, meaningful growth.. While always maintaining the sanctity of the highest mother of them all-MOTHER EARTH."

"All this happened during the transitions? *With women at the helm?*"

"Yes. While the world stabilized & evolved under the stewardship of women, they also played a key natural role as mothers-thus came forth a new breed of humans: *the offspring...*

It wasn't a new breed so much in the biological sense, as in the mental, emotional, social & spiritual sense. The 'offspring' took forward the wisdom of the transitions, to set the foundation for the NEW AGES..." Zenia paused for a while, allowing Dave to absorb it.

"Fascinating. Amazing! Sounds just like the emergence of humans from the Neanderthals; a new breed, a quantum leap..."

"Yes, exactly- the foundation for a new world was laid."

"You know what, as a child, I had read stories of several civilizations rising from the ashes, like the proverbial phoenix. And then, as economics students, we read about the rise of Japan after the 2nd world war, from the shambles; this somehow reminds me of that- of what human spirit can achieve..."

"In a way, yes, but this is qualitatively different. *This is evolution brought about by feminine energies, not the traditional masculine energies.* And this is about a civilization whose consciousness evolved to the next level. All technological & systemic developments were an outcome of this elevated consciousness, rather than distinct from it. Material progress came on account of elevation of collective consciousness, and hence was sustainable this time."

"You know, endower, this sounds a bit too utopian. I can understand a society rising from the ashes, materially-*but can an entire civilization evolve in its consciousness, collectively?*"

"Yes, it can rise collectively, though obviously not equally." smiled Zenia. "That depends on every soul's individual journey. But the evolution of consciousness at a collective level is not that impossible. *There are signs...*"

"Signs?"

Zenia ignored the question. "If entire societies can rise materially, why not spiritually? A new consciousness governing an entire society has happened periodically throughout history- especially in societies materially or technologically *more advanced & equitable...*"

"It's not *that rare*- come to think of it, all it takes is a critical mass!" Ikona added. "After all, a leading thinker of your time has propounded the theory of *tipping point*-a concept equally applicable *to any social norm as well, right?*"

"Including elevation of collective consciousness?"

"Absolutely! All it needs is a critical mass of evolved souls, and once the tipping point is reached, collective consciousness rises to the next level..."

"Sounds a bit like the emerging human potential movements in our time. Read about Noetic sciences in one of our bestsellers." Dave reflected.

It wasn't that farfetched as it initially seemed, with a lot of realization & research having started at the end of the 2nd millennium. Many thinkers were unanimous that human consciousness was at a turning point, and evolved collective consciousness could do wonders...

"Remember, the transitions were not normal times- the world had just seen its bloodiest catastrophe. If there had to be a start, it was bound to be from a clean slate."

Still slightly unsure, Dave decided not to interrupt the flow. What they were saying had factual basis, as utopian as it seemed. He *was* in one of these utopian lands!

"So what happened after that? How did the transitions morph into the NEW AGES?"

"The 'offspring' developed advanced communications, computing, commuting & materials technologies, along with a giant leap in the understanding of energy dynamics. Aided by these developments, they managed to create the first human settlement outside of earth, on the moon... *FOR THE FIRST TIME IN HISTORY, MAN SET UP HOME OUTSIDE HIS HOME PLANET!"*

"This was one of the most significant developments in human history, and gave further impetus to human development. New resources, unspoilt environment, a new wisdom- the stage was set for a further leap in human consciousness.

After this, **the Charter of the New Ages** was officially unveiled, with the blessings of the 'mothers' who gave humanity rebirth. The charter was an extensive constitution, laying down the roadmap for a new society, basis the fundamental principles of harmony with natural laws, and a dissolution of outwardly fragmentation, leading to a more holistic society."

Dave's mind flew to the Magna Carta, a similar landmark charter that became the harbinger of modern civil rights & rule of law.

"Since all these developments came about because of feminine energies, the council accorded a special place to the 'sacred feminine'- its rightful place, lost in history.

After all, it was feminine energy that gave the world a new life, a higher reality...

So while women were no longer the leaders of these institutions, they always find a special mention as the 'mothers' who guided the world through the transitions into the NEW AGES..."

"As always, women gave life where men brought forth only death & destruction.." Ikona concluded, leaving food for thought...

13. The New Worlds- Zen and Kaizen

Dave lay there on his floating bed, lights dimmed by mood control, soft music playing in the background. In the corners, aromatic candles added to the deeply soothing mood, ready to induce the recipient of its sensual fragrance to sleep... but a restless Dave was wide awake, fidgeting with the disk, occasionally staring at it...

He was reflecting upon his journey so far, as well as what endower Zenia had shared with them earlier in the day- so profound, yet so apparent...

Why couldn't he perceive it earlier? After all, his own companion was the embodiment of all those feminine qualities...

Lost in thoughts, the disk fell out of his hands onto the floor, and it momentarily flashed the image of the crop circle, along with its clue, onto the floor:

Trinity within trinity within trinity; he who truly seeks, finds...
The core and the outer governed by the one that binds...
Three connected by the union of four..
The outer, the three new and the core..
The trinity of worlds, civilizations & friends..
A new order emerges while the old one ends..
When the trinity morphs into the quartet,
A new fellowship shall be set...
As the layers are unraveled,
The Messenger would be revealed to the one who has travelled...

Just then, there was a beep on the far wall, indicating that someone was at the 'door', rather the connecting glass; it was Plutus.

"Come, come buddy.."

"Just dropped by to check on you. Not slept as yet?"

"No. contemplating."

"About what you heard today?" Plutus had sensed this in Dave's eyes when they left the museum.

"Yeah, that and everything else. The endower's words have left a deep imprint- *we men ruin the world and women lovingly nurture it…and yet we continue to live in a world dominated by masculine energies? Why?*"

"One of the many flaws of your world!" Plutus remarked in a lighter vein, but the underlying sting unmistakable.

"That's why the sacred feminine is understood, experienced and held in the highest esteem here; and no, not in the way your novels or fancy theories or occult practices suggest, with a certain ethereal or historical perspective- but rather about the true nature of feminine qualities…

Dave, the sacred feminine is not merely about Goddesses; it's about the magic even ordinary women bring forth, which makes creation so resplendent- they give birth to life, nourish it, and provide it with the loving anchor & compassionate balance needed to keep it an evolutionary state. That love & compassion is the essence of feminine divinity, buddy…"

Dave sighed. "We need that magic; and bloody desperately, given where we are today, and where we've steered our civilization to! Oh, and by the way, after today, I am compelled to think that the messenger may well be female- don't think men deserve to!"

"Interesting hypothesis, though not necessarily correct." Plutus spoke with a maturity that gave a true glimpse of the level head he carried on his shoulders.

"Instead of yo-yoing from one extreme to another, get a sense of the underlying essence- it is not about genders really, my friend. It's about the nature of energy, and the perennial conflict & equilibrium between them…"

Dave gave a blank look.

"Am sure you've seen the Taijitu, the Tao symbol of Yin-Yang?" And he projected one from his wristband micro computer onto the far wall.

"Yes, I have." Dave smiled. His foray into the world of oriental mysticism & philosophy had introduced him to the concept of balance, something he assiduously endeavored to practice now. "The coexistence of opposites- the circle of life, of night & day, good & bad, joy & sorrow..."

"Yeah, but it also has many other interpretations & secrets- one of them being the harmonious amalgamation of masculine & feminine energies, each existing in equilibrium; but more importantly, there is a little bit of both in each other- visualize the small black circle in the white space & vice versa..."

"Interesting; never thought of that! So basically even in men there is a bit of the soft feminine trait, and if that can be consciously cultivated, there is no reason to believe that men can be only demons; comforting!" he smiled.

"Yes, that's the secret of androgynous viewpoint, and that's the core philosophy of the offspring..That's how we are different from the humans of yore; We are a more conscientious & aware breed, having consciously cultivated the feminine energies within.."

Just then, the clue flashed again in Dave's mind, as a fleeting image...

"Hey listen, I was reflecting upon this whole thing when the crop circle clue reappeared-as if it somehow relates to what I learnt today, as if something more needs to be understood. And now, while we were discussing about the offspring, it appeared again..."

"So that's why you are kind of tossing & turning, huh?"

Dave smiled in assent. There was something struggling to emerge from all this, but somehow not there yet...

"Ok, let's see- probably more needs to be understood. But what about it? Let's reflect... hmn...

Trinity within trinity within trinity..." Plutus remarked, stroking his chin in a gesture of deep thought.

"The trinity has so many connotations, such a lot of significance, as I discussed with the endower today. But I feel the spiritual connotations had their relevance in guiding me to meet the curator. Here, somehow, the trinity seems to be alluding to something else- *another level of interpretation*...and, not a single trinity, but rather a series of trinities..." Dave spoke, his mind trying hard to decipher it.

"OK, so within this series of trinities, one is ours, the trinity of friends, as we have deciphered; *the trinity morphing into the Quartet..*"

Plutus smiled at the mention, the truthfulness in his eyes shining through.

"So what could the others be?" Dave gazed at Plutus.

Without much thought, Plutus answered. "I think the clue itself answers it- the *trinity of worlds, civilizations & friends*... It's apparent!"

"I don't quite follow it.."

"Let me explain; the endower explained about the offspring settling on the moon, right? And how critical this was, as humans set up colonies outside of earth for the very first time."

"Right."

"Over time, the 'offspring' created settlements on two more virgin worlds- Columbus & Einstein."

Dave was surprised! so far, he had still not realized that the 'offspring' had settled on worlds outside of the moon too! And, of course, the names of the worlds struck him...

"Did you just say Einstein & Columbus?"

"Yup. Surprised that they sound unusual for the names of worlds? Not Greek or Roman gods?"

"Kind of. But more than that, actually- these were the same images I saw during the crop circle clue...

Now I get it!" Dave said with a thrill, figuring out what those supposed disparate images were trying to communicate. *"Those visuals of celestial bodies along with Einstein & Columbus represented the outer trinity!"*

"So that makes it the outer trinity-the trinity of worlds! The moon, Columbus & Einstein..." Plutus said, summing it up.

Dave stared into the distance, as the associated image flashed in front of his eyes, and more clarity emerged...

"Now I get more- the middle circle represents earth, so the inner circle most likely represents its satellite- moon. And the outer circle the solar system...*Trinity within trinity within trinity...and the three other smaller circles represent the new worlds...*"

"Brilliant!" Plutus exclaimed. "In terms of code cracking, you could give Robert Langdon a run for his money!"

"*Langdon??!* I see you are well connected with our world, including its best sellers..." Dave genially remarked.

"Have to be buddy- heaven has to keep a close watch on earth!" Plutus winked convivially as well.

"But why three circles? Two other worlds, Einstein & Columbus. So why three? And are these colonies are fully functional, with people living there?"

"I can't answer about the first part; but I can tell you about the latter half of your question. By the 25th century, there were settlements on Good old Earth- very different now, almost recreated to its pristine, pre-industrial age glory; the beautiful moon, now beyond the realms of poetry to actual habitation; and two other satellites, discovered recently in the solar system- **Einstein**, primarily a colony of cyborgs- half a billion strong & a centre of great technological innovation, and **Columbus,** located beyond Saturn- a favorite vacation spot for humans.

So you see, four different worlds, four different atmospheric & surface conditions, but similar simulated living conditions!"

"Wow!" Dave's mind traversed the entire expanse of human history, when humans settled in different lands, explored new worlds & conquered them. *"Here is the next level of conquest!"*

"Not conquests buddy, alignments! The new age settlements are as much a reflection of the boundless human spirit of determination, innovation & enterprise, as a manifestation of symbiosis with nature and natural laws. They aren't just mega cities or concrete jungles, but colonies planned and built on the basic principles of sustainable, green, equitable & natural habitation. Yes, they are ultra modern, can accommodate, feed & sustain large populations, and have amazing connectivity, both in terms of communications & commuting, but are also models of natural & simple living."

"Sounds like an interesting coexistence of contradictions."

"Actually, not. In essence, they are the true embodiments of the NEW AGE philosophy-one of seamless integration between science & nature. This is true ZEN! Humans have finally understood Zen, and are living it!"

Dave reflected... true Zen... one with the flow, with nature...

"But how? What about the challenges of settlement?" he queried after a while.

Plutus went on to explain that there undoubtedly were colossal challenges in creating habitable environments & developments on three different worlds, both in terms of technology & master planning; but the planners, technologists & engineers of this new era saw these as opportunities to start on a clean slate, rather than impediments...though long gone, memories of abuse of mother earth were deeply etched in human consciousness, and there was complete determination to never allow it to get repeated.

To begin with, there was the basic challenge of creating an earth like atmosphere, so that human, plant & animal life could survive & flourish. The answer to this was the creation of giant 'atmospheric domes', using advanced materials & NANO technology. These were not solid, but rather gel like, allowing for free transit in & out for passenger & freight vehicles, while at the same time shielding the habitations from outer atmospheric disturbances, potentially violent storms etc.

This was achieved by breakthrough advancements in super light, super strong materials technology, creating a gel like substance- Gelass...

Gelass reminded Dave of something...something familiar...

The Gelass was based on aerosol technology, and could just be 'sprayed', to create 'atmospheric shields'. Invisible to the naked eye, it was controlled by billions of 'nano bots' connected to & regulated by the Intelligent Interplanetary Network (IIN). These little machines, or 'nano bots' controlled temperature, pressure, gravity, ambient light & oxygen-CO2 balance, to simulate earthlike conditions on these worlds, without altering the inherent characteristics of that world.

The second challenge was the abundant supply of oxygen & water, in consumable form. This was made possible by advanced mining, refining, processing and distribution technologies, allowing for extraction, purification & supply of these natural resources. Moreover, since these resources were being explored & produced on different worlds & terrains, they had the blueprint of recycle & reuse. On the moon, for example, the soil was rich in oxygen, especially a compound called *Ilmenite*. *Giant processors were set up in non habitation areas to extract oxygen from the soil, for both interplanetary fuel as well as human consumption.* To aid oxygen supply & atmospheric balance within the domes, a huge forestation master plan was drawn, based on extensive soil & seed research, which would, in the course of time, add to sustainable oxygen sources, apart from augmenting the natural beauty & simulation of near earth like conditions.

Similarly, the other two satellites were rich in frozen water. Apart from mining in those, another potential source was the asteroid belt between Mars & Jupiter-the largest known of these, Ceres, had earth like properties, and was already being studied during the 21st century, supposedly containing more fresh water than earth itself. Advanced space drilling technologies allowed the extraction of liquid water from frozen underground lakes. This was then used for both-consumption, in liquid form, as well as for oxidation, using advanced electrolysis. Both these processes were carried out in massive central processors, and then sent to the respective worlds' refining hubs, from where they was supplied, collected back & recycled.

Conversely, lunar & earth oxygen was also partially used for water creation by combining with hydrogen, using newer catalysts. Since this reaction in inherently exothermic, it had dual advantages- creation of water for consumption, & the generation of substantial clean energy, which could be used to drive reactors elsewhere.

Dave saw a delicious irony here- water & oxygen, the most commonly available resources on earth, were the most precious commodities here. *It was mother nature's way of reminding us that while the best things in life come for free, we should not take anything for granted- neither the love of our beloved, nor the gifts of mother earth. What we abuse, we have to pay for...and that's when we realize the worth of these little things!*

The third challenge was the interplanetary distribution of these elements & compounds. Here, the answer lay in huge advancements in commuting technologies, which ensured that interplanetary freight was 'commercially' viable; though, as Dave would learn later, this concept had a very different meaning here...

The fourth was the challenge of harsh, unstable and, at times, fluid & volatile surfaces on these worlds- how does one create huge colonies on such an unstable, non solid surface?

Here again, Gelass was the answer. It created a super strong, super thin, fluid, and pre designed opaque surface, thereby creating an 'illusion' of stable ground! On this simulated 'surface', all superstructures could be created, apart from placement of soil for vegetation & forestation. Moreover, since these were gels, they were extremely flexible & mobile. Hence any sub-surface disturbances, from earthquakes to volcanoes, were never transmitted inside the habitation areas, but rather absorbed by it, creating a 'shock absorber' layer.

The fifth was the challenge of feeding the population on diverse planets- here, urban farming & green house technologies, built on vertical, not horizontal farms, was the answer. Advancements in crop research, irrigation & seed technology meant that richly organic food could be grown by minimum consumption of surface area, water or fertilizers. Moreover, a special technique called 'energy focusing' was widely practiced in the farms here, giving the foods a different level of nutrition & energy.

However, there were special pockets & farms, where truly exotic stuff grew, having a different energy, nutritional & healing qualities altogether. Dave recollected his first morning here, when he was fed special herbs from the healing gardens of the moon, and cereals from the farms of Columbus...

The final key challenge was the actual housing and 'town' planning. Here too, the approach was radically different from what was followed in the past.

The master plan was based not upon advanced urban planning, or even an urban-rural balance, but rather on creating sustainable 'communes'. With the advancement of intra & interplanetary commuting, there was no need for the concept of urban mega cities. Instead, people chose to live in communes, either in large super structures, or mobile, flexible housing, spread across open spaces, based on ideological proximity & personal choices...

In the mass, commune based housing, complete mini-cities resided in a cluster of ultra tall, gigantic towers. This is where Plutus & his friends stayed, and this is what he was fascinated by the first time on this plane. Using carbon nano-tubes as the structural skeleton, instead of conventional steel or iron, gigantic skyscraper over 2000 stories high were created. Since these were anyways housed inside atmospheric domes, there was no issue of high altitude temperature or pressure variation, and the consequent forces & their impact on their mega structures. The dome itself regulated the environment.

Back on earth, however, these giant towers used super thin, super strong carbon isotopes to build the surfaces. Their superior strength, along with super thin & flexible surfaces, allowed them to withstand natural forces- as also to regulate oxygen supply, temperature & pressure at very high altitudes. This was especially relevant considering that manmade structures were now higher than the 'roof of the world'.

And on worlds like Columbus, igloos and ice colonies made of special ice of its surface were both popular & exotic for mass based housing. On the other hand, for non mass based housing, since distances no longer mattered, and infrastructure was not a constraint, people could live as 'far' or as 'close' to the central districts as possible. Infact, spread out communes rendered the concept of central districts & suburbs pretty fuzzy, even redundant.

Add to this the development of flexible & mobile housing, and a whole new, integrated model of housing emerged, where individual pursuits could seamlessly merge with community based services. This was suited to the needs of the seekers, free souls and those who extensively traveled with their 'backpacks'. This kind of flexible & mobile housing allowed 'virtual communes' to congregate and disperse as per their individual choices. NEW AGE housing, along with the new economic model of this world, became a key factor in facilitation of individual creative energies proliferating freely...*basic instincts no longer needed to be at odds with social life...*

Dave's mind flew back to the congregation at Woodstock... if only commune could be merged with comfort & modern technology...

Well, here it was...

****

Dave paused to pore over the astounding information he had just garnered. It was amazing, almost fairy tale like, how so many challenges were surmounted, so many obstacles overcome...He then learnt further about the key advancements which allowed for overcoming these gargantuan obstacles:

The first was the advancement of mining & materials technology. This gave the offspring access to completely different compounds & minerals, each one having a special value. There were super strong materials, lightweight materials, materials viable for nano bot construction, oxygen & hydrogen rich materials, & materials rich in precious & isotopic compounds. The more materials technology advanced, the more it facilitated interplanetary travel & settlements, thereby allowing for further research & development.

Supplementing it was the breakthrough advancement in propulsion & commuting technologies for intra & interplanetary travel, including PATs & CATs. This allowed for freight & commuter travel across the world at speeds & efficiencies hitherto unimaginable.

Then there was the great breakthrough of this age- ***The Intelligent Interplanetary Network (IIN),*** *along with holographic projection technology;* based on advanced Artificial intelligence (AI), fuzzy logic and whole new interplanetary protocols, *the IIN was the super advanced, interplanetary version of the world wide web- the 'multi world web' or 'mww'...*

But it was not just an advanced, interplanetary communications platform; rather, the central nervous system of the NEW AGES, controlling, coordinating & communicating across most aspects of life & administration, through modules & sub modules. It would be no exaggeration to say that *the IIN was probably one of the most significant developments here...*

And finally, another key development at the heart of all this progress was a higher understanding of energy and huge leaps in energy technologies. This not only created material abundance and made space travel possible, but actually was central to the creation of a radically different society & NEW metrics, as Dave would learn later.

Of course, all of this was meshed with the wisdom of moderation, both in population & consumption. A wiser human race managed to keep the total population at an "equilibrium" level of three billion, spread over these four worlds. At an individual level, there was an onus, a recognition of regeneration exceeding commensurate consumption, so that no future generation would ever be bequeathed a world depleted & unhealthy...

"So this is what the equilateral triangle connecting the three circles represents? Balance...three worlds in true equilibrium, harmony..."

"One more brilliant act, Professor Langdon." Plutus smiled.

"Yes, it's a message for balance & harmony, not to strip & recklessly consume.. and do note that it's an inverted triangle, so wanna take a guess as to what it denotes?"

"Feminine energies??!!"

"Exactly. Balance through feminine, not masculine energies. And you thought the shape of the crop circle was accidental?" Plutus spoke mockingly.

Dave responded with a mock salute of his own. "Man, there are just layers upon layers..."

"Yeah. So the next layer is that as a tribute to the new found human wisdom, along with the innate ability and desire for exploration & innovation, the two new worlds were aptly named: *Einstein & Columbus! Symbolic, yet significant..."*

"So what's the third trinity?" Dave asked after a while. They had now ventured onto the deck outside, to enjoy the crisp, fresh breeze. Dave, now aware that it was all a simulated environment within a dome, nonetheless felt the same freshness here as on a beach.

"The trinity of civilization: three new races..." Plutus replied, gazing into the distance, resting his chin in his palms, and his elbows on the ledge.

"Three new races?"

"Yes-another key social development of the NEW AGES *was the evolution of the 3 races;* socio-techno-ideological units, based neither or biology, nor on the dogmas or false compartments of the past, but on new age ideological affinity.

So there emerged the organics/puritans, commonly referred to as the offspring, the hybrid 'cyborgs', and the Genrefs- a race of genetically refine offspring, based on advancements in genetic & cloning technologies."

"Clones? Genetically refined race? Sounds dangerous." Dave soaked in the beautiful 'night sky', engaged in a stimulating discussion with someone who could have been a stranger, yet destiny chose as a special friend.

"Yes, in a low energy, low consciousness environment, very dangerous. If such developments are used to distort nature or its flow, then unethical. But then, so is the case with all technological advancements in your world. It's not technology itself, but the application of it, that really qualifies it. *Technology, by itself, is neither moral nor immoral, but rather 'amoral', much like energy.* In an evolved, spiritual society, the hybrids and Genrefs simply use the powers of genetic technology in an ethical fashion to further human development, to create better, healthier cells. To that extent, they aren't very different from the borgs, except that they have chosen the organic route instead of the synthetic route. *In our world, adding to the evolutionary process to understand the mysteries of creation are not seen as impeding god's plan, but rather as aiding it..."*

"So the Gen-refs aren't a race per se? And not full-fledged clones?"

"No, no- there is no race of millions of carbon copies. That is against nature, and we would never take that route; of course, there are selective cases of people or parents taking to the cloning route for specific reasons, but mostly for some sort of cellular enhancement." Plutus spoke in a reassuring tone. Dave still seemed concerned, though.

"Don't worry- all technologies are closely governed, and made to pass the seer test, before they are made available for mass consumption; clones are strictly a quasi-race, not a cult of replicated copies, as some of your movies would scare you into thinking. All races here have the same core values-those of evolution & harmony of spirit. It's just a difference of routes to the same goal. Proof of this is that there is a special community here called the seekers, who are drawn from all the races. They are NEW AGE equivalent of the mystics."

Silence for a while, then Dave queried. "So what about the *'Three connected by the union of four'*...?"

"Think it refers to the Quartet."

"Quartet? Yes, that too is mentioned. '*As the trinity morphs into the Quartet...*' But I thought that referred to your trinity morphing into a harmonious melody of four friends, thanks to me." Dave smiled.

"I thought so too; but in your own words, this clue operates at multiple levels." Plutus turned to look at Dave. "On one hand, it talks about our trinity & quartet, and on another, it seems to metaphorically allude to the Quartet- *three new worlds & races connected by the Quartet; a union of four...*"

"So what exactly is the Quartet? It's some institution?"

"More like a new system of Governance. As our society evolved, newer institutions took roots, and a new establishment of administration, called *the QUARTET,* was formed."

"So the Quartet is a form of governance?"

"Yes. but more than just an advanced form of governance- it seamlessly combines the four establishments, forming the bedrock of an integrated system. Concurrently, a GRAND COUNCIL of Masters was established, to maintain balance & harmony between various aspects of life & governance. This Council comprised evolved beings from all races."

"So, the Quartet runs things, while the Council regulates it? Like a watchdog?" Dave tried to encapsulate it.

"In a basic sense, yes. But it is much more than a watchdog- it is the moral compass of the administrative system."

"Brilliant- so you are basically telling me that you are an advanced civilization, having three ideologically oriented races, residing on three new worlds, facilitated by feminine energies & advanced technologies, resting on the platform of higher consciousness, having a whole new system of Governance called the Quartet, and regulated by the Guardian Council ..."

"Well summarized dude!'

Dave lay quiet for a while, taking in deep breaths, absorbing the entire significance of their conversation, and of more mysteries unraveled- the three circles of the crop circle pattern, the equilateral triangle & harmony, the images, the clue itself...*It was now apparent that the clue & pattern were a poetic & pictorial snapshot of the world he was being guided to. Brilliant, he couldn't help admiring; what he thought to be meaningless, cryptic words & images back then, were the most beautiful renditions of this amazing world...*

It was falling into place, bit by bit...

But beyond the thrill of further unraveling the clues, he was feeling good about something else as well, leading his energies to be super-elevated! After the scarring images of war, which remained etched in his subconscious, this is just what was needed to reinforce his faith, his pride, in humanity again...

So much 'true progress' was possible when collective energies were channeled in creative & technological pursuits, not in destruction. The exponential growth of information & networking technology (which was, in some way, the harbinger & precursor to the IIN) was one such living proof of our time...

And sadly, the growth of nuclear weapons technology was another example of significant energies & creativity gone terribly awry...

While Dave was enjoying his new-fangled understanding of the higher worlds, apart from the unraveling of the crop circle clue, the Council was getting concerned- *apart from the earth, they now also had to worry about the heavens too...*

Signs of energy turbulence were emanating from Einstein. Something was at work there, something which was beginning to worry them...*the Clairvoyants could sense it...but there was nothing conclusive...*

What started off as a potentially breakthrough energy experiment that could further propel the NEW AGES, was now seemingly going astray. And while no one openly spoke about it, there was whisper that these clandestine experiments were covertly supported by some members of the Quartet. Clearly, something was not very transparent, and the Quartet didn't seem to either know or care enough...

The Council then decided to take matters in their own hands by keeping a close tab on these developments- they weren't the conscience keepers of the NEW AGES without reason, and decided to depute someone they trusted to this remote planet...

Unknown to Dave, this is what was delaying his meeting with the Council...

14. HUMAN BEING, NOT HUMAN DOING...

It was now over three 'moon months' since Dave had been 'teleported' here. In this time, he had learnt quite a bit about this world (rather worlds), its advanced technology, its new 'work ethic', and it's evolved social ecosystem. He also saw a wonderful example of the synergy of science & spiritualism in every aspect of life here, having briefly learnt about a new system of governance (the QUARTET).

In this period, he also felt increasingly comfortable about his stay here. He loved the huge floating houses, the sight of flying PATs everywhere, and significantly, started liking the food as well!

He acquired three new, special friends, with whom lasting bonds were being formed: Plutus, the ever graceful, gracious & calm young man; Ikona, the epitome of feminine energies- strong yet gentle, in control yet tender, intelligent yet humble, her unconventional beauty reminding him of 'another life', another love; and Lyon, the cyborg- cocky to the point of being arrogant, super intelligent, sharp witted, even brusque at times, but with a heart of gold. As he drew closer to them, jointly exploring this world, he sensed that this trinity had indeed morphed into the quartet...

In this entire period, there was no fresh clue, nor anything eventful; but the questions did keep recurring- *about the 'meaning' of his journey, the mystery of the 'MESSENGER', and how exactly did he fit into the overall scheme of things...* this led to occasional bouts of skepticism & anxiety...

And then there was the issue of 'withdrawal pangs'- having spent a large part of life working by the clock, he found it difficult to adapt to a life of 'doing nothing', except 'observing'. *The longest vacation of his life, he would joke later!* but witnessing such a fascinating world, where people 'lived' life, made him a bit more comfortable with the idea of just 'being'…

And by observing his buddies, he deduced that *the concept of 'work' in this world was radically different from ours...*

In this world, people usually worked on 'projects' or 'assignments', as per their own inclinations. There were no conventional organizations, no fixed hierarchical structures; instead, there were loosely bound 'project teams', which came together on specific projects, completed them, dispersed, & then moved onto the next 'project'. Huge advancements in commuting, computing & communications technologies meant that the vision of 'virtual' work & 'virtual' offices was a reality.

Add to this, there weren't the usual kinds of professions- in fact, there were no preferred professions! So there was no premium on 'getting a degree from Ivy League' or being an 'MBA', and no parental or peer pressure. What was important was to gain knowledge & wisdom, to continually grow as a person, to upgrade oneself, and to follow the inner calling...

Dave, the 'steeped-in-structures-and-processes' manager, initially found it difficult to digest the fact that organizations could exist & survive in such an unstructured & flexible environment. But somewhere, this concept touched a chord within- after all, in many ways, he now held work pressures, the race for survival & rigid organizational structures, responsible for his losses…at least partially! If things were different in his workplace, maybe his realities would have been different too…*Grappling with these conflicting emotions & philosophies, he got more clarity at the promenade one evening…*

****

Almost every evening, Dave would visit the promenade to watch the 'earth rise'. Out of the many 'viewing decks' on the moon, the 'earth point' seemed most popular. Built on top of a beautiful 'mountain range', it was frequented by thousands of visitors every evening. But unlike a simple viewing deck, this was a huge promenade, spanning miles on end.

In front was a large, placid, water body stretching on for miles, giving it the feel of a pine forest merged with a tropical beach promenade. It had live music, several roadside bistros, and a carnival like atmosphere extending into the wee hours of the morning...out here, a multitude of people spent hours just sitting, catching up with friends, indulging in adventure & water sports, walking, running, painting, serenading, composing music, meditating, reading...basically doing whatever they liked...

This place seemed to be having something for everybody...

In fact, it seemed that people here had lots of time 'outside of work'. Yet, no one seemed deprived-no poverty, no scarcity, no great disparity...the whole place seemed to thrive on an 'abundance mentality'. People seemed to have access to whatever resources they needed, or wanted...

This meant that there was an abundance of artists, literary folks, explorers, R&D guys in the NEW AGES- anybody who was the creative or exploratory types-and nowhere was this more apparent than at the promenade, where they converged, electrifying the place with a pulsating energy...

While observing them, Dave invariably remembered the 'rues' of Paris, where street painters, singers & musicians dotted the sidewalk, pursuing their avocations with gay abandon. But unlike those artistes, who usually lived as paupers and died broke, the creative & exploratory types here seemed rather 'well off'. They came in fancy PATs, were always smartly dressed, had high-tech accessories & gizmos, and most likely had comfortable dwellings...

It was almost as if they all had some hefty inheritance left behind, or that the government here had a super generous social welfare system...

Making a mental note of this apparent contradiction, rather aberration, Dave was sitting in deep introspection one evening, when he felt a sudden vibration in his trouser pocket, much like that of a cell phone. As he instinctively reached his hands out into his pocket, it struck him that he had no cell phone here- the vibration was from something else, something unexpected- *his relatively tiny disk!*

After weeks of stillness & silence, it was suddenly buzzing to life, in yet another beautiful but unexpected location, words seemingly forming, inscribed in the gel like object- but not the normal script, *rather like calligraphy...graceful curves, flowing lines, all in a bright golden...*

As the words finally acquired a distinct shape, he held the disk closer to his eyes, peering in to read them…

The fourth clue…
In the present of the future, not in now's past,
Beyond the vestiges last..
Beckons the original mother
To an institution nurturing her…
The revered, the wise, the conglomeration sacred
The harmonious connecting thread
Where the spirit is nurtured & wisdom bred
Seek them if the message you have intuitively read…
Past the chant, through the black gold, rock & dust,
Move with understanding & trust,
Where the life giving snake slithers & winds
The worthy there his destination finds…
Answers more then will flow
If one's true self can one show…

Dave felt a surge of adrenalin-it had been three months of living & 'being', but no further 'action' with regards to the clues; the original vision had suggested seven clues, but here he seemed to be stuck on the third, leading to restlessness at times. But here, at the promenade, sitting in silence & contemplation, the next clue presented itself when least expected…

There was something about the place…and the timing…

Still holding the translucent disk close to his eyes, something else struck him- beyond the intricately contoured words, through the disk, he noticed a man staring intently at him across the street. Dave squinted slightly, trying to get a better view, and saw that the stranger's gaze was unblinking & intense. A sudden feeling of discomfort came over him, and he immediately moved the disk away, tucking it back absentmindedly in his pocket. As their eyes met, it vaguely hit him that this was the same guy who had been staring at him for several days now, though he had never really bothered about it earlier. But now, just when the next clue presented itself, the stranger's gaze seemed a bit disconcerting…and beyond a random coincidence…

So who was he, and why was he staring at him? And how should he respond? Now, these questions suddenly welled up within him, and Dave's discomfiture increased when he noticed that the gaze continued, unmindful of the fact that he was looking back too- almost as if he were being scanned by a pair of deep green eyes having some kind of X-ray properties.

But before he could react, this man, seemingly about fifty (by now, Dave had stopped guessing ages here), with a slightly balding head, cigar like object in his mouth, and stylish shades, walked right upto Dave. He was smartly dressed in what looked like cargoes & tee, and had a tough frame- the kind one would associate with ex-army officers. Standing next to Dave, he stared at him with even more intensity, almost a glare...

Just as Dave was about to blurt out something, the balding man broke into a warm smile, offering his hand. Dave feebly shook a tough hand, his own grip rather tentative by comparison. While he continued to be momentarily blanked out, at a loss for words, the stranger sat next to Dave, and chewing on the stub, came straight to the point.

"I see you have questions about how these folks here manage to live so comfortably, by supposedly doing so little- there are no structured organizations, no fixed professions or 'vocations', no 'day jobs'; yet this place chugs along like a well oiled machinery, a fairy tale, and you don't know who runs it and how they get all the money for this, right?"

Slightly taken aback by the bluntness of this question, and wondering how he had figured it out, Dave nodded tentatively.

"Don't be so stunned- I have been observing you taking notes daily. Obviously, this place doesn't fit into your mental framework, so you are struggling to make sense of it, boy."

Boy! First a distinctly unsocial behavior, now a condescending tone...and a blunt admission of the fact that he was been watched daily! This guy was something...but Dave didn't react, just yet...

"You wanna know how this works, and from where they get all their money, right? The answer is: nowhere! 'cause there is **no concept of pay for work, or rather, working for pay** *here!"*

"What do you mean?" Dave blurted. He now regained some composure, realizing that this episode had entirely knocked the socks off his thought process.

Far from deciphering a clue which presented itself rather enigmatically, he was now discussing about the work ethic of this place, with a rank stranger- someone, who just a minute back, made him feel distinctly uncomfortable.

And yet, now seemed to offer him relevant answers...*interesting... intriguing...*

"What I mean is that the advancements of various technologies have altered material living substantially, making fulfillment of basic needs easier, personalized & more flexible. And of course, the system of the Quartet takes care of the basic needs of the offspring, giving tremendous freedom to pursue their inner calling; *as a result, the concepts of occupation, vocation & profession have altered radically...*"

"So are you saying that people *don't have to work for money*? The system takes care of their needs?"

"What I'm saying is that once human focus shifts away from working for survival, you realise the sheer tornado of human energy which can be unleashed for creative, constructive pursuits. Then the wisdom of *'luckiest are those whose vocation is the same as their avocation'* no longer remains a pipe dream; this is how grew our consciousness, our administration systems, and the whole focus of humanity shifted from survival to growth- both personal & communal. Alongside, the concepts of satisfaction & achievements got refined & redefined- now your social standing is no longer a function of what you do, what you achieve and how much you earn, but of what you are, what your **being is...**"

"C'mon, don't look so surprised, lad! After all, *isn't it the deepest desire of every individual in your world to work not for money, for survival, but for happiness, for self growth, for something more meaningful?*

All of this is possible only if you have a social, technological & administrative system based not on money fulfilling your needs, but on the system fulfilling it..."

"But how?" this was utopia zone once again.

"Lot of this started in your time, actually- the profound definitions of leadership propounded by your thinkers & gurus, from Peter Senge to Peter Drucker, have finally taken concrete shape.

People's success & stature is now determined not by their 'net worth', but by their 'self worth'; not by their 'network', but by their ability to contribute to the network...

Their sense of power comes not from their external influence, but by their "being", their ability, their creativity, their inner leadership & evolution...

When you hopefully understand the 'Energy exchange system' and the IIN better, you will realise that here is a classic case of the system modifying itself to eliminate flaws at its very core..."

Dave reflected use upon the words. Whoever this person was, he touched a deep, dormant desire & chord within. He could have been anybody, but spoke so much like the new age thinkers & management leaders he used to voraciously devour & religiously implement; who stated unequivocally about *the domain of leadership being grounded in a state of being, not doing...*

He was so right in pointing out that all of us would love to follow the calling of our heart, if we didn't have to pay our bills. It was an extremely liberating thought, with implications for the whole of humanity...

But Dave was not completely convinced- not just yet! Years of the manager's conditioning threw up questions on how such a place could work. *If all people did what they 'felt like', how could this place run smoothly & efficiently?*

How could organizations function in such an environment? And there could be no disputing that the foundation of a healthy society was its well oiled, flawlessly run organizations...

In response to this skepticism, the stranger reminded that such a structure did exist in his time too- *THE MOVIE STUDIO!! After all, one of the most popular & enduring institutions was built on a 'project structure'...*

While being a part of a project, diverse constituents were bound by a strong sense of belonging, giving their best. Myriad experts came together to create a product of immense beauty & class, such that it became an integral part of human life & flow. But then, at the end of the project, they moved on, to the next project at hand...ready for another passionate day's work...

Wow, this guy is sharp & articulate. Definitely a management thinker! If he were back in my time, we could have started a new age management consulting firm together, Dave smiled to himself...

"You still not completely convinced, right? *And you wanted to be a new age management thinker?*" the stranger now smiled warmly, as if reading Dave's mind.

"OK, so here's some more for you, something which was already gaining ground in your time. In fact, I'm sure, you would have either experienced it or participated in it in some form or the other. And you most certainly have heard the underlying management philosophy."

"What's that?"

"*Re-engineering*- process vs. functional management…"

"Don't tell me. Business Processing Re-engineering?!"

"I just did, kid! That is exactly what it is! The philosophy of re-engineering spoke about organizational changes as central to it, right?"

"Ye..ah.." Dave replied softly, as if he had missed something so basic, so fundamental…

"Away from functional management to process oriented management."

"Exactly. Your traditional organizations were structured around tasks and division of labor; functional management, which created silos! In this format, management had the dual job of supervising over both- the process itself, and the teams managing the processes. Then came about this management revolution, which spoke about a new structure- based upon cross functional process teams, working on specific projects. Governed by the process owner, not supervisors or managers...

Basically, getting together for a process project, delivering it, and moving on! Fundamentally changing the way management structures existed..."

Dave looked sheepish. How could he have missed out BPR. His own style, in fact, was so similar to its principles.

"Various examples have been given for this, including the classic case of football team, the rock band & so on. Now, tie in this understanding with a movie cast, and it becomes all too clear, aint it?"

Dave nodded. But he still felt some gaps….

"People on our plane still work in their domains of strength & expertise, there is still a tremendous entrepreneurial drive, but all of it is naturally aligned. And because there are no functional 'turfs' to be defended, people give their best in projects they are associated with, get 'credited' according to their commitment & impulses, and then exchange these 'credits' for 'buying', rather procuring, these very products & services for their comfort."

"Getting credits & using them to procure goods? Heard this earlier too- energy credits & debits; but I don't quite follow..."

"Forget it for now; if & when you understand the new metrics & economic model, clarity will dawn.

For now, follow that just because there is no money on our plane doesn't mean people don't 'work'- this aint no dole system! In fact, because the metric is energy, people actually get energy credits as per their level of commitment & spirit, so performance is much better, sincere & honest. And because it works as a process organization, with hugely superior technology, the output is significantly enhanced.

Let's just say that we have mastered the art of doing more with less- **the law of least effort!** "

"So this is what spawns so much creativity here?"

"Yes, creativity is inherent to the energies of this place. As I said earlier, it's primarily about self growth. In fact, you might be surprised to know that amongst the creative 'types' are a host of blokes who 'do nothing'! Literally nothing at all, as per your worldly norms! Some spend their time traveling, while others write memoirs. *And yet, they are highly regarded here..."*

Dave smiled, remembering the rues of Paris once again...

"Then there is another group you might find fascinating- the 'seekers'..."

"Heard about them..."

"What about them? They are an eclectic bunch, an assortment of folks drawn from various races, who have chosen meditation as their 'vocation'! Emerging from different walks & stages of life, they spend days at the various 'temples' & 'energy centers' spread out across the land, meditating, using a technique, or techniques, that suit them.

To your world, they might seem like losers or monks, but they are neither- *ask them, and they define themselves as 'energy explorers', at the cutting edge of evolution...*

As they raise their energies, they supposedly project it in both the NEW AGES and the 4-dimensional plane, attempting to maintain balance...that's why they are the favorites of the Council. In fact, most of the Council consists of erstwhile seekers..."

"So they offer prayers instead of material contributions?"

"Yes, and more- they also supposedly have some special 'energy contributions', which are known only to the Council. Now, what would you call such blokes?" the stranger asked, digging his teeth deep into the stub.

Dave could only smile. He had seen monks & monasteries back on earth, but the sound of these folks was unlike anything he had seen, or could even visualize. Far from being mendicants or celibates, these 'meditators' seemed more prosperous, stylish, and cutting edge than others, living life king size...

In fact, as the stranger clarified, some of them had rather 'lavish' lifestyles, traveling across planets in their glitzy PATs and living out of fancy mobile houses. But the underlying core was their desire & spirit of exploration & furthering growth.

"So *it is all about energy, not money*? And the energy & creative guys are rather affluent?"

"Now you get it! Look at your world: what is most sought after, most precious, is valued highest in terms of money. *Why should it be so?*

Why should money get access to the best the world has to offer? This is a *new world*, a *new place*! That's why it's called the NEW AGES, and not 'post something' ages- *it's the age of a NEW society, a NEW MAN!"*

And with that, the stranger abruptly got up, shook Dave's hand, and departed with a rather firm 'See you soon'; proceeding to the hangar where his PAT was parked...

But not before he had left behind two objects...

A miniature, glistening sundial, and an exotic looking sand clock- an hourglass...

He was not to be seen after that. *Not at the promenade, that is...*

Dave sat there, reflecting upon the emergence of the *'NEW MAN'*; yes, if our creative energies were freed from the rut of survival & money, a new man, a new society could emerge. Memories flooded him again, as he reflected back upon what might have been, had he not pursued corporate 'growth' so blindly. He could have enjoyed love, had a fruitful life, maybe even taken a shot at setting up a rock band...

Regaining composure, he picked up the two objects, pondering over the clue, which appeared after a long time.

What exactly did this clue mean, and why did a stranger give him yet another new perspective at the very same time? Not to mention two objects which seemed irrelevant, yet symbolic in equal measure.

By now, he had learnt to see the pattern in 'coincidences'...
In the present of the future, not in now's past,
Beyond the vestiges last..
Beckons the original mother
To an institution nurturing her...
The revered, the wise, the conglomeration sacred
The harmonious connecting thread
Where the spirit is nurtured & wisdom bred
Seek them if the message you have intuitively read...
Past the chant, through the black gold, rock & dust,
Move with understanding & trust,
Where the life giving snake slithers & winds
The worthy there his destination finds...
Answers more then will flow
If one's true self can one show...

Unsure of where to start, he did the *one thing* which came to him naturally now- a quick 'holographic call' to his friends...

****

Some pleasantries later, they were on the job, listening intently to the two apparently disjointed events, yet coming at exactly the same time. The *'original mother'*, Plutus surmised, was a reference to mother earth, the original nurturer. The others seemed to concur, though tentatively for now.

So did it mean going back to his world? To the original mother?

Diffident, they moved on to the subsequent lines. But not much clarity emerged, except that they referred to some special institution- there were several sacred conglomerations back on earth, be they religious, spiritual, scientific, even political, depending upon how one viewed and interpreted it.

So which one was this referring to? Which institution nurtured the mother, who in fact, was always revered as the nurturer for mankind? And was a connecting thread...

Heavens & earth? Yet another portal? A special place?

The next four lines seemed to both edify & baffle further, in equal measure- apart from vague references to black gold, rock & dust, it adverted to some slithering snake, beyond the chant...*and a life giving one at that...*

This is where the destination seemed to be...

So, what did these lines imply? Some strange, occult practice of ancient chants? Past that- something, some place, with stones & gold, holding some sort of a life giving snake? Chants related to Snake worship?

Putting the two pieces together, it seemed that he had to go back to earth, possibly find some place, even portal, having arcane connections with some hermetic, possibly esoteric ritual. Based on chants & snake worship...*Could it be?*

From the worldly plane, he was directed to a higher plane through an energy portal, and now, mid way into his journey, was supposedly being guided to go back, and figure out some other place back on earth!

A full circle, but seemingly disconsonant, incongruous...

Something was amiss...

Flummoxed, even muddled, Ikona moved their attention to the first line: *In the present of the future, not in now's past...*

But nothing immediately. Lyon looked at Plutus expectantly, and Plutus at Dave with hopeful eyes, but Dave was fidgeting absentmindedly with sand clock.

Staring at it, Plutus too seemed fixated at the simple, yet elegant & mysterious looking object, as the sand flowed from one end to the other, passing through a narrow constriction, time flowing along with it...

Change the direction, change one's perspective, and the flow reverses, yet time flows...

"I think this whole thing once again talks in allegory- change one's perspective, understand the flow of time... that's why you got this sand clock. It *tells* you something more..."

"I don't get it Plutus- you think the sand clocks gives a clue to decipher the first line?" Dave responded, suddenly more attentive now.

"Yes. Listen carefully- *In the present of the future, not in now's past...* What does it say?"

"That the future you are in is the present. That's why it reemphasizes- *not in now's past*. It means this plane itself Dave, and it obviously tells you that what you looking for is here & now, not in its past!" Lyon pitched in, making more sense of it.

"But it spoke about the earth- the original mother!" Dave protested. This now seemed oxymoronic, paradoxical...

"No, it means the earth in this plane- in the 25th century! That's why it calls it not merely the mother, but the *original* mother! It means the original planet of life, from the perspective of the new Ages." Ikona smiled, her hands moving outwards in a circular motion, like a magician signaling the parting of curtains to reveal the wonder hidden inside.

"So the institution refers to something of the New Ages? Interesting." Dave felt this changed the entire perspective...

"Yeah- something on earth, in the New Ages, and related to some life giving snake! Beyond some chant. Even more interesting..." Lyon's electronic voice was now harmonic. "Guys, if the sand clock gave a clue, so should the sundial. As Plutus said, this is allegorical in nature. Dave, you said the monastery prayer wheels acted as an ancient sundial, right?"

"Right, as also the amazing sundial I saw in Jaipur."

Lyon punched his wrist micro computer, and a large, holographic image of a map of the earth projected on the floor in front of them, reminding them of the first time the disk had projected such an image back in his tree house.

"So, what does a sundial do? Its shadow moves in accordance with the movement of the sun, rather the earth, right?" The others nodded.

"And, you saw special sundials in two places, one of which was the gateway in Tibet? The movement of shadow on the sundial configuration of the prayer wheels guided you to the gateway, correct?"

Dave concurred, unsure of what Lyon was arriving at.

"Now, let's locate these two points on the map, and highlight them. Let's say that the sundial which facilitated your journey is *here*." Lyon marked a point in the map near Xigaze, placing the little sundial there.

"And the other one here, in Jaipur, Rajasthan. Now, let there be light…*pun intended*…" He said in his usual ballsy way, as a small light source shone on the sundial, much like the sun casting its rays on the Xigaze Monastery pagoda. He held the light source at a particular angle, such that as the shadow lengthened, it moved across the map, till it crossed Jaipur.

"Now, we join these two points together, to depict their common significance."

"How and why do you join them? Rather random, like a force fit? There are many sundials on the planet." Plutus asked.

"Didn't you only mention that it is allegorical, just a while back?" Lyon shot back, politely by his standards. There was a certain calm reassurance in his demeanour, a confidence in the knowledge of what he was doing.

"*Beyond the chant…*" Lyon's electronic voice now became unusually soft. "Think guys… *chant??*"

Seeing blank faces, he made a mock expression of disgust, shaking his head in a what-will-happen-to-you-guys expression. "Linguistic skills, I see, are obviously none of your fortes! Chant in Sanskrit is 'Mantra'. So mantar…? Jantar Mantar?!"

There were low whistles of appreciation, as Ikona pouted her lower lips, nodding her head in mock appreciation. Dave was taken back initially, but then recollected his feelings at the Samrat Yantra.

"Well, buddy?" Lyon looked at Dave with anticipation.

"Well, I am both speechless and excited. When we happened to be at Jantar Mantar, I sensed that it had some significance, but it never struck me that this was the connection, the connotation! However, now I see that the flat tyre was more than just a tourist halt, and the Samrat Yantra was not called the king of instruments without reason." Dave smiled.

"Exactly- samrat literally means king, so *Samrat Yantra literally means king of instruments.* But now, coming back to our beloved shadow, let it continue further in a straight line, as it passes through Arabia, crossing by the holy city of Mecca. *Coincidence, anybody??*"

"Wow! Now it fits in: *past the chant, through the black gold, rock & dust...* obviously Mecca, the holy land; the land of the mystical black rock- the Kaaba; black gold- oil, and dust, as in the desert..." Ikona snapped her delicate, neatly manicured fingers, in a graceful manner.

As for Dave, he was getting more fascinated, even intrigued now. It was amazing how three supposedly unrelated, yet significant points, including one which was the holiest city for over a sixth of the world's population, were coming together on a common path. It was then that the true significance of the crop circle clue, and the raised points on the holographic projection back at the tree house, struck him- and come to think of it, their positions seemed to correspond to these points...

Wonder what secrets the other points on the pattern hid beneath the surface? A new perspective on 'holy' lands?!

"The shadow keeps extending, friends." Lyon continued, gently moving the light source downwards. *"Through the heart of Africa, then the Atlantic, and finally crossing the equator at the northern end of South America."* He stopped moving the light point, a knowing smile crossing his face.

"So?" Dave asked, not really expecting some place in South America.

"You ask so?? So, it means that this clue points to a location in Brazil!" Lyon said, pinpointing to the location, his index finger emphatically 'knocking' thrice, on the map, unmindful of the fact that the shadow was a virtual projection.

"And what is this location? *The answer is Amazonas, my friends, close to Putumayo, Peru. Yet another mystical land...*"

"Are you sure?" Ikona raised her eyebrow, sensing the line of thinking. *Was it indeed headed there? Guiding Dave there?*

"Absolutely lady! By now, we know that the clue has many layers. I simply apposed the sundial and with the black gold & the slithering, life giving snake! Not to mention the mystical locations the path of the shadow covers.

As for the life giving snake, well, it is right here!" Lyon referenced the earlier highlighted point rather matter-of-factly, but barely able to conceal his unabashedly smugness.

Dave raised his eyebrow at the mention of the snake in the same breath as the sundial- and in Amazonas.

In a corner of his mind, the mention of the slithering snake evoked the memory of the uncoiling snake, seen in the archives. *Were they co-related? Was there yet another pattern here? The snake in Brazil...*

But before anyone could prod further, Lyon explained with his trademark flourish. "Guys, the snake refers *not to a literal one* in Latin America- not Anaconda for sure! The slithering, flowing body of life means *the Amazon river,* whose journey through these parts winds like that of a snake. It's not uncommon to find it referred to as such in your history, Dave! "

The others were taken aback for a moment, but then Dave gave him a thumbs up. "True genius always shines." he winked.

Taking a mock bow, Lyon surmised. "So this clue is referring to an institution, back on earth, located in the *Amazon rainforest,* which nurtures both the individual spirit, and the new ages itself. Any prizes for guessing *which one*?!"

"The Guardian Council!!" Ikona & Plutus responded in unison. "Incredible! *The institution nurturing her, the sacred conglomeration, where the spirit is nurtured & wisdom bred... the harmonious connecting thread between the new ages & the old world, technology & spirit in the New Ages!*" Ikona's hunch turned out to be correct.

"Indeed, ladies & gentlemen!" Lyon took a final bow, akin to that of a performer post the grand finale, responding with a swish to the enthusiastic applause of captivated audiences.

Clearly, this guy was the centre-of-attention material, the born showman- and without any qualms about it...

"That's where the Council's temple complex is, back on earth, *in the present of the future.* And, oh yes, notice the poetic play here- *the present* of the future connotes that the Council is not merely in the present, but a present itself- a *gift* of the New Ages **(present *of the future)* to mother earth...*"*

Plutus & Ikona were still awestruck- this was not just another planetary Council station, but the base station- the original council complex on the original mother, housing the much venerated Seer Temple, or *the Temple of the path of light.*

The space of the highest echelons of the Council, only select apprentices, apart from Masters themselves, had the privilege of walking in its hallowed precincts- that too after years of dedication to the Council & its cause.

And here, a supposed novice was being guided to enter its consecrated portals...

Dave too felt a wave of excitement pass through him- the Guardian Council?! And it's base station?! Just moments back, he was given a sneak peek into the organizational systems & work ethic of this plane. And now, the fourth clue, along with the stranger's 'gifts', was leading him to the Guardian Council. It not only meant an opportunity to meet Master Aleus again, but to interact with the highest spiritual body of this plane- one that regulated a multi-planetary, cutting edge system...

In the same breath, he was also enthused at the prospect of getting more answers, now that the clue unraveling spree had begun again- about his journey, the elusive Messenger, and the 'New Man', now that it was 'coincidentally' revealed to him.

Answers more will flow,
If your true self can you show...

But before he could even agonize over arranging a rendezvous with the Council, an official holographic message followed- an invite from the Council itself. Amazing timing, as if just waiting for Dave to figure the clue out:

The chamber beckons, o man of the journey,
Seen this world, now the inner world awaits thee...
The masters and a higher understanding of energy,
Experience the next step in your destiny...

Synchronicity & coincidences at their best, he smiled. Just when he thought things were drifting along came a new clue, a random meeting with a stranger who explained new age management better than any management guru himself, and now an invite from the Council itself...

He was reminded of the events leading upto his journey to India, in all of twelve hours, and smiled heavenwards...

15. THE GUARDIAN COUNCIL

Ever since the formation of the NEW AGES, the Guardian Council was a central institution, the pillar on which so many of its systems were supported- it had been varyingly described as the soul of the NEW AGES, the conscience keeper of the new systems, the moral compass of the QUARTET and the custodians of the values enshrined in the CHARTER...

And not without reason- it was the apex spiritual body whose sacred task was to ensure that the balance & harmony of the NEW AGES was maintained, and the general direction of the QUARTET was in line with the charter at all times...

The Council also had another sacred charge- of maintaining the balance between the heavens & earth, by projecting 'uplifting energies' to the 4 dimensional plane. Apart from 'projecting' energies, they also operated through chosen souls, who would be the 'bridge between the two planes, between this world & the next'. All this was to ensure that the earth didn't hurtle onto the path of catastrophe & self destruction, and followed its natural progression towards evolution...

The Council itself was made up of evolved beings from all races- seekers, seers, synesthetes & clairvoyants; from *among these were chosen a hundred masters-* men & women co-opted after years of evolution & contribution, and who were the brightest & wisest stars in the NEW AGE firmament, collectively having the ability, wisdom & foresight to ensure that the sacred charge of the Council was always attended to.

Among these were also naturally gifted folks, who were identified by the council after a series of tests.

These were the clairvoyants, who had a special ability to see, or rather sense the future- *ESP, if one were to say so*; and the synesthetes- the ones blessed with another special gift: *synesthesia, or the ability to have multiple senses awakened by a single response...*

While this concept was understood from the 19th century, and some research done, it was never fully understood or appreciated. Varyingly seen as enhanced neural responses or some form of neural disorder, synesthesia was said to be induced by either psychedelic drugs or by a stroke or seizure. Yet no one understood its true creative potential, as the those who harnessed its potential were invariably more gifted than the rest, being able to merge sights with sounds to create some interesting phenomenon of the New Ages- sensory zones. With time & training, these gifted apprentices learnt to harness their 'tools' to 'sense' the energy balance across the worlds at all times, guided by the wisdom & the sensitivity of the Masters; and to highlight, even respond appropriately in case they sensed deviations or imbalances...

As the clue indicated, the Council base station was back on earth. Being Dave's first visit outside his 'new' home- moon, and back to his old home, this felt nostalgic & special. From the moon, he boarded an earthbound CAT, and made it in slightly less than two hours (earth hours! He adjusted his watch to account for a different duration of the day). The CAT was shaped futuristically, reminding him of Starship enterprise of Star Trek, as it traversed the empty space between earth & the moon- but, in reality, was more like a huge, luxury cruise liner; individual suites for the passengers, various decks & lounge areas, at different levels, apart from umpteen recreation rooms. And the decks were unlike what he had ever experienced...

Since the craft was traveling at abnormally high speeds from Dave's perspective (several times faster than any rocket designed by the 21st century), the viewing decks were safe only in a pressure regulated, inertia neutralized, gravity controlled environment. Here again, Gelass was the answer, giving passengers the feel of actually being in 'space', while creating conditions as normal as possible. All this was fascinating, being adding to his excitement, which was already peaking at the thought of meeting the Council.

After dropping him & the other earthbound passengers at the 'space port', the craft proceeded onwards for its next destination, Columbus. The 'spaceport' was the central disembarking point, like a super modern airport built high up in the air. It was located at the prime meridian point, from where passengers could 'hire' their own PATs & proceed onward, by programming their coordinates-latitudes & longitudes. In the port was an 'acclimatization' area for transit passengers, so that they could get adjusted to the conditions back on earth. Dave chose to 'rent' a simple, two-seater PAT, the size of a luxury car. He instructed the chauffeur to go slow, so that he could see the earth in detail...*and observe how it looked 500 years in the future...*

In the present of the future, not in now's past...

As they flew low & slow, Dave sensed that the earth seemed different, more radiant...it was greener, the mountains & soil more vibrant, the oceans deeper blue- almost as if the earth had been healed & regenerated after all the abuse...*Mankind's obligation...*

Soon, the indicator suggested that they reached base station of the Council- it too seemed much greener and richer than the Amazon he remembered...and teeming with life energy...

****

The base station itself was rather unassuming- a vast complex of intricately set buildings, seamless camouflaged by the thick forest. Hidden by dense foliage, the buildings were hard to spot with the naked eye.

The base station of the Council in a dense forest- very interesting, Dave surmised. *But then, that was the theme of the place; human progress in harmony & communion with nature...and energized by the aura of the dense forest... a network of energy...*

As he touched down upon 'home soil', Dave was flooded with emotions-love, nostalgia, collective anguish, blessings...He had felt deep love & longing when he saw the earth from the moon the very first time; but to be back on it, half a millennia ahead of his time, was truly like the magical homecoming of a weary traveler, taking refuge in the bosom of a mother he had been long away from- in her arms, all fears, pain & anxiety dissolved as tears, long waiting to flow...

And the fact that he was here to meet the highest spiritual body of the new ages made this even more special...

On venturing inside, guided in a self navigating 'new age golf cart', he saw the beauty of the forest- multiple levels of vegetation, from tall trees acting as canopies, filtering sunlight & rainwater, to the midsized trees whose growth they facilitated, to ferns & vegetation at the base level- nature was yet again demonstrating the beauty of coexistence...of how each piece in existence supported the other, with pure energy & giving...

Even within nature's own 'pecking order', there was harmony & sharing of energies...

****

The main structure in this complex was the **seer temple, the temple of the path of light**- a high energy synthesis of various religious architectures. So the gothic cathedral, the intricately carved temple, the mosque with its exquisite tiling & symmetrical domes, the monastery with its bright red murals & thangkas, and the red brick synagogue, all seamlessly merged into each other...not to forget the original shamanic influences, a tribute to the land of the Amazon!

Along with these influences, there was the influence of some other structures- which he couldn't exactly place, but which seemed like ancient prayer sites...

The beauty of the place was captivating, emanating the most soothing of vibrations...

The temple complex had several outer rooms, courtyards, galleries & passageways in these various styles, leading to an inner sanctum. Behind the main complex, up the slopes, were the chambers of the masters. They had distinct shapes, each reflecting the 'style' of the respective inhabitant.

Master Aleus' was shaped like an 'igloo', while some others were clustered together, reminding Dave of the 'shire' of the hobbits. All these 'dwellings' were mostly made of natural materials- seemingly not a common occurrence in the age of 'nano engineering' & advanced materials- and hidden from normal view by the dense foliage, giving the impression of a quaint, 16th century Victorian village in tropical settings...

As he entered the temple, another interesting phenomenon caught his attention- right from the outer courtyard, there was the humming of various chants, akin to the vibrations he felt in the forest just before his teleportation- *and it seemed to lift his energies in the same way it had back then...*

Crossing the various rooms & chambers, each having a distinct purpose & style, he entered the inner sanctum- a vast space with a high ceiling made of stained glass & tiles, intricately carved walls & columns, and long rows on either side. These had arrangements for simple seating for fifty masters on each side, with a large, raised altar in the center. Just in front of the altar was a gilded podium, on which rested a resplendent chair in all its magnificence & glory- **the resplendent 'space' of the Grand Master...**

Between the 'space' of the Grand Master & the assembly, were several rows, like pews. However, instead of being seating areas, they housed 101 candles, 50 on either side and a large one in the centre- akin to the seating arrangement of the assembly. *But they were no ordinary candles...*

These were the connection of the Masters to the Grand Master, with the 'flicker of the candle' denoting the subtleness of the energies each of the Masters, allowing the Grand Master to 'see without seeing'...

Above the podium were bas relief images- some familiar, like Pyramids (not only the great pyramids of Egypt but from various parts of the world, and across civilizations) and places of worship like the black stone of Kaaba, St Peters Basilica, Angkor Wat etc, while some unfamiliar- like celestial bodies, 'flying objects' and more crop circles patterns...

Perfectly mystical settings for the perfectly mystical Grand Master...

In fact, the enigmatic Grand Master was not 'seen' by anyone- he was said to be of 'pure spirit', belonging to the highest plane, *the realms of the Buddhas.* Like all the subtler things of nature, he had to be felt & experienced, his message interpreted by intuition, his apparitions viewed by the third eye...

However, since the Grand master periodically gave messages for collective welfare, 'it' would communicate to the council via a medium. Whenever 'it' chose to 'manifest 'its' blessings & guidance, the 'select' master would *just feel it*, and then be either seated on the chair on stand aloft on the podium, acting as the conduit through which the message flowed from the plane of pure spirit unto this...

As Dave made his place in the sanctum with the hundred greatest men of this plane, there was a sense of awe, a deep happiness & calm. Awaiting with open arms the message intended for him...

The Council commenced the assembly with the twin hearts meditation, a meditation of the heart & crown chakra. The atmosphere was serene, the energies uplifting, the vibrations subtle, as the gathering blessed mother earth. For an hour, all masters & their apprentices meditated in pin drop silence, after which the apprentices respectfully bowed & made their way out of the sanctum, onto their key tasks, leaving only the masters behind, as *Master Aleus then declared the conclave open...*

****

"Suppose you had a world run by not men, but by women. A world without boundaries, without the barriers of geography or religion...a world having armies not of war, but of peace & development...where resources are allocated to development, not destruction...*imagine...*" Master Nobius Shengdon smiled.

Dave smiled back, studying Clairvoyant Nobius' features-yellow skinned, probably of East Asian origin, moderate height & build, and dressed in white robes, he seemed like a normal oriental guy- quite a contrast to the flamboyant Aleus.

Something familiar about him...something about the way he looked...and spoke...but Dave couldn't place it just yet...

"And suppose you had a world where nobody had to work for money to survive, and everyone was free to pursue his/her dreams, avocations & deepest desires...where money wasn't the currency, but human impulse itself...where whatever one needed to live comfortably was provided by the system itself- basis this currency, not money!" Added Master Zeut Etrusci, his deep eyes fixated on Dave, giving him a familiar look.

As Dave looked in his direction, he was zapped by what he saw- *the stranger from the promenade!* *X-ray eyes*...yet another coincidence, he smiled, bowing low, paying his respects. He had not expected to meet the cigar stub chewing stranger again so soon, least of all here in the capacity of a revered Master of the Council!

As annoying as the stranger's ways had seemed back on the promenade, his gifts had helped in unraveling the clue, not to mention their stimulating discussion on a world without money!

Different Masters, different ways, he was beginning to understand...

"Yes Masters, now I am a believer. If someone would have told me the same thing a few months back, I would have been skeptical-as would most of us, in spite of the whole wave of the human potential movement, and the undercurrent of a spiritual renaissance. But then I came 'here', guided by synchronicity, and saw a whole NEW WORLD... *not utopia, but reality...*

A world where individuals do work hard to grow in life, but where growth itself acquires a different meaning, a different dimension, a pursuit of a deeper inner dream..."

"And am sure you keen to know more about how this fascinating system works, sonny?" Zeut winked at him, chewing his stub.

"Yes Master. You explained well last time. Though I didn't remotely guess for a moment that I was talking to such an exalted soul..." Dave nodded, his mind drifting back to his previous encounter with Zeut, and whether he had said or done something possibly offensive to a seeker of this stature.

"Focus on the here & now; young man- the only exalted reality is in the present moment, so experience it fully..." The soft & delicate voice of Lady Sinetha El Magdal brought Dave back from his thoughts.

Another Master, she too seemed remarkably young for someone having a son older than Dave. Both mother & son were highly regarded in scientific circles, with Sinetha having been a leading energy physicist & inventor in her earlier avatar.

'She has quite a few energy breakthroughs to her name, apart from being a champion in PAT racing in her younger days- 'Ace of race' is what they named her club. She looks simple & calm, but is a woman of great depth. Some years back, she was inducted into the council, a testimony to her contributions & wisdom, and is now a master.' Ikona had briefed Dave about beforehand.

"Oh, I am sorry ma'am." Dave said. "I had sort of drifted off, thinking about my journey here. And then, some strange thoughts & feelings occurred."

"Be aware of those feelings, but be centered only in this moment..."

"And it is in this moment that we were discussing about our systems- systems that are a model for your world." Zeut steered the conversation back on track.

"But before we talk about the systems here, shouldn't we first discuss your journey, your life purpose? After all, one has to first know about the inside, before contemplating the outside." came the husky voice of a very tall, robust man, seated in a corner.

Dave looked in that direction, and was equally bemused & surprised to find a huge hulk sitting on an oversized chair. Dressed fashionably in a leather jacket, tight pants and dark shades, that was Master Atlas, yet another 'character' of the Council! If Master Aleus was the proverbial rock star of the Council, Atlas was the literal one!

Seemingly in his mid 50s, eight feet tall, rock hard biceps bulging out from a shiny, sleeveless jacket (*Dave thought these were the biggest biceps he had seen, bigger than even Arnold!*), tattoos covering his forearms & neck, long, snow white hair neatly tied into a pony, and a thick bushy moustache, he seemed like a cross between the middle aged, harley gang types and Hulk Hogan-a personality which could floor ladies, anytime, anywhere! But beneath this flashy personality resided a man of many parts- unknown to most even within the Council, he was their point man & chief trouble shooter- the trusted one Aleus could rely on for the most critical & secretive of assignments...

This 105 year old master was also the lead guitarist of a new age, fusion band, one formed on his 75th birthday. This had him traveling across the worlds for his gigs (which were a big rage with all races, especially the female audience), and gave him the chance to seamlessly juxtapose his Council duties with personal passions. *Yet another example of no dichotomy between basic instincts & social obligations...*

"Yes Master, I would only be too glad to share my journey. After all, there are so many twists in this story." Dave smiled.

"You think so? Then lemme tell you the tale of a bandit who became a master..."

Dave raised his eyebrow questioningly. The only such tale he had read was about an ancient Indian seer, Valmiki.

"Over a century back, a boy was born to a brilliant cyborg father and a 'seeker' endower mother. Born as Cedar the 3rd, this boy ought to have considered himself lucky to have such an illustrious lineage; but instead, he faced a traumatic childhood on account of problems between his parents, who just could not reconcile to each other, as 'racial' differences kept on building up. What should have been a union of differing strengths soured into an ideological battle, causing progressive bitterness & acrimony."

Dave's mind flew back to his own relationship with Shakti, of how they built it, not inspite of, but because of their differences; and how he blew it towards the end. A golden opportunity to bring together two streams of thought was mindlessly squandered at the altar of a singular worldview. A tinge of regret entered his mind, but he quickly brought himself back to the present.

"The acrimony got so stinging that they finally parted rather bitterly- his mother leaving home for her seeker commune in search of lasting peace, while his father retreating to a cyborg commune. Both sought their own tranquility, not realizing the impact this had on this young, impressionable mind."

"And so it happened that this setback in formative years led to Cedar's disillusionment with the NEW AGES & its systems. After all, synthesis of opposites was supposed to be the guiding principle of the NEW AGES, but all that he saw was a disruption of his childhood. This disenchantment soon welled up into pent up anger, acquiring the shape of anti-establishment feelings.

He began to hold the system's idealism responsible for his mess. And in the absence of stabilizing forces, his powerful energies started getting channeled on the wrong side, in unwholesome activities. By late teens, Cedar had established his own band of interplanetary 'pirates'- likeminded angry teens, who found their sense of identity & rebellion in 'beating the system'. To make this point loud and clear, he took on the name of 'Blackbeard', the most notorious pirate in history, and grew a beard, just like his hero..."

As fascinating as it seemed so far, Dave wondered why he was being told this...

"Starting with petty crimes, this renegade group soon graduated to piracy of key technologies, and came in touch with some critical advancements in network algorithms.

As notoriety of his acts spread, Blackbeard's life soon turned into a cat & mouse game with the law enforcement authorities- a race to beat the system at its own game, on its own turf. And it saw him improvising, mastering the art of beating the 'law enforcement' algorithms with improvisations of his own. While this added to his notoriety, select few among the wise actually saw this as a sign of his genius- one of them being a gem called Aleus.

And so, after years of failure on the part of the authorities to stop this genius pirate, Master Aleus took it upon himself to 'redirect this genius energy'. Where the authorities failed to exactly pinpoint him, Master Aleus used his ESP powers to track down & meet Blackbeard; and that meeting in the forest of Columbus was a watershed...

They say that a true Master's energies touch you in the deepest & most unexpected of ways; and this is what happened with the rebel too. That one meeting changed things fundamentally, the touch of the master bringing a stream of tears in even the most hardened of eyes; unlocking layers of conditioning, freeing the soul to experience its true nature. *And a transformed soul was now named Atlas- the one who would support the heavens...*

Master Aleus introduced him to meditation, and after a year of solitary refuge, the rebel emerged as a calmer, wiser person. No, he hadn't lost any of his fire, but he was ready to direct it for the realization of higher goal, in the service of humanity, as per the guidance of the Council."

Dave again smiled inside. Some of it sounded familiar.

"The next 25 years of his life & talents were dedicated to contributing to the various sub-modules of the network, especially the one on law enforcement. Poison kills poison, and the Council couldn't think of a better mind to improvise the law enforcement module than him. Statistics ratified this faith, as crime prevention rate was up by a whopping 80%! Not merely by detection technologies, but the humane approach. Towards that, he traveled extensively, counseling youth afflicted by rage & anti-establishment feelings, helping them channel these in constructive projects. The renegades of society became its active force. This development made the Council sit up & take real notice- he was turning out to be quite an asset.

But his first passion was always music, unknown to most except his mentor. So, after 75 years of a roller coaster life, dedicated to both anger & helping people overcome it, he decided it was finally time to pursue some unfulfilled personal dreams-the BIG M! And in typical style, he got together with his erstwhile 'partners in crime' to set up a new age band, dedicated to venting the pent up energies of the youth into productive, uplifting endeavors. As the years passed, the BIG M expanded into Ms; 3 **Ms to be precise- music, muscles & meditation***...*

So now, the high energy Atlas hit the gym & guitar with equal gusto. For the third 'M', he chose the solitary path, retreating within for six hours a day, in between his workout & jamming sessions! Flamboyance & zest for life could have had no better ambassadors…

His 3 Ms helped build his body & soul (the mind was always razor sharp), and on his 100th birthday, he was officially inducted into the Council- that too as a Master- on the recommendation of his Mentor. Of course, there still were those who had reservations about inducting such a 'character', but Aleus argued that wisdom needed to be balanced with zest & energy- and Atlas brought both these qualities in abundance, apart from unwavering loyalty."

Atlas sat in a brief silence for a while, as if absorbing the entire significance of what he just narrated. And then, turned towards Dave again. *"You see it, Dave? The pirate sitting in front of you, sharing his life wisdom with you?* Remember the bit about the karmic cycle spanning more than what you can see? A bandit can become a saint, and a 'normal middle aged executive' can be drawn into an adventure across heavens & earth…"

Master Aleus smiled. "Life's mysteries are to be savored, its unpredictability to be welcomed with an open heart & alert mind. That is what builds wisdom…"

"Yes Master, I welcome it with an open heart, as I have done so far. Though the wisdom bit still eludes me at times."

"We realise that. You've understood the circumstances, factors & reasons of your journey, seen this world, learnt & understood quite a bit about it, and are a wiser man. But you are still confused about the BIG PICTURE, the whole chain of events; and most importantly, WHY YOU…"

"Right, Master."

"Hey, just call me Atlas, dude. Don't you guys have a first name culture in your society?" he smiled mischievously. Atlas, was loathe to anybody using glorified terms to address him.

"Oh, we do, *Master*." Dave said, slightly taken aback. Instantly correcting himself, he stammered. "Sorry, uh, Atlas... We do use first names!" He smiled at Atlas.

"And yes, I still harbor questions. I know the masters have been instrumental in guiding me here, right from the dreams to the clues to the disk to the circumstances leading to the Himalayas. And I am deeply thankful & indebted to you for that. *But why am I here?* Some of it still seems spooky... incongruent...as much as I try to reconcile myself to it, I still can't fathom this whole messenger bit? And I am told it's my dharma to seek him..."

"Yeah. so?"

"So I am no skeptic. I am a spiritual person, and by now a believer in a lot many things. But sometimes, it all seems so strange, so surreal, so unreal- *prophecies, UFOs, messengers*...As soon as the logical mind takes over, questions abound- what's their role in a normal, modern world? How do they correlate with a middle aged executive? Especially a 'messenger' emanating from a supposedly high tech world; *and why & how do I find him?* It seems everything around the periphery, including all that I have learnt so far, is beautiful, amazing, enlightening...solves so many of my doubts, gives me so many new answers & perspectives, both for self & my world- *but the core question itself remains unanswered..."*

"Why does it seem so illogical that it fills you up with such incredulity? You have seen our world for quite a while now, and how advanced our systems are. You have also seen how science & spiritualism are seamlessly integrated here. So why the doubts, kid?" Zeut spoke a bit brusquely. "I mean, we had such a long discussion the other day."

"I'll tell you why." Atlas spoke sharply. "Because you are still unable to completely shed your past conditioning, inspite of seeing & being here. If your conditioned mind can make you seek divinity 'up there', why not here? Why are you still uncomfortable with the idea of exploring inner divinity? After all, who is a messenger? Simply an individual who has realized inner divinity, and has a message to share. *That is your quest, Dave. That's what your dharma is guiding you to..."*

"I don't doubt that the messenger is for real, and indeed has something profound to offer, as also being the reason for my quest. But I also can't completely fathom this dharma bit. Sometimes it seems synchronicity, but sometimes so random."

"Even now? After my story? After receiving so many answers?"

"Unfortunately yes. Like the exact bit on UFOs & crop circles in my dharma? I have figured out the clue & the pattern- truly poetic. Figured out the disk is a precious gift, guiding me to the gateway, elevating my energies. Also understood that such shocking statements were needed to jolt me out of complacency. *But what exactly was happening?* How can synchronicity be connected to *aliens*? Who really is guiding me? The Masters, ethereal 'beings' from heavens, or aliens?"

"Synchronicity has many ways to inspire & facilitate. So don't bother beyond what you know- and, you have deciphered a lot. The moot point is that human beings have always needed higher guidance, or shall we say, guidance from the 'heavens'. What you refer to as 'alien' is simply that- *alien to your mind at this stage.* So focus on the message; the messenger is simply a conduit. *Anyone divinely guided is a messenger,* communicating the message of the 'heavens' on earth. You are here not only because of your karmic journey, *but because of your choices along the way-* that is the key! In times of despair, when skepticism could have swayed you, weakened your resolve, clouded your vision, you stood firm and chose to go with the flow. So just accept it- with the faith that the highest intelligence knows better than you, just as it has guided you thus far. Bother not about details unknown, but focus on what you have understood. *Do your karma, continue to make the right choices, and leave the rest to synchronicity*!"

Dave was reminded of a similar line from the Bhagwat Gita-Krishna's message to Arjuna the warrior...

"And if synchronicity so chooses, you may see, rather 'sense' more answers in the clairvoyance chamber." Atlas smiled. "Where incidentally, you'd be headed next, before we discuss any further about the systems of this place. As I said before, first understand the inside, before you try to master the outside. "

"Clairvoyance chamber?" Dave recollected Master Aleus having mentioned it in their meeting, but understood little of it.

"Yes- call it technology or a gift from the higher planes, or a 'karma scanner' beyond space-time." Master Aleus smiled. "But the essence is that it would allow your sub-conscious, your higher mind, to project images in a directional sense, correlating the past with potential future choices, allowing you to fathom your journey more holistically."

Dave nodded in deference, but was as confused as before. Nonetheless, some memories came back- things he had read in scientific journals, and seen in a couple of sci-fi movies...

"It seems strange Master, but some of this technology, or at least something similar, was being researched in our time too- *brain wave scanning using MRIs* allowed for defence establishments to try & probe 'thoughts' at a distance. No one knows whether this project indeed went through or not, but I recollect having read that intelligence agencies saw a serious potential here." He smiled, surprised at how this journey, this place was awakening his dormant memories.

Atlas contorted his facial muscles, the expressions leaving little doubt about the sheer disgust he felt. "Just what are we talking about, Dave? We refer to a profound, universal gift, to help guide & nurture souls; and you talk about military technologies in the same breath?"

Dave recoiled, not anticipating that his response would elicit such a sharp response. Sensing this, Atlas relented, the smile back on his face.

"Yes, brain wave scanning was being piloted in your plane. But for what, Dave? To create a big brother who could keep tabs on you, even more? Anyways, this big brother turned out to be a monster who operated from the plane of fear, and was already too big for the comfort of individual freedom? And your men of science created an even bigger monster to snatch away your little remnants of freedom- and your world calls it a technological breakthrough?

Ever thought of where will this vicious cycle of paranoia lead you guys? Just when will humans stop piloting cutting edge technologies to snoop or control, rather than empower? For God's sake, stop this regressive use of technology to create a cycle of fear- all in the name of security & liberty! Is this the kind of freedom & liberty your founding fathers envisioned?" disgust had now given way to anguish...

"There is much fear in your world, Dave. So much distrust, causing so much anxiety. Hence, so many of your technological breakthroughs either feed these emotions, or stem from them....

You spoke about brain wave scanning & its potential use in defence technology, or in prevention of terrorism. But just look at this: they developed lie detectors, and criminals got smarter to beat it; they put in place more surveillance, thinking that they were fortifying their defenses, but in reality, they were simply generating more information than they could handle; they thought they were securing themselves by probing ever more so, and in cases, using these technologies to bomb them to smithereens-but they were simply spawning more terrorists, who in turn led to an ever proliferating overload of intelligence to process. Bringing things nearly back to square one...

A never ending, ever spiraling cat-and-mouse game...

Clairvoyance, on the other hand, goes much beyond brain signal imprints, penetrating deep into one's soul journey. The projections in the clairvoyance chamber are personal, for an individual to get more clarity or sense of his journey, for a higher purpose, not for control or manipulation..." Master Aleus spoke with his usual wisdom.

"When humans see this truth, their use of technology will change, for ending this crazy game, not looping it further; a loop, which has no end, only knots...

Anyways, for now, it's your turn to experience this wondrous inner technology...out of pure love & faith, devoid of all fear & anxieties...so go forth..."

16. Clairvoyance chamber

When Dave entered the clairvoyance chamber, clad in pure white, he was expecting something high tech, behooving this plane, or at least a crystal ball gazing sort of mystical environment. Instead, what he saw was a simple, small room with white walls and a comfortable couch in the centre. As he sat upon it, soft music started playing in the background, and the white room started getting awash in different swirling colors, deep & intense- the white walls turned into screens, as hues of different colors appeared as concentric circles, chakras, and different patterns. This, he would realize later, were meant to cleanse & awaken his internal chakras...

A gentle female voice then appeared, asking him to take three deep breaths, & completely relax. gently guiding him through this process.

"Lie down supine, & completely relax. Let go of everything- your worries, fears, anticipations...everything... Just relax & feel your natural breathing. Don't influence it, just be aware of the natural rhythm, as your breath goes in & out. Observe it, without attachment or judgment..."

"Your breath is the most beautiful, intimate, personal thing, and yet the most universal...it is the gift without which you can't survive for a moment, yet in every breath you take in the entire universe...it is the bridge from individual consciousness to cosmic awareness... just feel it..."

As Dave focused on his breathing, he felt going deeper inside. The voice continued. "Now relax every muscle, every joint, tissue, cell in your body. Start from the head, going down to your toe, feeling the flow of energy; and then from toe to head. Experience your solidity dissolve; feel yourself as an energy system..."

Dave felt more & more relaxed...

"Now observe the circle in front of you, as it changes colour. Just be aware, & feel, but don't think…silence your mind, and feel your energies rise as you enter the higher realms through the portals of colors & sounds. Be aware of the music, the sounds, the vibrations…as you go deeper, be aware of the silence within, and in between the sounds…"

As Dave relaxed, breathing becoming softer, calmer & more rhythmic, he drifted into an altered state of consciousness, a higher state operating from his centre. But unlike his energy lift of the past, this time he was aware…centered…

The voice continued. "Do not allow thoughts to enter. Just feel, be aware, but do not think…be aware of your thoughts, your feelings, your emotions, but do not think or analyse… just be aware of those feelings… become the observer…give birth to the witness…"

Dave continued to go deeper in his centre, his balance becoming more robust. As he drifted further into this state, he could just 'feel' the observer...

In that altered state, he started experiencing visions- unknown to him, he was experiencing clairvoyance- sensing his past & future as a continuum, a holographic movie…

As these visions kept appearing & dissolving, the screens around him started projecting these images, though hazy…as if reading & projecting his feelings…

This screen was also visible for 'experience' by certain clairvoyants of the Council…*based on their experience, they would interpret it in the light of the prophecy*…

The voice gently guided: "Continue to see & experience with the eyes of the beholder, the observer…the inner eye...

Be aware of these visions & thoughts as they arise & fade away…if you feel any kind of discomfort of anxiety, just shift your awareness to your navel, and you shall be centered, anchored again. Then gradually come back to your thoughts, feelings & visions…"

As Dave's state became even deeper, the images became more pronounced. In these images, he 'experienced' the President & the war cabinet, not as a dream, but as an energy tussle. *And he 'sensed' that he had some role in this energy 'combat', which would precede the real combat*...

Then he 'sensed' the identity of the master in his dream- *momentously, it was the Grand Master himself...* guiding him, sending energies...through a manifestation...through means... a channel...

The scene then shifted to the stormy night when Dave was headed to his forest lodge. The ball of light appearing in the sky...the brief moment of seeing those images...and then blacking out...

Or did he?

As Dave saw this scene from an observer's perspective, he realized what happened that night: the *ball of light* was actually an advanced PAT from the higher plane, or as people commonly understood, a UFO...very simply, an *unidentified flying object- unidentified in the 4-D plane*...trying to *give the gift* to Dave, to help him teleport...

And teleport he actually did! *Dave made his first 'journey across the gateway' then, briefly entering the NEW AGES!*

But his energies weren't high enough; he wasn't ready for this 'leap'- this called for a 'leap of faith' too, which he lacked at that point. So, soon after the teleportation, his energies dropped, as anxieties became predominant. Not ready for advancing further, *he was 'thrown back' to this plane*...and 'blanked' out when he came back! But with faint memories of 'another place & time'...

The Masters who had facilitated this leap realized that Dave wasn't ready yet. In such a state, he could neither absorb the message of the higher plane, nor seek out the messenger. *The journey would have to wait...*

But they would help him. So, they left behind the disk, a *very special gift*. This, they 'prayed', would lift his energies soon, prompting him at the right time. At that time, Dave interpreted the 'gift' as pointing to a new beginning in his life, without realizing that *the 'new beginning' also referred to one more chance to make the leap...*

Now it all made sense, the first clue:

'From the heavens, came the beings,
To help us rediscover our wings...
Leaving behind gifts to help us fly,
Scaling new peaks, to reach the sky...
To help with a new start,
Provided we look deep inside our heart...

Help it did indeed- to rediscover his wings, by abetting his energies, as Dave continued to evolve on the path of self realization. But along the way, complacency and doubts kept creeping in, so the masters realized he needed another jolt- a LOUD message. Thus came the sign of the crop circle pattern, directing him to the Himalayas- the most mystical mountain range in the world, and a preferred gateway of the beings…

The pattern and its visions also gave more clues about this new world- the visions of celestial bodies along with Einstein & Columbus; the references to the trinity of worlds & civilizations, and the Quartet…

Trying to awaken Dave's deeply buried memory of this place- hoping he would remember it, and be in high energy to make the leap once again.

But Dave was not yet ready- *a high energy gateway was needed for his ascension…*

The observer watched all this with amazement, yet equanimity; understanding the events unfold bit by bit…

Then came the flash visions of pyramids- various pyramids across the world, including the ones at Peru & Egypt…

And then a silver black pyramid with a dazzling capstone…

At this point, some clairvoyants seemed surprised. But Master Aleus smiled, in knowledge…

Dave's visions, however continued…

He then sensed something important…something related to the quest itself…

Vague images…like a tree…a book… a sword…a scroll..

Then a bright flash, and the moment of clarity-**THE PROPHECY OF THE NEW AGES!!**

Like certain select souls, he was experiencing the prophecy, albeit only the initial part of it, first hand;

This, he would realise later, was a very special occasion- for the prophecy, having a mystical, rich & secretive history, manifest itself only to the truly deserving & chosen…

'A soul there shall be, a leap in consciousness which shall make,
By transcending in the NEW AGES, to higher knowledge would be awake,
With knowledge, his higher self shall he align,
And experience his DHARMA, his purpose divine...
In dharma, the Messenger of the NEW AGES he shall seek to find,
Whose wisdom would be the key when the world has lost all its mind,
In this dark night, create he shall alchemy,
Guiding the world to its emerging destiny!
When all is at stake,
The right choices he would have to make,
In the soul's dark night,
The Messenger's wise choice will lead to the light...
His wisdom shall not have gone in vain,
As the whole of humanity stands to gain,
Divine blessings shall then rain,
Healed and guided in the New Ages, without the pain...
His dharma achieved, his karma done,
Balanced would be the karmic equation,
Darkness dispelled, rising a new sun,
Then it would all be One- the ONE...

The observer was astonished! *His coming was prophesied in the NEW AGES...as the soul who would find the Messenger, the one who would then carry the message of the NEW AGES back on earth...much like the messengers & prophets of the past...*

And once this wisdom was received & understood on earth, the destiny of mankind would change...

Now it all made so much sense!

Like a self fulfilling prophecy, he was being 'guided' towards its fulfillment, albeit mysteriously...and once he was ready, the prophecy revealed itself to him...

The prophecy then ended with a vague vision about the meeting a 'companion'...a blinding light...

THE DISK...

Something about it, which would be revealed at the right time...

The observer smiled at these...they were beautiful...

But somewhere in this symphony appeared a jarring note- a fleeting image of a warrior snatching a baby from his wailing mother's arms...and then smashing it on the ground, killing it...

Dave seemed to experience pain at this point. But before it could expand, the vision switched back to the President & his war cabinet...*followed briefly by a calm looking President making an announcement...*

What, he couldn't fathom...

The Masters watched this with bated breath- the President seemed calm...
But it could mean anything...they could only pray...
And then it all vanished...the visions stopped...

Dave lay there in that state, till the voice then slowly brought him back to the outer conscious state, with a gentle count of ten to one .As he slowly got up, he felt refreshed & energized...light & relaxed in every cell...as if he had woken up from the deepest possible slumber...

After sitting in pure silence for some time, Dave realized that he had 'sensed' missing pictures from his memory, by delving deep into his subconscious...

And he remembered it, unlike previous experiences...

He was now clear about what exactly what happened on the night of the UFO experience, and surprised to learn that he had actually been to the NEW AGES before, but was 'thrown' back- not ready for a momentous journey...

The subsequent chain of events, from the disk to crop circles to the Himalayan vision, to the actual journey itself, were all further links in the chain... preparing him for a higher energy state, so that he could make the final teleportation into the NEW AGES, fulfilling a part of the prophecy...

'*When something momentous & noble has to happen, the whole universe conspires for it...*' he smiled.

But along with the answers were new questions...and some jarring visions...

What was it about a child getting killed? He could feel a troubling sensation when he saw it...

What about the pyramids? The capstone? The companion?
And what about the President about to make an announcement?

Till now, his dreams ended with the president & cabinet in heated discussions. *This somehow seemed to be the next step...maybe even the culmination of those discussions..*

But he would not trouble himself with these...*we all know what we need to know...no more, no less...*

As for the Masters, these visions confirmed what they had sensed all along- *the stakes were high!*

It was all about finding the Messenger, his message and his choice in the key moment...and it left them with both hope & worries!

****

"So, what does it all mean, Masters?"

"What does it mean to you?" Sinetha smiled back. Enigma was the way here.

"Gives me more answers; more blocks fall in place..."

"And?"

"Gives more meaning to this whole adventure. Including how I came here...*I mean, I was here before?!*" he smiled.

"Indeed you were! And what about the '*why you*' bit?"

"Partly more clarity than before." Dave paused to put his thoughts together, recollecting the prophecy.

"Though questions still remain. This journey started off with a dream- about a President & a disastrous war, and then came the quest for a Messenger. But after this experience, I think I have some clarity- I am no longer skeptical about the messenger- guess you were right about the Messenger simply being a higher soul out to share a message with the world."

Atlas smiled at Dave's admission.

"Masters, if I correlate what I saw now with my visions about the annihilation, and the evolution of the NEW AGES, *it seems that the quest for the Messenger is somehow linked to the dream & the war.* In fact, the prophecy takes it further- it actually refers to him 'spreading the message' back in my world; as if spreading this message would have repercussions on this disastrous war; and the NEW AGEs..."

"But what?" Dave pondered to himself. "What exactly would he do on earth which would change its destiny? Bring about a *new religion?*"

"Why religion? A new awareness, a new consciousness- the seed would be sowed, a new foundation could be laid." Aleus said metaphorically.

"But *who* is this Messenger? And where would I find him? I still don't have definitive answers…"

The Masters looked at each other & smiled. "That's for you only to seek, since you are chosen for this quest."

"I have tried, but rather unsuccessfully so far." Dave shrugged as he smiled at the image of a failed Indiana Jones.

Nope, Dave Jones couldn't morph to Indiana Jones…

"Remember, in a spiritual journey, success is the journey itself, not merely the outcome…someone thus spake? " Sinetha uttered wisely, reminding Dave of his pronouncement.

Dave nodded with a smile- after all, this is the same thing he had said while replying to the code question at the Holographic History museum. After a brief pause, he asked: "Masters, I saw some new images today- some surreal, & some disturbing. What could they be?"

"What is shown to you must also be known by only you!" *There was something in the way Sinetha said this.*

"As for disturbance, all we can say is- be fully aware in the present only, and don't let negative energies find room in your mind…be they fear, anxiety, anger, guilt, hate…anything!

Remember, *no one has become a bodhisattva without observing these, however deep the negativities of the past or all around… and yet, no one has ever become a bodhisattva without transcending these…*not by attaching to these & disturbed, but by transcending these…"

Dave attempted to observe these words of wisdom, heavy as they were at times. A few moments later, he expressed his befuddlement. "So what now? Where do I go from here…"

"As usual, wherever the flow takes you. Just keep your heart open."

Then suddenly, Zeut got up and headed towards the altar, speaking in a heavy voice. The Masters all rose in unison…

"This conclave stands dispersed. Relevant answers has Dave found, understood his gift and the reasons for his ascension. He must now continue to focus on the journey…the masters bless him…Amen…"

With this, the Council dispersed, as the Masters left one by one, leaving Dave alone in the sanctum, rather surprised and somewhat disappointed at this abrupt, even spasmodic conclusion to the conclave...

He was expecting more...
About the systems of this place, and what significance it had in his journey...

17. THE ENERGY EXCHANGE SYSTEM

Hey, that's it? I was expecting more about this unknown Messenger & my quest. At least somebody...something...where and how to find him, in the light of the new revelation...about his message...

And what about a world without money, based on energy? Shouldn't I have been told more about how exactly it work?

As if on cue, five masters turned back-Aleus, Atlas, Nobius, Zeut & Sinetha, flashing a knowing smile at him...

Energy connections, Dave smiled back....

"The conclave may have been formally dispersed, but the flow of wisdom need not be, son. We sense that you want more answers, so let's get them- back to our discussion before you entered the clairvoyance chamber." Aleus smiled. His smile, his words, his soothing tone were always so comforting.

"Forget the messenger bit for now, as it will only make you more anxious- it will come in due course. For now, having understood the inner world, focus on understanding this world better. After all, it's as much for you to be aware about the NEW AGES as about seeking the Messenger." Nobius gestured to Dave, in a way that seemed vaguely familiar. *But what...??*

"Now that you have lived in a world without money, let's understand its base- *THE ENERGY EXCHANGE SYSTEM!* "

"Hmn...heard about it. Keen to know how exactly it works?"

"In simple terms, it means that the basic metric is energy itself."

Not that simple for me, Masters...

Sensing Dave's uncertainty, Sinetha suggested that they go out into the open. "What better way to understand energy dynamics than in the midst of nature? Where it operate at its purest level…"

As they were stepping outside, Master Aleus stopped for a brief moment near a pillar at the entrance and made a quick, strange gesture with his forefinger, continuing to walk immediately afterwards. Dave noticed from the corner of his eye that it was an ornate pillar, intricately carved, bearing diverse bas relief images– that of Shiva as the dancing Nataraj, the laughing Buddha, ancient warriors bearing all kinds of weapons, from the bow to the lightning bolt, Hercules carrying the world on his shoulders et al. But somewhere, amidst these bountiful images, tucked away inconspicuously was another image, which seemed to flicker faintly: something familiar, something gifted to him, and something teeming with interpretations & possibilities…

The hourglass…

In the course of the previous clue, Dave & friends had deciphered it to represent the passage of time, the ephemeral nature of things. Since it needs to be turned over periodically, it has also been depicted as a symbol of the cyclical, ever changing nature of things- day followed by night followed by dawn, the changing of seasons, and at the deepest level, of the circle of life & death itself. The Vipassana philosophy of *'this too shall change'* could not have found a better ambassador…

Given its rich symbolism, the humble hourglass found a mention both in secret traditions like the Masons, as well as advanced technology- the common icon on PC screens, thanks to MS Windows! In the current scenario though, it was depicted with straight edges rather than gentle curves, glowing with myriad colors from within- the colors, the ethereal hues fleetingly reminding him of the UFO experience– PAT experience, he corrected himself with a smile…

There seemed to be something else around it, like an inscription. *More like hieroglyphs & symbols, actually*-shapes he couldn't fathom...

However, before he could study any further, Master Aleus' quick gait compelled him to hurry, in order to keep pace with the group. At that instant, he felt something jingle in his pocket, but had little opportunity to turn back & notice- the group had moved far ahead!

Outside the sanctum, the group entered a beautiful garden, bearing breathtaking flowers of all hues, like a riot of colors- extraordinarily bright, with a splendor, a radiance he had not experienced in a long time- some of them in full bloom, some yet to 'open out', and some wilted, on the ground…

The symphony of nature at play across the entire spectrum of life & death...creation & destruction...all an interplay...

"See this- *energy exchange in its purest, unalloyed form...*" Aleus pointed at the garden. "Take in sunlight, soil & CO_2, and give back fragrance, beauty & oxygen. Basically, take in pure, universal inputs and giving back elements of life...*pure exchange*...in both bloom & wilting..."

This was an amazing & simple way to start...

"Contrast that with how humans have operated. Throughout history, they have progressively had different metrics, or systems of exchanges, but all of them man made. *None of them were pure exchange, like these beautiful flowers.*" Aleus said, picking up a wilted flower from the ground.

"In its earliest, most basic form, the mode of exchange was barter- natural & simple. I give something in exchange for what I need; life was simple, needs were simple...

Then came the platforms of exchange, the metric, the medium of exchange- first gold, then gold backed paper currency, pure paper currency, and finally, e-currency...

But come to think of it- what was it all about? The same fulfillment of needs, except that now it was with a 'uniform', universal measurement platform- this allowed for more complex trades, allowing more complex commercial structures to evolve. However, they key thing to bear in mind is that money is nothing but a form of energy, a metric of exchange.

Each of these 'currencies' was a derivative of energy itself, depending upon the evolution of the socio-technological systems & human consciousness of that time. So, for a basic society it was gold, while in an advanced society, it was e-money! *But it was all derived, not pure energy...*"

"There were inherent flaws with these metrics, including money- they tried to quantify, to assign value to, to grade things in life based on a lower metric like money, not the underlying energy behind it. Why should the rich have access to the most rarified, not individuals high on energy, character & virtue? The ability to acquire should be a function of one's being, not doing. That is how it should be in a logical, evolved society. So the next big leap, the natural quantum jump for an evolved society was to move away from the derivatives to pure energy itself." Zeut added, building upon his discussion at the promenade.

"And this big leap is Energy Exchange?" Dave asked, unsure of how this was unfolding.

"Exactly! One of our biggest breakthroughs has been to transcend from *currency to energy itself*, as a metric, a system of exchange. From *the derived to the pure...*"

"But how? How's that viable?"

"For that, we have to go deeper into our understanding of energy- let's take a step back and go to the early 20th century. Then, a maverick physicist came up with a path breaking equation, something which was *a quantum jump in human consciousness, apart from being a scientific breakthrough.*"

"You are referring to Einstein's equation, $E = mc2$?" He looked at Master Aleus & gave a knowing look."We discussed Einstein earlier as well."

"Yes, but that was about his theory of relativity- this one is about his other landmark equation- the foundation of a higher understanding of energy."

"The genesis of Quantum Mechanics? Energy & matter are interconvertible. And within matter lies a huge quantum of energy?"

"Exactly- but there's more."

"More?"

"Yeah. Fortunately or unfortunately, this equation was so far ahead of its time that most thinkers never realized its complete depth, its other implications & applications. *But to us, Einstein is the father of New age economics.*"

"Actually, he should have won a Nobel prize in economics too-given the path breaking implications!" Atlas winked

"*Two Nobel prizes always better than one...*" Dave engaged in some repartee of his own."But in economics for a physicist?! Next you'll say medicine or social sciences... " he smiled

"Why not? All this seems farfetched only to a fragmented mind. *To us, this equation is a combination of physics, metaphysics & economics*, depending on how you look at it."

"Must say you guys look at things rather *tangentially*."

"Straight & tangential are relative to the observer's perspective. Mystics have always known it experientially." Sinetha added. "We have simply taken this equation as a theoretical framework, upon which we formulated a deeper understanding of energy. And more importantly, built an application of this."

"And the application is to have energy itself as both, a source and exchange medium? Why have a derived platform like money when you can have the basic thing itself, right?" Dave queried, trying to make sense, but still uncertain.

"Right."

"So what's this application? And how does this work?" Dave had an undercurrent of impatience in his voice.

"Patience, young man!" Atlas said rather sternly. "Don't rush towards answers. Let them come to you. First, understand the concept better. Remember, energy has many forms & manifestations- this far your world already knows.

But our wisdom is that energy has many more forms- subtler forms beyond potential & kinetic energy, or even 'newer' forms like nuclear energy- forms immensely powerful, in abundance, and unknown to your world as yet!"

"Like?" Dave was curious now. This was pioneering, heck, leading edge stuff...

"Like *pranic energy or chi...kundalini...or a newly understood form of energy which can counter decay on account of free radicals...and more...*"

Dave raised his eyebrow.

"But that's a discussion for later. For now, what's important is to realise that we are in a constant exchange of these subtler energies, both with each other and the Universe. New age physicists & thinkers have come to agree with the mystics' view that every human impulse in the universe creates a ripple in it- just as the whole affects the parts, so do the parts impact the whole...*like the ripples in a lake when a stone is thrown*...

Depending upon the intensity of the pebble thrown, the ripple created is strong or weak. Similarly, human impulses create strong or weak ripples in the fabric of space-time, *the intensity of the impulse being the 'quantum of this energy'.*"

"Hmn..."

"From your worldly plane, you observe & experience only the ripples in the 4-dimensional plane. But at higher levels of consciousness, one experiences these ripples in higher dimensions as well. *This is energy in its higher, purer form...*

Once you understand this, the concept of energy gets expanded, acquiring many 'non material' forms- subtler forms like knowledge, love, wisdom, spirit etc..." added Aleus. "Forms that you know, but can't completely comprehend as a higher kind of energy."

"So imagination is energy, idea is energy, intent is energy, words are energy. In fact, consciousness itself is pure energy…

And this is the constant 'energy exchange' we are involved with continuously with the whole. This is akin to what new age thinkers like James Redfield, Peter Senge and Deepak Chopra have proposed- the unfolding of the Universe is not an ethereal, preordained process far beyond the control of ordinary mortals like us, but that *we are active participants in this process, through energy interactions with the whole...*"

"But this is still at higher planes?"

"This applies at all planes, including the 4-D plane."

"How?"

"Heard about the concept of *'reflectivity'*? Propounded by another leading thinker of your time, George Soros?"

Dave shook his head. He again felt embarrassed not having read a great trader & thinker of his time; and he called himself a man of the industry, of commerce, of capitalism!

"In simple terms, reflexivity is the relationship between thought & reality- *basically, what we think about the future has a bearing on the future itself. That's how human history, capitalism & markets behave…*"

"So reflexivity says that we contribute to…"

"…shaping our future!" Atlas completed. "Whether at a higher plane or the 4-D plane! Another example is creative visualization, affirmation or prayer energy that thinkers like Shakti Gawain & Marc Allen have adduced- reflexivity is simply a derivative of this on the 4-D plane. Either ways, the fact agreed by most thinkers is that we are in an active energy exchange with the whole, which in turn reciprocates in equal measure. Now tie in all these understandings- that there are higher energy states, that we are in a constant energy exchange with the whole, and that matter & energy are inter-convertible; *the Einstein equation $E=mc2$…*"

Dave arched his eyebrows, as if to say unbelievable…

"So what do you get in essence? If we are in an exchange with the universe, then just as we give energies, we should get back. And if matter & energy have a correlation, then the Universe should pay back for our material needs, on the basis of this energy exchange- *not on the basis of lower, derived metrics like money...*"

"*The basis of the energy exchange system?!!*"

"Indeed! If this is how the universe interacts with us, then why shouldn't the same be replicated in an advanced society? *If energy is the core metric, then all human endeavors & activities should be directed at maximizing this 'wealth', not derived metrics of wealth! And this 'higher wealth', this energy, should take care of all your material needs.* That's New age economics for you! Or natural economics, if you should like. Inspired by Einstein. Would you now agree he should have received a Nobel prize in Economics too? " Sinetha smiled.

Dave was left gaping...

"This, this is truly mind boggling! You have combined the higher understanding of energy with the exchange system to create a natural, energy exchange system! *It all seems so obvious, so apparent, and yet so distant, so ethereal...*"

"That's the crux of human evolution. What is higher or better, even if seemingly ethereal today, is worth striving for!"

"But how? Even if we can internalize this understanding, how do we create the platforms? I mean, we have an entire system- banks, capital markets, corporations, markets, trade- all based on money as a medium. "

"Let's just say that *we have a platform which can read individual impulses & energies...*" Master Aleus smiled enigmatically.

"The IIN controls, coordinates & regulates all processes of production, distribution & consumption, so that all needs are met basis energies, in the most optimized ways."

"And what's that platform, Master?"

"That's it for now. Don't bite more than you can chew, and chew only what you can digest. Before seeking more, assimilate what you already have." Zeut said with an 'apparent' swagger, chewing his stub as if he were chomping gum. But by now, Dave knew enough to trust them fully. Beneath their supposedly tough, and at time brusque exterior, lay a soft core based on deep compassion, every Master having his own style of...

Dave bowed low, in obeisance. *This was an enlightening session, a liberating feeling...*

He thanked the Masters once again, getting special blessings from Aleus, as they headed back to the sanctum- from where the Masters would retire to their respective chambers, for an afternoon of meditation. Along the way, Dave had a heady feeling- *amazed at learning a whole new economic model based on a cutting edge energy equation, and trying to correlate it with what he had learnt so far...*

His mind flew back to his observations at the promenade, and his conversation with Zeut- now he understood even better why the creative folks in this place were so 'well off', and why this place had an abundance mentality. Not only did the Quartet system guarantee fulfillment of basic needs, but the ones with higher energy actually had more 'currency' in the system...

All thanks to a physicist...

****

After bidding the Masters goodbye, Dave was about to head for the hangar to board his PAT, headed for the space port, when Master Aleus turned back, smiling at him, hands in his pocket, and said rather enigmatically: "*As above, so below,* Dave. That's the essence, the distillation. See beyond the apparent, understand the reflection. And yes, for every lock, there is a key...to be found & used by the worthy...

Understand the true nature of things... *all hinges upon it...*"

Dave wondered about this latest pronouncement from the Master- in a way, it seemed to reaffirm what he learnt, that energy ripples at lower planes affect the fabric of space-time, thus higher dimensions, and vice versa. But, he also seemed to be suggesting something else beneath, beyond this...

*Understand the reflection...for every lock, there is the key...all hinges upon it....*What, he couldn't fathom, and started to move, shrugging his shoulders. But then, in an instinctive replication of Aleus' gesture, he too put his hand in his pocket. *Why, he didn't know. It just happened...*

And not without reason...he felt something...
Rather, the absence of something. The disk wasn't there...

Now he figured out the jingling he had felt in his pocket earlier- *the disk must have dropped off somehow...*

But how? There wasn't even a hole in his pocket! And where?

A moment later, he quickly headed back to the sanctum entry- that's where he felt the jingle- that's where it should be...

And rightly so! On reaching there, he found the disk lying on the ground, at the base of the pillar.

Not bad...

So, Master Aleus indicated for me to come here to find the disk. But why? And how did he realise what I didn't?

As he saw the disk, it was flickering from within, not unlike the way it had glowed the very first time- but it was different- more like a filament gleaming from within a light bulb...

Nonetheless, he picked it up. Just as he rose, he had a chance to see the strange, yet familiar image, up close:

The straight edged hour glass...but not merely as a flat image- rather, it was raised...3-dimensional, rather than two...and flickering, much like the disk...

I thought it had served its purpose when it guided me to the Council. So, what's it doing here, amidst all these images & symbols...

And why is it glowing, just like the disk? Why did I come back here at all? And what are these images around it? Possibly hieroglyphs? Or just a random assortment of shapes- lines, curves, dots...?

Dave looked closely, and sensed that it wasn't a normal hourglass image- something was different about it. It seemed somewhat fluid rather than solid, *as if waiting for something...*

Instinctively, his hands were drawn to it, touching it gently, almost caressing it. It was a smooth but gel like surface, with the inner glow intensifying in line with his caring caress.

The smoothness was uniform- no jagged edges, no inscriptions, no clue if he were looking for one...
Except at the intersection point...
In the centre, there turned out to be a small gap, a small notch. Tiny, almost imperceptible, yet seemingly significant- as if indicating something...
As above, so below...for every lock there is a key...
All hinges upon it...
All hinges upon it???
Gotcha! All hinges upon it! Upon this point...
This tiny, nearly invisible notch was the 'hinge'- an actual hinge on which 'it all rested'! Revealing the true nature of things...
All it needed was a key to unlock it...
But what kind of key...?
He didn't have to think much, though. The key lay right in front of him, glowing with the same radiance as the lock...
The disk as a gift...and now as a key?!
Dave gently touched the tip of the disk to the little notch, and the true nature of things- *of the hinge*, became evident... there was a faint click, and the hourglass first turned 90 degree, to become horizontal...

And then, the two parts seemingly snapped at the hinge, collapsing to a form a new image altogether...
That of two pyramids- twin pyramids- now flickering in unison...
Unhinged from the centre, and now joined at the base!

Pyramids? Dave's first reaction was that he was encountering too many along his journey, to be mere coincidences. Rather, they were more like an enigmatically recurring theme- *in the crop circle pattern, the holographic image back at the tree house, the bas reliefs above the altar of the Grand Master, in his clairvoyance chamber vision, and now on this pillar...*

As he considered it, he realized that mankind's fascination with pyramids was almost as ancient as recorded history itself! It was understandable therefore, that such an enigmatic form found a revered presence in this evolved land, what with the shape itself arousing so much curiosity & spawning so many theories; but somehow, it seemed more than a mere tribute to one of history's most enduring & enigmatic mysteries- *it seemed to be a pattern, a series of clues yet again...*

No sooner did the thought of clues cross his mind than the hieroglyphics & shapes around the twin pyramids started glowing brightly, and began seemingly unhinging too- moving like the teeth of a gear, in a harmonious, orderly fashion. What seemed like a strange, unknown assortment of images just moments back, rearranged itself neatly, to form an English verse, revealing the next clue, *the fifth one*:

'Seek the heart,
Where it all made the start...
Based upon the union of the four,
It shall open many a door...
In your quest, this is an important key,
Free your mind, and this heart you shall see...'

Wow, Dave exhaled, though he didn't really figure it's implication. Fascinated, he attempted to run his hands as affectionately on the alphabets too, but instantly, they disappeared once again, rearranged back to the original hieroglyphics, like a clock unwinding.

As if on cue, the twin pyramids softly clicked again, and in a seamless motion, their bases unhinged, tilting towards each other, till the vertical surfaces facing each other touched in a smooth fashion. The anti clockwise motion continued, hinging once again at the tip, till the two pyramids were joined together in the shape of a horizontal hour glass once again.

And, in a final, synchronized motion, the whole shape continued its anti-clockwise motion by another 90 degrees, till the shape was back to its original position. *Hinging around the tip of the disk...*

On cue, the glow of both the hourglass & the disk disappeared too, leaving behind a static image. Tucked away in the midst of hundreds of images... *Concealed... inconspicuous...anonymous yet again...*

18. Seek the heart where it all made a start…

"There is something important I wanna discuss with you guys. Come ASAP! Let's meet at crater Apennine. Coordinates being sent shortly." appeared Plutus' rather cryptic holographic message to Dave, just as he was about to board his PAT, headed for the moon bound CAT station. He had not even fully savored his meeting with the Council, and all the new knowledge he was a recipient of, when this message flashed simultaneously to the trinity. At the time, Ikona was on Columbus, doing research on new age organic farming, while Lyon was spending sleepless nights on algorithmic upgrades for the next version of the travel module, aimed at further optimizing it.

Incidentally, Plutus himself was immersed in a special cross functional mission at the pole of the moon, carrying out materials & energy experiments there. A cold, inhospitable place back in our times, the poles were a source of significant water ice in the new ages, used for fresh water supply as well as to create hydro energy. Teams of scientists first created a hospitable environment using Gelass and associated technology, and then set up several base stations all across the poles, till they became hotspots of scientific activity. Plutus had volunteered to join this project a few months back, especially passionate about the potential impact of it.

Therefore Dave wondered as to what could be so important & urgent that Plutus had to abandon his project mid way? Not that he would mind this rendezvous one bit. It had been a while since the four of them had met, and he was pretty excited to share his experiences at the Council…

'And the earth becomes my throne
I adapt to the unknown
Under wandering stars I've grown
By myself but not alone
I ask no one, & my ties are severed clean
The less I have the more I gain
Off the beaten path I reign...'

Dave was humming his favorite Metallica chartbuster as he strolled around the crater, trying to find an opportune spot to set up his tent. The place, the milieu, the company of the trinity- it was all beginning to make him feel so liberated again...*soaring like Jonathan Seagull...*

Feelings he had last encountered as a teenager...

Then, as life caught up, this freedom slowly got wrapped up in layers of conditioning...about life's 'realities', about 'responsibilities'...*conditioning, which told him that life had to be stable, not nomadic...serious, not lighthearted...in the known zone, away from adventure & the unknown...*

Eventually, most people gave in & gave up- on their free spirit, their passions, their nebulous but profound dreams... on everything which once mattered...

And it was no different for Dave- the 'realities' of life triumphed, as the process of living morphed from a thrilling adventure to a mundane routine...

But, coming here had unconditioned him, layer by layer, bit by bit...and as he stood there, in a remote campsite in a different place & time, he was feeling like the energetic & rebellious teenager he once was...*free to dream, free to roam around, free to just be! And free to make a difference, not just to exist!*

Feeling light, he went back to building his *dwelling*...

****

"Ok sir, here is your house. Please enjoy your camping experience in your modest little house." Lyon joked, while handing over a small box to Dave. On it was written *'home sweet home!'*

Camping kit of the NEW AGES, Dave thought...

Modest little house...

"A personal vehicle, a modest little mobile house, and a free spirit. What more could a simple man want" Dave smiled back.

"See what awaits you...*a small gift* from your buddies..." he was told then, with a wink. Now, while opening it, he had a sense that it wasn't going to be exactly small...or simple...

And rightly so! Far from being a simple tent like object, the box contained an individual, foldable, mobile house...

But foldable had a slightly different connotation here...

The box contained 'folded sheets' or rolls, somewhat like a tent. But, on placing the kit on the ground, and giving the necessary commands into the micro computer, the *assembly began on its own...*

The super strong, ultra thin, carbon isotope sheets opened up to a giant mass- assembled quickly by nanobots and supported on carbon nanotubes, which acted as the 'pillars'. Moreover, the whole thing came preprogrammed basis size, surface & ambient conditions. One had to just give the necessary commands to the micro computer, which itself was suitably connected to both- the mobile housing module of the IIN, as well as a Personal Energy Device (PED), for all the power requirements. *Thus, in a matter of minutes, a complete dwelling was ready, self sufficient & well connected...*

But it wasn't merely a functional dwelling...far from it...the unit was both aesthetically appealing & super intelligent. Since the material was ultra thin & malleable, the nanobots could be programmed to give the structure any shape- igloo, tent, castle etc, depending upon the material quantity and property. Moreover, the inside surface could be sprayed with a special colloidal paint, consisting of carbon nanotubes. This had multiple functions: as a paint, creating the desired texture & shade; as a temperature controller; and as a projection screen, from where the individual could reach out to & communicate with any part of the network...

Dave remembered his conversation with Plutus about flexible, mobile housing, which allowed for mobile communes to flourish. No wonders, seekers blossomed here. *It was so easy & comfortable to allow for instant communes to be assembled & dissembled... truly flexible housing model...*

As Dave sat in his 'simple house', he smiled, reminiscing that his first passion had been to be an architect; to design high tech, yet 'natural' houses...

And here he was, once again living a long lost dream...He then remembered his tree house, and *how building an eco friendly, yet charming abode, was possible right in our time, our world...he felt good about his tree house...*

After his buddies had set up their 'tents' too, they spent the day catching up, having casual conversation about the past few days. For Dave, this was the most unconventional 'camping' trip of his life- nothing like the boy scout camps, yet the same feeling of thrill, exhilaration & youthfulness...

Hours passed as another stunning lunar evening set in, covering the crater in a twilight zone...but no high tech mega structures, no symphony of flying PATs, no dazzling lights here- just nature, pure & unalloyed...

As the evening set in, they strolled along the crater, simply experiencing the evening... In this utter, pure silence, they could better experience the inner voice...

What words couldn't do, silence could, as they felt special about themselves & each other...

With the lights getting dimmer, they came back by the crackling campfire, taking stock of their lives & journeys, especially Dave's- the momentous changes & discoveries of the past few weeks, and how life felt so different in a new world...

Yet, when Dave looked at the flame, heard the familiar crackling sound, and felt the company of the three most special people in his life now, he realized how similar, beautiful, things were...he also realized that the more accepting he was of the universe, unconditionally- allowing life to flow 'through' him, the more his sense of adventure was awakened. His fears dissolved, and the childlike joy & innocence returned. The basic joys of life were the same across space & time!

"So what is this urgent thing that you wanted to discuss?" Dave finally broke the utter silence, asking Plutus.

"I have a *special announcement* to make..." Plutus replied with a sheepish grin, glancing towards Ikona. Inside the atmospheric dome on this remote crater, a soft, simulated wind blew, hissing in the silence.

"What?" Lyon asked, somewhat uncomfortable. For a fleeting moment, Dave too felt a butterfly in his stomach...

Why, he couldn't sense though...

"Rein in your horses, pal. Before the special announcement, yet another special something..." and he went inside his 'tent', only to emerge with 3 guitars. "Let's jam!", he excitedly remarked, passing on one each to Dave & Lyon, while retaining the third. "Let's express through music what our souls feel..."

For a moment, Dave looked at the other two, a bit tentative. A nod from Ikona did the trick, and he readied to strum, tuning the high tech electronic guitar, made of an advanced alloy, but strangely not connected to power connection. "Mind you, the sounds could be a little different from what you are used to...this is *our version* of an electronic guitar..."

Dave nodded, gently twitching the strings with his thumb- the act of an artist trying to achieve oneness with his music, and all that which created the music...

After a brief thought, he decided to play a rendition of *'Nothing else matters'* by Metallica.

'Forever trust in who we are, and nothing else matters...' and Dave sang his heart out, after a long time.

"Why this buddy?" Plutus asked, a bit surprise, at the end.

"I thought about which one to play on this occasion, and then arrived at this...it used to be something that would keep the embers burning bright while I was chasing glory in my world, especially at times when I was beaten & bruised-from education to sports to Corporate glory, competing always...

Now, months into a different world, that part of life seems so different, so alien...yet my faith is reinforced more than ever before, my belief in self unshakeable after this magical journey; this, my friends, is my dedication, my attempt to keep that memory alive-to remind myself of how faith can move mountains, be it in a different or sanitized environment, or in the rough-and-rumble world of mine...as long as I believe, there is always magic at the next bend!"

His buddies gave him a thumbs up. Yup, faith could move mountains and part the seas...

Next, it was Lyon's turn. But while he was readying to sing in his high pitched, electronic voice, Plutus suddenly came to the centre and started singing in a smooth voice: *'Can you feel the love tonight...'*

As his surprised friends gazed up, he walked across to Ikona, guitar in his hand, down on his knees, and continued with his mellifluous rendition of an Elton John classic. And as soon as this song was over, he started off with *'you fill up my senses..'*, all the while staring intently at Ikona…

Utter silence…no applause, no reactions…just blank faces! Finally, Dave gathered the presence of mind to raise his fingers in a *'what's this'* gesture.

Plutus' eyes twinkled. "Buddies, *this* is my special announcement. Ikona and yours truly have decided to cement their childhood friendship into a special bond."

"What??!!" Ikona blurted out. By now, the discomfiture was palpable, and unnerving…

Dave & Lyon, on the other hand, looked confused…

"Yes, Ikona and I hereby declare that we are madly in love, and wish to spend the rest of our lives together…"

"Now, wait wait wait. Just what kind of a joke is this??" Ikona reacted with a combination of shock & irritation.

"*Joke*? Isn't this why we are all gathered here, pretty lady? Didn't we decide jointly honey, that we would get all friends together, and then break the news? But now you back out? You're breaking my heart…" Plutus said, his throat seemingly choked, yet his voice betraying the slightest hint of mischief.

"Stop at this very moment, Pluty, else I am going back! What nonsense is this?" Ikona was nearly grinding her teeth.

"OK, *stopped!*" he replied with a straight face. Lyon and Dave were thoroughly bewildered by now, not knowing whether to feel happy, dismayed, relieved, or nothing at all… Finally, the normally cocky Lyon spoke, rather timidly. "What's going on? Are you guys really getting hitched or what?"

"No way!" Ikona reacted sharply, quite unlike her soft demeanor. "This must be one of his silly tricks!"

Plutus burst out laughing. "OK, ok, *mea culpa…*"

"So *this was* a joke? And you called us all the way here *for this*?" Dave asked, incredulous.

"Je *suis vraiment desole…*" He smiled, making a baby like face. *I am really sorry…*

"You bum! Is that really why you called us here? Do you realize we left important projects?" Lyon said, agitated. "I have timelines to meet, a new version of the module to be launched.."

"I realise." Plutus turned serious. "OK, this was just a joke; but I called you guys for two special reasons..."

"And now, *what are those, sir?*" Ikona's prolonged sarcasm was quite unlike her.

"One, that our lady Ikona's birthday is coming up in a fortnight, so I wanted to give her a surprise-a special celebration with all of us together...

After all, it's been a while since we've met, so what better gift than all of us celebrating together?"

Suddenly, all of Ikona's anger dissolved, and she gave a tender smile to Plutus. "Oh my Pluty, you are such a sweetheart. I'm sorry I lost it on you this way." she said, back to her soft, delicate voice, pulling his cheeks softly. Plutus blushed. This was the demure, feminine touch any man would fall for...

"But why now?" Lyon said, still flustered. "We have a fortnight to go dude. And oh, by the way, *we* remember her birthday *too, you see*." came the trademark Lyon snide remark.

Competitive populism among friends, Dave smiled...

"Because I will not be around then, folks...that is the second announcement I have to make...*yours truly is going to Einstein for a special assignment, personally mandated by senior members of the Council...*"

"How come?" Dave asked.

"I have to meet an elite group of cyborg scientists there, ostensibly for a first hand status update on an energy project they are working on, and report it back to the Council."

"That's cool dude." Lyon said, finally smiling. "So now you work on special reviews for the Council, huh? *Big man!*" he said with a mock sarcasm.

"What project is this?" Dave enquired.

"This group is working on some energy amplification & distribution enhancement technologies- *supposedly* an official project mandated by the QUARTET. "

"*Supposedly?*"

"Yeah, the distribution efficiency project is supposedly just a front. The Council suspects that the real deal is some other covert, high-tech, high impact energy experiment, which has been surreptitiously carried out for the past few months."

"Past few months? And nobody's noticed it, or is keeping tabs on it?" Ikona sounded surprised.

"Yes ma'am, it's been on for quite a while now. Initially, most folks ignored it, since *this was a purely private* research. But now, it comes out that apparently these experiments can have larger ramifications. *Potential collective consequences...*"

"So that's where you come in, huh? As a scientist trusted by the Council. Hmn...which means that they are obviously worried about something." Lyon tried to make sense of it.

"Yes, they are concerned. For a while, they deliberated on direct intervention as a possible option, vs. merely keeping a close watch. But prudently, they have chosen the latter, 'cause there's more to it..."

"More?"

"Yes- grapevine has it that some high levels Quartions are covertly supporting these experiments, without any official sanction or mandate."

"Serious?"

"Yeah. And that's bothering the Council even more. *Especially since they alone have knowledge of this...*"

"Are you telling me that the Quartet has no knowledge of such extensive experiments? In such a high tech society, where information flow is so seamless?" Dave sounded surprised.

"No *official knowledge*...and that's worrying the Council."

"So that's why they can't trust a nominee of the Quartet?"

"Yeah."

"Sounds murky..." Ikona raised her brow.

"Any idea on what exactly is this experiment all about? And just how much does the Council know?"

"Knowing the Council, I am sure they have reasonable knowledge, else they would not jump in. Not in such an involved manner at least! Even though it's mostly secretive, I've heard that these guys are working on some technologies & devices which can fundamentally impact the basic energy exchange system...*under the guidance of some ultra-secretive genius*, whom nobody knows about. The Council wants me to plug the gaps, to fill in the missing pieces..."

"And just how would that happen? If something clandestine is at work here, you can't just barge in."

"Not barging in, exactly. Since I have credibility in energy circles, the Council has positioned this visit as a 'exchange program'. That makes it sounds quite normal- at least for the official project. And once I entrench myself, it's up to me after that! Of course, there is Master Atlas- he would be doing lot more gigs on Einstein, I bet! And, guide me along the way..."

"Interesting..." as Dave made a mental note of the bandit who became a 'rockstar saint'. "So, will you be gone for long?"

"Frankly, I don't know. Let's see..."

"Take care, partner- this doesn't sound straightforward." Dave said, genuinely concerned about his friend, as he got his first sense of the challenges of the NEW AGES.

"I will buddy, I will... so, how was it with you?"

"Amazing. The Council is so different from what I had imagined or envisaged. The masters are unlike anything I have ever seen- in all shapes & sizes...they defy any stereotype!"

The others smiled. "So, you had your experience in the clairvoyance chamber?"

"Yes; and it literally took me 'across time'..."

"And, what was the outcome? Any new answers?"

"Yes- lots of clues & visions. I now know more about the role & goal of the Messenger. Apparently, it seems related to the President & the war, but I can't exactly pinpoint what. And frankly, I have no clue of any such President, nor any apparent conflict in my world. And even if there was, I can't see what a messenger can do about it..."

"Hmn...maybe the answers will come. What else?"

"It now seems that there are *two more characters* in this whole chain."

"Two more characters?"

"Yes- some medieval knight I saw, slaughtering a baby; and something about *finding the companion...*"

"Interesting; strange..."

"So, what do you make out of this?"

"Hmn...can't really say. The first one could be anything, but the way you describe it, sounds like some knight from the crusades. Maybe a templar knight."

"I thought so too; but what could it possibly mean to me? I mean, I ain't even no regular churchgoer...more like an agnostic! So what do I have to do with medieval religious history and a medieval knight?"

"As if this mysterious President & the Messenger aren't enough dope for a treasure hunt..." he smiled as an afterthought. "And what do you think about the companion bit?"

"*Find the companion*...it could mean so many things, in so many aspects, both here and back in your plane."

"Like?"

"Like the fact that we are your companions, in a way. But we are three companions, and already found. So this one's ruled out..." Lyon deduced.

"Maybe *someone else, someone special,* whose company you seek; whom you have to meet, to find.." Ikona gave an impish smile.

Instantly, the image of Shakti flashed, and Dave gazed at Ikona in a way he had not looked at a woman in a long time-*unblinking, deep, penetrating...*

Ikona squirmed slightly at this, while Lyon seemed stunned yet again...*today just wasn't his day...his own buddies...??*

Sensing the discomfiture in the air, Dave instantly retracted, veering the conversation elsewhere. "Hey, there's something else too. After my meeting with the Council, I got another clue from the disk. And in *yet another enigmatic way...*"

"Enigmatic?"

"Yeah- through an innocuous looking shape-the *hourglass.*"

All three of them perked up at the mention of this. "Again?"

"Oh, wait wait- there's lots more. Master Aleus tells me some supposed words of wisdom, and it turns out that they are clues to unlock this hour glass. As I insert the 'key'- the disk in the 'hinge', the shape morphs, and twin pyramids stand where there was the hourglass a moment back..." Dave's excitement was peaking, as was that of his pals.

"Then, this changing shape leads to some unknown hieroglyphics transforming into neatly arranged alphabets; and before I can even 'feel' the words, it all goes back to the original shape, nestled inconspicuously among hundreds of bas relief images. *What else do you call this but enigmatic?"*

"All part of your learning, Dave...*our learning*..." it was the endower in Ikona talking.

"So what's the learning here, apart from the clue? That pyramids have a special place in the New Ages?"

"Aha!" Lyon replied rather nonchalantly. "There are so many here, so many throughout history, that it even ceases to surprise or fascinate us beyond a point. But yes, *they are special*..." And he left it at that.

"And?"

"And what? *Nothing!* Let's focus on the clue?" Lyon responded as coolly, trying to assess if that, along with its context, conveyed something. Dave smiled, understanding that he would get no further on this piece. The significance of the pyramid would probably have to wait, if there was indeed one...

He closed his eyes, trying to remember the exact words. After a moment, he put his forefinger on his chin, as if still pondering, and spoke. "It said something like:

'Seek the heart,
Where it all made the start,
Based upon the union of the four,
It shall open many a door,
In your quest, this is an important key,
Free your mind, and this heart you shall see...'

"Interesting. What could this mean, especially in the context of your meeting with the Council?"

"It refers to keeping an open heart. "

"Which you already are, since the beginning." Ikona smiled. "So why *now*?"

"Maybe I have to be more open hearted. That's what the masters kept emphasizing too."

"So which is this *other heart* you are supposed to seek? Where it all started?"

Dave was silent for a minute. This reference to *another heart where it all made a start* once again brought back old memories. Then he said softly "Beats me."

Ikona immediately sensed his anguish, and squeezed his hand to comfort him. Inspite of his discomforting gaze earlier, they were special friends, and shared special energies- Ikona let her awareness of this fact guide her.

Lyon made a mock face, and broke the silence after a while. "Guys, what's this about the union of four? Didn't we already solve it in the second clue*? So why again? Pluty, what do you think?*"

"Huh, you said something? Sorry, my mind is still stuck in the assignment. Wondering about the role of the Quartet..."

"*Of course* I said something." Lyon hated being ignored. "I was asking what you think about this 'union of four' bit? Why is it getting repeated?"

"Sorry, but am finding it real difficult to focus. This Quartet bit is preoccupying my mind too much..."

But then, with some effort, he pondered over it. "Ok, so there is something about the heart and the union of four. Yeah, sounds like our fellowship. In a way, Dave's journey here started with us, so this seems like the heart where it all made a start...based on the union of us four?"

"Na, I don't think so. This has already been deciphered. I think it refers to *some energy system having four points,* which, when in harmony, could facilitate an open heart."

"Maybe. But I think it refers to *something which has four dimensions*, and where it all started." Ikona added.

"Eureka! Why didn't I think of this before!" Dave suddenly exclaimed. "*It obviously refers to the Einstein equation-meeting of the three dimensions of space & one of time-the Union of four...* the foundation for the energy exchange system!"

"Man, you could have run naked on this. After Archimedes, this is *the next big* Eureka moment!" Lyon remarked in his trademark jest. Dave continued, nonetheless.

"Now it seems to tie in- while I was disappointed that I didn't get much information from the Council about the Messenger, in retrospect, I learnt quite a bit about the energy exchange system...*which is the heart of this plane.*

And its starting point is the understanding of Einstein's energy matter equation, as well as the theory of relativity. *Hence the reference to the union of four...*"

"Brilliant buddy! You are getting better and better at cracking the codes." Lyon flashed a thumbs up.

"Not without reason have I progressed so far." Dave replied, taking a bow, mocking Lyon.

"No attitude, *human*! Remember what Master Aleus says: Arrogance leads to ignorance." Lyon winked. Momentary silence, and then, as if on cue, they all broke out into an uproarious laughter.

"Quite a rowdy bunch we are turning out to be." Dave said, remember that the last time he had such a boisterous bunch was in his early days in sales. And they were quite a handful...

"Human, you are impeding our evolution by infecting us with crass, unevolved behavior!"

"No cyborg, I am teaching you the lovely human emotion of laughter!" And, with that, they burst out into another animated mirth.

"Ok people, come back & focus." Ikona interjected. "We still have a clue to unravel."

"Already done, ma'am. It refers to the Energy exchange system, and Einstein's equation."

"OK, so it is referring to the Energy exchange system, and asking you to build upon your understanding of it. But how? You gonna study Quantum physics & relativity in detail now?"

"Dunno. And we still haven't figured out the companion bit." Dave said. Silence...the euphoria of the previous minute was replaced by contemplation...

"There has to be *more* to it..." Ikona said.

"This is to be interpreted *at more than one level*, like the other clues. We were right about our understanding of the Energy Exchange system so far, but there has to be another layer...Plutus, any thoughts?"

"I'm sorry, I just am just not able to focus on this; somehow my mind keeps going back to the role of the Quartet in my assignment..."

"*ROLE OF THE Q-U-A-R-T-E-T...*" Lyon repeated slowly.

All eyes on him.

"Quartet-*union of the four*; four key aspects of society- administration, governance, technology & religion! How could we miss it? We have to be dummies!!"

"I don't get it." Dave queried with an air of anticipation.

"In a way, *isn't the Quartet the heart of the NEW AGE* systems & society?" Lyon smiled. "So, *seek the heart* could mean the heart of this plane- *the administrative heart! based on the union of four...*"

"Where the energy exchange system started-and from where it is all managed, in an integrated manner! So, at one level, the Einstein equation and the Energy Exchange model is the heart, based on the union of four dimension; and on the other, the Quartet is the entity which actually applies this knowledge, being the administrative heart of the New Ages." Ikona added excitedly.

"And in an institutional sense, it is the *companion* of the Council; while one governs, the other regulates." Plutus added, about to put together all pieces of the puzzle.

"Bingo! So that's it! The whole experience, the clue, is basically guiding you to move from the Council to the Quartet-*its companion*; this tells us what the companion is, too."

"So my next progression is from the Council to its companion institution- the Quartet?"

"Yes, 'cause there, you will get to see the energy exchange systems- *THE HEART, and all of its modules first hand.*"

They raised a toast to celebrate their deciphering of the latest clue, by sipping yet another special herbal brew.

"And what about the Messenger? That still remains."

"Maybe something about the Quartet...*someone there*?"

Dave pondered over it, and then looked at Plutus. "This sounds funny, almost a weird coincidence about you & me- *you are going away on an assignment related to the QUARTET, while I am being asked to go to the QUARTET. You go at the behest of the Council, while I get this clue just after meeting the Council.* And both of us head in the quest for something unknown as yet...yet, on quests, which could have an impact on both the heavens & earth..."

"Coincidence?" Plutus smiled, his eyes glittering, as he looked at Dave. "There are no accidents in the Universe, only meaningful coincidences..."

Dave smiled back, sensing his connections with Plutus...

****

"So, how do I take this forward? Can't just barge into the QUARTET and tell them-hey, show me how it all works around here. I am here 'cause some mysterious disk told me so."

"You can't just barge in, but you definitely can be sent; assigned..." Plutus smiled. "If I can be sent on an exchange program, you certainly can be sent on a special project...*as an intern...*"

Dave understood the reference-with the blessings of the Council, an internship would be arranged for him in the QUARTET, across chambers; after all, it wasn't uncommon for aspiring seekers to be assigned to projects in the QUARTET.

"So, will I see you again?" Dave asked Plutus, a certain emotion hitting him; as if this was it...

"I dunno buddy. I guess maybe...hope so..."

Dave gave Plutus the bear hug of his life, his eyes moist now.

"I still don't really know why I came here, but I do know what I found here- right at the top is your friendship guys. We've known each other only for a few months, yet I feel we have been connected since ages, and will continue to do so.

Plutus, Lyon, Ikona: I still can't fathom how and why someone would be so considerate and loving towards a stranger, from not just another land, but another world. I know you guys feel mine is a special journey, and I also realise that this place has special energies-some inherent values; but this is not merely altruism or kinship- *this is a special bond, so free flowing yet so deep.*"

Ikona gave him a loving hug, followed by Lyon. "Don't worry, bud, we are with you, always-whether here or back in your world. *History will remember us as the other 'quartet' of the New Ages...*

Four special friends on a special journey..."

19. The quartet and charter of the new ages

Dave could barely sleep the night before, both excited & anxious about his assignment. He was visiting the central complex of the QUARTET as a special intern, personally recommended by Master Aleus- *and looking forward to the doors it would open...*
Based upon the union of the four
It shall open many a door
In your quest, this is an important key
Free your mind, and this heart you shall see...'

His assignment, spread over a month, would encompass stints in different chambers, meeting key administrators, subject matter experts, principal Quartions & network administrators. However, the *piece de resistance* was his scheduled meeting with *the Chief Quartion & the Chief Network Administrator (C NA), both central figures in this system...*

While Dave was personally reluctant to make this visit high profile, Master Aleus insisted that he meet the highest authorities. He went ahead with the master's instincts, though his own felt that a more discrete, anonymous presence would make the task much simpler- a low profile visit would give him the time & space to figure out how this correlated to his journey, the messenger, the questions... and at his own pace...Nonetheless, he was excited at the thought of seeing the *heart*, firsthand...

Since it was a rather 'formal' visit, Dave decided to do some homework before the actual meeting. He figured out that the peak coordinating body combined the 4 pillars of society:
- Administration (Governance/bureaucracy/judiciary)
- Industry (trade/commerce/economic & monetary systems)
- Technology
- Religion & spirituality

Since known history, these pillars have operated as discrete entities, with clearly laid out domains & boundaries; so the government oversaw governance, administration & judiciary, the trader ran commerce while financial institutions ran the money markets, scientists & technologists developed newer technologies and focused on R&D, while the clergy 'ran' religion...*The domains & fiefdoms were clearly laid out, the boundaries clearly demarcated...*

Of course, there were phases when some, or all of these, were under a central command, but that was only when one of the entities assumed a 'supreme status', thereby controlling the other entities...

Always, one pillar controlled the others...

So there were monarchies, where the 'God King' controlled administration, and often religion & commerce; the church- which, for most part, extended significant control over not only the administrative establishment, but also issued diktats regarding science & technology, apart from introducing the first banking system in the world. Then, there were dictatorships, where the establishment drove technology, primarily as a military tool; and, of course, communism, where the state controlled industry & banned religion...*However, never in history was there a central, coordinated system where each found its rightful place, but with inherent synergies..*

****

With the advent of modernism, democracy & capitalism, there was fragmentation once again, as decentralization, demarcation of domains and devolution of power became guiding principles. *While this was fundamentally progressive, humans once again lost the holistic approach to life.*

Individual freedom led to fragmented systems, each of which existed for the good of the individual & society, but within its own domain, functioning without any synergy or coordination. As time passed, everything from science to education to medicine to the four pillars got more & more fragmented, everything became verticalized, with humans venturing deeper & deeper into each vertical. It required the wisdom, systems & technology of the NEW AGES to bring about a natural convergence of these, without the negatives associated with centralization of power. Just as the individual became aware of the concept of multiple identities and their inherent co-existence, so did society. *Convergence of various facets was no longer about centralization of power, but about natural coexistence...*

With this as the backdrop, in the NEW AGES emerged the QUARTET-an apex coordinating body that oversaw the harmonious & natural cohabitation of various aspects of human life. But it was not a supreme body in the sense of a central control & command institution; rather, it was more of a coordinating & optimizing institution, a *platform designed for facilitating the seamless & integrated functioning of each of these aspects, towards overall wellbeing & harmony.* This was achieved by having individual chambers- each designed to not only specialize in their respective aspects, but also have an overall view of society. Each of these were manned by domain experts as well as offspring of overall credibility- R&D experts, network administrators, social scientists, technocrats, entrepreneurs, thinkers, philosophers, even seekers; *at times, varying points of view, but mostly working in conjunction, towards common objectives.*

While the actual representation varied, one thing was mandated as per the Charter: *Women & 'artistes' together needed to have at least a 26% representation, both in individual chambers and the overall Quartet composition.* Maybe not representation enough to take important decisions by themselves, but with 'veto' rights, whereby they could at least scuttle any proposals which were not based upon the New Age values. *Yet another of the inbuilt systemic control...*

The actual running of these chambers was largely automated, thanks to the various IIN modules, connected via a *'loose network'*. Each of these chambers was connected via the IIN to the various functional entities of the NEW AGES- new age corporations, R&D organizations, spiritual societies, space expeditions projects, energy enhancement organizations, defence establishments etc. Farfetched as it seemed initially, all these were held together by cutting edge technology, apart from high energies & wisdom ...

And, of course, monitored by the conscience keepers- the Council...

When Dave actually arrived at the HQ, he was expecting to see an imposing, high security complex. Instead, what he saw for most part was a maze of beautiful gardens, in the midst of stunning, snow capped mountains. The whole place was breathtakingly beautiful, yet apparently far too simple, even vulnerable, for a peak administrative complex.

Located in a sprawling valley on the satellite Columbus, surrounded by ice and snowcapped glaciers, the complex layout was like a giant maze of gardens. While this made it aesthetically rich, complementing the snow white surroundings, it also had security connotations- it was designed such that getting in & out was possible for authorized personnel only;

A layout akin to the 'Chakravyuh' formation in the Indian epic, Mahabharata. Just as it was virtually impossible to penetrate into the chakravyuh formation, or to escape out from it, so too with this maze...

Since the layout was controlled by the advanced, highly classified algorithm of the defence chamber, it kept periodically changing its formation, making it virtually impossible for intruders to predict the formation, even if they has somehow managed to successfully decipher the last one...

Another amazing part was that most structures in this complex were made of ice & snow, making it seem like a winter resort rather than an administrative complex. Moreover, at no point was there any frisking, which Dave found strange for the highest security zone in the galaxy. Sensing his amazement, the escort clarified: "This is not ordinary ice, but frozen ice, made of a special compound available only on the mountains of Columbus. The glaciers that you see around you are not merely scenic, but special."

"What's so special?"

"Their high energy states, due to the energy trapped in this compound. It is very high in oxygen, and its molecular structure gives it remarkable strength, lightless & malleability-all at the same time.

This enables us to teleport the entire complex to any desired locations with relatively less energy, while at the same time, managing the high oxygen & energy state inside- making it both robust & mobile; a key requirement of the highest security complex. Imagine if you could just transport the White House, the Pentagon & Capitol hill, almost instantly, to any location, without impacting its functioning, how 'high security' would it be?" he continued, trying to speak Dave's language.

"That's why you don't see a *high security* installation from your perspective." He tried to make it as apparent as possible.

Dave got the point. Moreover, as he was to realise shortly, the actual HQ itself was set way below the surface, at a depth no structure or mine back on earth could survive.

The access was via a series of horizontal & vertical escalators, which automatically synchronized in a varying pattern each time, but which would be invoked only for authorized personnel. This was like an sub-terrenean safe, with a hundred number series combination, meaning zillions of permutations & combinations, randomly originating each time. To crack something like this was virtually impossible, even with super advanced technology, and for the smartest hacker.

He also realized that apart from this super advanced access system, there was also the IIN security sub module at work, with its sophisticated biometric scanning & tracking system- this meant that even if someone hypothetically cracked both the maze and the escalator code, there was near zero probability of beating the twelve variable biometric scanning, including retina scans, finger scans, heat scans, brain wave scans, energy scans & so on, making unauthorized intrusions virtually impossible. *Wow! That's the coolest security system I have seen, and supposedly on a flower bed in a valley!!*

****

An amazed Dave lost track of the depth they had traversed, when they finally reached a giant cavern, much, much bigger than what he could have ever imagined...

Within this unbelievably massive underground cavern existed virtually a mini city, fully functional & self contained!

Far from being a dark, dingy mine or cave, this place was a lively township made of the same ice and snow as on the surface, in a Gelass bubble. A completely simulated, regulated environment, providing all the comforts & technology for smooth functioning & living...

However, underground, the ice had slightly altered properties, shimmering even more radiantly, giving the whole township the look & feel of a crystal city.

Icicles, stalactites & stalagmites looked like crystals of various shapes, sizes & hues, prompting Dave to nickname it 'underground chandelier city'! The complex itself was in the shape of a spiral, representing the milky way. At the centre, the core, was the federal chamber- where the key members, including the chief Quartion and the chief NA had their offices, along with their key staff.

The chief Quartion's chamber gave the impression of a super advanced command centre combined with an ancient Egyptian temple. Next to it was the chamber of the Chief NA, where the central servers of the IIN were kept. Access, of course, was restricted to level 4 secure personnel only.

All around the 'core', in spirals, were the various 'arms'- the diverse chambers of the QUARTET-offices, labs, recreation areas, hangars et al. Along the edges were the high tech staff quarters & guest houses for visitors, apart from an extensive entertainment & social infrastructure, which included learning centers, recreation zones, meditation & energy centers etc.

But what really stood out was the fact that the entire circular periphery was dotted with amazing natural beauty- little mountains, water bodies, lake fronts serving as community areas etc. There was nothing to suggest that they were operating at great underground depths, as a combination of Gelass technology, surface ice with luminous properties, and a simulated environment created the most comfortable & warm living conditions- ideal, not only for productivity, but also social contact...

Dave now felt comfortable spending an entire month here... he would have an eventful time, he could sense!

He retired into a luxurious suite in the visitors' guest house, to recharge for tomorrow, when he was scheduled for an appointment with the Chief Quartion himself...

CHARTER OF THE NEW AGES

"By now, you would have seen & learnt quite a bit about the NEW ages, its systems etc, right? You would have also figured out that we have a system of administration by the QUARTET, which functions in accordance with the *Charter of the New Ages.*"

"Yes sir, I am aware."

"Good, so you understand that the NEW AGES is an era of higher consciousness, of advanced technology & radically evolved systems, in all walks of life? Therefore, a valid starting point would be the charter itself-the bedrock of all that our world is based upon." said the chief Quartion Mirdad, in a deep, baritone voice-his words measured, his personality powerful.

Named after a 20th century spiritual classic, Mirdad was a radiant man in his early 90s, with an illustrious & versatile background- entrepreneur with a flair for analytics, materials researcher, able administrator, ace mathematician, and most importantly, an explorer and adventure traveler. While most of these facets were commonly known, as it is for anyone in public life, the adventurer bit remained private- known only to his closest friends & associates, yet being one that he most relished...

'How can one do justice to such a huge responsibility without being utterly brave & fearless?' was his refrain to his friends. *'And only he who has the spirit, the passion, to continuously venture into the unknown, keep conquering subtler layers of fear, can be truly brave. That's why, of all the things needed for this role, being an adventurer is most critical...'*

"Let's just say that the Charter is like a constitution. However, unlike your constitutions, which have become largely symbolic, the sanctity of the Charter is paramount. It is not only a book on which we take oath, but effectively ingrained in all our administration, via the IIN modules. The whole process is closely monitored, not only by the concerned administrators, but also the Council itself." Mirdad continued, pacing around in his large, high tech chamber.

It was a huge circular room with a high, dome shaped ceiling made of a special material, which could turn reflective, refractive or opaque depending upon the need. Within it, various interesting objects were spread out all across-tens of holographic projections playing at different points, displaying everything from various charts & graphs to actual holo-conferences, apart from a life size gyroscope in the centre, rotating on both the axis. The gyroscope was illuminated from within, emanating a reddish haze.

In Mirdad's gait was a sense of purpose, as he moved from chart to chart, stopping briefly to study it, before moving to the next one.

"Before I dwell into the charter itself, let me tell you a little more about its genesis- you would do well to know that."

"Sure sir."

"The CHARTER is fundamentally based on *2 principles:*

- *Harmony with natural laws, and*
- *Dissolution of unnatural fragmentation.*

These two form the bedrock of everything, all the systems; remember, we are in a plane where the wisdom of the *underlying unity all in the Universe* is deeply embedded in our consciousness, and manifest in all our systems & institutions. You understand the principles of the energy exchange system?"

"Yes sir- Master Aleus & the Council explained it to me."

"Very well then, I can't do a better job." He smiled in a certain knowing way, as he reminisced his old-time friends. Years back, Mirdad had let go of the chance to be a Master in the Council to attend to his 'material duties'. Now, in hindsight, even the masters felt glad about that trade-off- the Quartet couldn't have had a better Chief Quartion.

"However, let me reemphasize that the underlying principle of the energy exchange platform too is the inherent integration of human & cosmic impulses. And that is the principle on which all our systems evolved, thus initiating the NEW AGE."

"I understand, sir."

"Everything, from our education to our healthcare to our commuting to our recreation to our culture, is in some way, based upon these principles. All the chambers are based on the same foundation."

"I have seen the common thread of an integrated approach run through most things here, in the time I have been fortunate to spend in this world, sir."

"Indeed. History has shown that a fragmented system can never look at the holistic picture, or have synchronized goals & functioning. This is all the more true of a high intelligence, high energy system.

You will, of course, spend time only in select chambers, so that you can quickly grasp the overall functioning of the Quartet, for your thesis. What paper is this, by the way?" He said, standing next to the gyroscope, peering intently at it. "Aleus tells me that you are a bright young man, aspiring to excel in social sciences?"

"Uh, well, um…it is about, well, how some of these systems can, you see, replicated on earth… about…uh..."

"Good, good…nice. Do well and make the best use of your stay here." Mirdad nodded, seemingly focused somewhere else. He was still absorbedly gazing at the gyroscope and its hues. Then, turning back, he moved to one of the other consoles, punching in some commands.

"Figuring out my next adventure holiday, you see." he beamed at Dave.

"Anyways, let's get back to the point. Let me explain with some examples. Science & religion have been always distinct from each other, in fact at cross purposes, most of the times, in your history. True, towards the end of the 20th century, there was a serious thought on the integration of Physics & metaphysics, but that was still largely in the realms of the intelligentsia & thinkers. It is only in the NEW ages that physics & Metaphysics are no longer contradictory, a battle between faith & reason, but more like two sides of the same coin. *These are simply two approaches to understanding & experiencing the realities of our being and the universe-approaches, which are not at odds, but complementary...*

Another example of this innate amalgamation is the Zen Holiversity-a superior institution based upon holistic learning, since that is the formative plank on which rests the edifice of a holistic society."

At the mention of the Zen Holiversity, Dave's mind reached out to Ikona. Although he had not yet been to holiversity, he could visualize her in one of the New Age, open air classrooms, in her role as the endower…

Feeling drawn to her…but not fathoming why, though…

Mirdad continued, bring Dave back. "Similarly, most problems of your world are because of deviation from natural principles in the name of progress. Align with the functioning of nature, and you have a seamless synthesis of higher consciousness & cutting edge technology. *Then technology & systems become tools, not to conquer or abuse nature, but to explore & harness its hidden gifts."*

"Absolutely sir."

"Good." Mirdad smiled. "Come to think of it, both these principles are actually complementary too. When fragmentation between technology & consciousness dissolves, society automatically becomes more naturally inclined. And the more aligned we are, the more gifts the universe opens out for us. As we are able to sense the gifts of nature more clearly & subtly, technology helps us to harness these for our true, collective welfare, while consciousness evolves to place the right checks & balances on technological & material growth. This, young Dave, is the basis of the Charter, the fundamental root, from which emerged the concept of the QUARTET-defragmentation of the four pillars of society."

"Yes sir, I am aware- the seamless synthesis of governance, commerce, technology & spiritualism."

"Full marks-young man has done his homework well."

Dave smiled at this-it was only here that so many called middle aged Dave 'young man', 'kid', 'lad' and so on. *Good, they make me feel so much younger; people don't grow old, when they stop growing, they become old,* he remembered...

"When you look at human history, the evolution of its systems and their collapse, you will understand why this is so important, and how the time is ripe for a Quartet type system of Global Governance." Mirdad paused, making some strange gestures with his hands & fingers, seemingly rotating them. Then, with a smile, he continued.

"In the old times, during monarchies, quite a few of these pillar were integrated, but back then, the state, was all powerful- the pharaoh, the empire, the church- all had tight control over governance, religion, and, to a fair extent, science & commerce too. *Things were integrated but centralized.* So the Pharaoh was the God King, while the church decided that the earth was the centre of the Universe. Individual freedom was limited, and within the bounds of this tightly regimented system. Any trespassing or circumvention meant overstepping of boundaries- a gross violation of the norms.

Then, as humans evolved, empires gave ways to early nation states, within the broad framework of imperialism. Democracy then took roots, more and more nations gained independence, and the concept of nation state got firmly entrenched, governed by democracy, collective will & rule of law.

This was a great system, lasting through a large part of the 20th and 21st century, and seamlessly effected the transition from imperial blocks to sovereign nations. *This was the primary sense of identity in the 20th century, the primary anchor...*

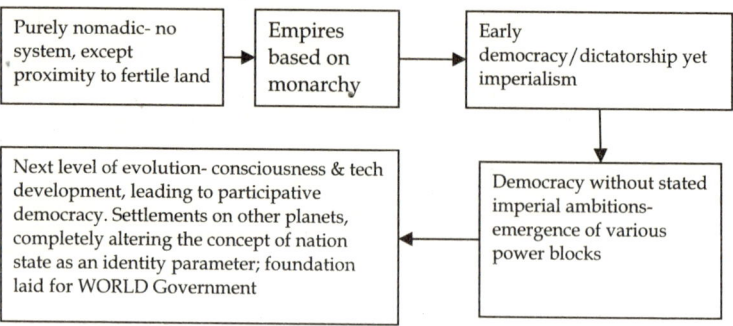

As nation states took roots, governments established the public sector, with focus on basic, heavy industries & capital goods. This was the first time in the modern world that administration & industry found some convergence again. The public sector had scale and access to a national market, thus phenomenal distribution; but it lacked speed & efficiencies. Thus emerged the private sector in secondary & tertiary sectors. More goods & services emerged, and newer breakthroughs started happening at an exponential pace. The capitalist manifesto took firm ground, manifesting as profit motive.

The refined called this ambition- an inherent human urge for growth, for upward movement, a desire for creation, while the blunt called it greed. Gradually, the private sector started participating in the primary sector too, as newer, lucrative revenue models evolved. Thus, governments again migrated towards the business of governance-focusing on social welfare, healthcare, education, infrastructure and cultural development- while the task of wealth creation moved back primarily in the domain of the industry.

As both governance & industry 'evolved', fragmentation set in again, and the divergence became more pronounced. Basic facilities & industries initially became fragmented, only to be consolidated across national boundaries by Multi National Corporations, building global networks & creating scales.

So you see the whole historical cycle, Dave? From aggregation during the monarchical period to fragmentation during early democracies, to a gradual move from Government consolidation to private consolidation. You see the whole migration of society from the ancient to the modern world?"

"Yes sir, I see." Dave replied, attempting to making sense of this whole cycle of thousands of years of human history.

"Thus emerged the new order of the modern world, after millennia of empires, where an equilibrium was reached between the nation state, the public sector and the private sector, representing Multinational Capitalism. And with this came the metrics and institutions of this new system-*currency, inflation, GDP, banking & markets*. These emerged because of the need of the modern world to quantify, to have measurable, *objective* systems-everything now needed to be measured, from education to vocation. *That, which couldn't be ascribed a tangible value, was seen as fringe, and not core to progress.*"

"So true sir. In the old world, we were so much more comfortable with what was qualified, not necessary quantified. Everything didn't have to be measurable. We were comfortable with a higher power, hence didn't need to measure everything."

"Exactly- your modern world spawned newer systems and a 'refined' world view, *one comfortable with fragmentation, as long as it could be measured, labeled*. So the nation state gave us identity and charged taxes, while the private sector gave comforts and made profits. But then something changed in the late 20th & 21st century, disturbing this new equilibrium...

Humans were evolving, democracies were evolving, and so were individual aspirations. In societies where the growth in consciousness & easing of material needs was substantially achieved, the abstract started being more clearly perceived. The analog system found a new expression, and not everything needed to be digital, measurable-*the realization that the tangible was not the only real thing came to be accepted; that there could be abstract, 'softer', higher realities...*

With this, and partly because of this, people started having a better understanding of *multiple identities*, which bred & fed multiple aspirations- which, at times, were at odds with this new equilibrium of national identities and multinational capitalism. Suddenly, the equilibrium between individual & collective identities & aspirations was stirred, jolted.

This was accentuated in the 21st century, when, as you have seen, resource depletion and disparities exacerbated the fault lines further. A certain restlessness started brewing, and what was once an anchor, became bondage, suppressing aspirations based on other, softer identities. And, as this happened, there was a backlash, mostly violent, unfortunately."

"I relate to it sir, but don't quite follow..."

"See the history of late 20th century onwards? You had a nation state formed on the basis of an ideology, but breaking up on the basis of ethnicity. Why? Because newer, dormant identities were surfacing. Similarly, you had a nation being born out of religion, but getting split on the basis of language. All these were signs of restlessness, identities & aspirations pent up for far too long. They had to explode, rather implode, sometime...

Where you had mature & reasonable political leaderships and democracies, these transitions were smooth. But in most cases, they were brutal & violent, as the aspirations were viciously suppressed in the name of 'national integrity & sovereignty'.

For long a pillar of your social & collective identity, the nation state was also responsible for mind numbing bloodshed & harsh repressions. Your elected leaders became the new despots, forgetting *that a nation is not merely aggregation of geography, but of its people.* And aggregations ought to be on the basis of freewill, not compulsion."

Dave's mind flew to his India trip, and the questions that had arisen when he compared the conflict in Kashmir to the common identity in Sikkim. Now, some of these were being addressed head on, threadbare...

"As the world saw so much suppression in the name of national sovereignty, there was progressive disillusionment with the whole concept of nations & boundaries. Anyways *technology made the world flat & aspirations mobile,* so individual aspirations found expression more than ever before, thanks to the internet, a vibrant media & cell phones."

Wow! An adventurer with an anthropologist's view...

"At the time that nation states were beginning to losing their relevance, yet another counter force was at play-an undercurrent of disillusionment was building up towards the other venerable institution of the modern world-Multinational capitalism."

"I don't get it."

"See the historical perspective, Dave-visualize how it all began, and how it evolved. Trade, in its most basic form, was a classic manifestation of naturalism-as natural as the wind flowing from high pressure to a low pressure zone. Similarly, trade fulfilled a human vacuum by facilitating the flow of goods & services from a point of excess to need- basically an exchange of one set of goods & services against another, seamlessly. That's how it all started, and that's why & how it grew across the millennia.

But then, as other social developments took shape, larger Corporations came into existence to take advantage of economies of scale, and with it emerged sunrise industries like banking to support the growth of these Corporations. So far, so good, leading to a new revolution- *the industrial revolution...*

However, dilution, confusion, and a loss of direction gradually set in. What started off as a great leap of growth during the industrial revolution, resulting in a positive sum game ecosystem by way of true value creation, got corrupted along the way.

The system of Multinational Capitalism, which had its relevance for over two centuries, lost the plot. The basic philosophy of seamless exchange got replaced by the mantra of *'growth for growth's* sake, and with it emerged the absolutely juvenile concept of Corporations existing primarily to make profits, to achieve growth at any & all costs. All wrongs were justified with the sugar coated talk of 'creating shareholder value', and a negative value ecosystem was gloss wrapped to make it appear more palatable! The Corporation then moved from being driven by innovation to deceit in name of street smartness: a fundamental win-lose ensued, be it between vendors & customers, management & stake owners, corporate & social goals, profits & environmental consciousness, professional vs family commitments etc. The original philosophy didn't merely get diluted- it got totally corrupted!

"You make it sound that growth per se is bad. *Real bad...*"

"Not at all! Read my lips. I am simply asking a fundamental question: *What is growth itself, and for what purpose?* Funnily, most of those so driven by the mantra of growth don't seem to have any inkling of this question, much less an answer. And for something as fundamental as this. Ironic, isn't it?"

Dave paused to reflect at his own life, his experiences, his tradeoffs: driven, aggressive, passionate...

But for what, exactly? To get people to guzzle more sugared water? Now this question seemed loud, even stinging...

"In your current capitalism, the feeble answer, wherever articulated, usually is: 'growth for growth's sake'. And that is where the problem starts, the dissonance sets in! Growth is fine, even welcome, as long as it leads to satisfying of lower level needs, so that human creativity can be freed for higher pursuits. That is higher capitalism, or naturalism...

But the vanguards of this your Capitalist system were so caught up in their own creations, that growth did not become a means, a tool, but an end in itself. How many of your managers and business 'leaders' ask: Is this worth doing? Does it add any value to our stakeholders or society? To overall human pursuit? Or am I doing it because this is what has been done, or what we are supposed to do? Or worse, this is all that we know to do now. And that success in this task is beneficial for my career, irrespective of whether it makes my life fruitful or not..."

It was a scathing indictment of the system that Dave too was a product of. But wizened with a new perspective, he couldn't disagree now! Not one bit...

"See it in context now. As individual aspirations grew, 'softer' aspects of life started becoming more central. While initially, every society enjoyed the fruits of unfettered capitalism, the disillusionments started building up: against the new form of cross border imperialism, against its effects on our spirit, against its willful rape of our environment. True, MNCs made tons of money, but the tradeoff was simply not worth it; and a higher human consciousness sensed it more sharply..."

Dave grasped the larger picture, as Mirdad summed up succinctly. "As these dual forces acquired momentum, this equilibrium was fundamentally jolted."

"And?"

"And what? Nature abhors vacuum. So, as these twin pillars came to a point of redundancy, it was time for the next level of democracy, a new system- *A new, post modern society...*"

Dave pondered over. Mirdad was showing him a new vision, a potential future based on a new society, the next level of democracy; and a capitalistic system rescued from the clutches of its own stinking corruption...

Now he fully absorbed the significance of Master Aleus' rejoinder to his original premise- that the New Age was not merely a metaphor, but a *new reality indeed. Yet, some doubts persisted...*

"But it's not as easy as that, sir. Breaking up nations into smaller units & yielding to popular aspirations is far simpler in theory than reality. Being a separate nation is one thing, *running it altogether different.* And that too in sync with the collapse of the other anchor- capitalism..."

"Indeed- that's where our system of the QUARTET makes sense. As consciousness rises, and when fragmented identities dissolve, at least for administrative purposes, you have a true 'WORLD GOVERNMENT', instead of repressive boundaries or boundary less profit seeking vultures-a model of living based on harmony with nature- our twin pillars. " He smiled.

"So geographical aggregations have no raison d' etre?"

"They can, as is in our case. Geographical aggregations are simply aggregations based on logistical & functional efficiencies, but no longer anchors of identities. True bonding can only be basis ideology- one that transcends geographic, racial & religious affiliations. And with the disappearance of the nation state, civilizations can start thinking more in terms of holistic welfare, rather than narrow, parochial, 'self interests'.

When you integrate this with the other important institutions, facilitated in a seamless manner by rapid evolution of technology, you get a *global system* which takes a truly holistic view- an integrated mechanism of governance, industry and technology which constantly evolves, ensuring better & more natural ways of fulfilling material needs, so that human endeavor is freed for higher pursuits. Add to that evolving views on religion & spirit, and the integrated Quartet is complete." he smiled, again moving his fingers in a strange, circular way. Suddenly, in the background, a mellifluous tune started playing, a complete symphony.

"This, my friend, is our anthem of humanity, replacing national anthems."

Dave stood up in deep respect while it played. Inspite of certain questions & doubts, he felt privileged, fortunate, to display his reverences to a World Anthem, an anthem of humanity...

"Now if you shall excuse me, I have some important work to attend to; you may meet Quartion Che in the next room. He shall continue the discussion on the evolution of democracy & the Quartet governance system."

20. The new 'ism'

"Sir, from whatever I have learnt so far, I must say I am an unabashed admirer of your system of Q*uartet governance*. It is different from anything else I have seen or read about, and feels like a breath of fresh air from our world." Dave opened the conversation on a positive note, trying to break the ice with Quartion Che, a respected anthropologist, now in charge of the module on administration & democracy.

Che smiled & nodded. He seemed of African origin, with close cropped hair along with a French beard. Dressed in a traditional two-piece suit, he sat on his desk, spinning a little 'moon globe'.

"We've experimented with so many systems, so many 'isms'- capitalism, socialism, communism- yet each seemed to offer only part of the solution. Theoretically, I like the fact that your system combines elements of all these." Dave expressed one of the most bothersome dilemmas of modern society, and about how the solution seemed so simple. *In fact, too simple to be true…*

"*Theoretically?*"

"Yes sir. Actually, this is one part that I am still not able to completely relate to. In some ways, it seems like a refined, sophisticated, new age version of the old, & apparently failed model of communism, where the state controls the resources, the bureaucracy & much of the industry, providing for the needs of its citizens, while they go about their pursuits within this framework. If centralized aggregation of resources could work, then why did communism collapse?"

"The ostensible reason is because it left little room for human endeavor, creativity & initiative, not rewarding initiative proportionately; and, of course, authoritarian regimes weren't exactly models of public welfare, purging their own citizens. Let's also not be naïve and forget the significant investments made by rival blocks in aggravating this discontent." He smiled at a veiled reference to the role of western intelligence agencies.

"However, the system of the QUARTET incorporates the best of both. It is compassionate & egalitarian to the point where basic needs are met in the most comfortable way, where a good quality of material life is neither a concern nor a pressing preoccupation, while at the same time, having a proportional rewards system, albeit based on the higher pursuits of life. *The system itself is based on pure energy & impulses. Therefore, wholesome, natural & higher endeavors get rewarded commensurately. We call this 'Naturalism'*...

In the context on your world, let's put it this way- while technological & commercial leapfrogging ought to happen, safety nets should be in place to take care of basic needs of those impacted & deprived; that's the only way sustainable growth can coexist with social development.

This could be through individual compassion or government policies, or both- *but the moot point is, not out of compulsion, but compassion.* Those impacted, or rendered redundant by newer technologies, should get basic sustenance support and development infrastructure, so that they can grasp newer, higher skill sets. If not them, at least their children can participate in these advancements. This is how collective growth is combined with the uplift of the lowest sections of society-as individual initiative combined with systemic skill building.

To us, this is capitalism with compassion-Naturalism! Outside of this, the cowboy, unregulated, greed driven version of capitalism is as much of a failure as communism."

Dave remembered the economic collapses of the 20th century, and felt ashamed at the excesses of capitalism. He may have been a man of the corporate world, but this wisdom was making him mortified of those excesses. The world definitely needed a new model of capitalism, a new economic model...

"Dave, this is not communism. There is a fundamental flaw in trying to compare communism with naturalism. Socialism is forced redistribution by the state. *Naturalism is voluntary reallocation*, driven by a systems & technology that everybody is part of. This is the epitome of an evolved democracy, a higher society- a far cry from the authoritarianism of communist regimes. *It simply is the conscious awakening & aggregation of the basic human instinct of compassion..."*

After a pause, and some more spins of the globe, this time that of the earth, he continued.

"You see this globe spinning? It spins, yet remains in balance, because there is an inherent symmetry. What would happen if one part became too heavy, while the other too light? The globe would stop spinning & collapse! *The same it is with the real globe, Dave. Balance, you see, balance. It's all about equitable growth, equity, balance..."*

"Do you think there is disparity & dire poverty in your world because there aren't enough resources? Do you genuinely believe that? Nah, I don't think so. Even in your world, you have enough resources & technological wherewithal to satisfy all needs, without emitting tons of smoke! The problem is that they are so unevenly distributed. That's why, naturalism, unlike capitalism, focuses not only on creation, but distribution too. Balance...equilibrium...harmony...your systems will never change till your society evolves, till individuals evolve..."

"When that happens, hoarding dissolves. True joy comes from nature, from within, from creating, not accumulating. You have seen our world, Dave. Thousands of creative people, scientists, artists, explorers simply follow their inner calling, finding true joy in that. They all have comfortable houses, PATs and everything else they need for contended living. Millions live in remote locations, forests, hills, away from the crowd.

We have invested in commuting technology, mobile housing, distribution technologies etc, so that there are no mad cities, no urban chaos- only individual settlements or communes, ensuring that there is no 'prime real estate', no asset bubbles!

Everything is so natural & seamless, and that is what gives us our happiness. No one stocks or consumes in excess, even though we have the most advanced technology, the resources of four different worlds!

We don't need to horde money or possessions to be happy. *Continuous flow of energy is how the Universe remains in balance. Any form of energy, including money, only stagnates if hoarded- that's the law of entropy."*

"Right sir, I get it. A welfare state model, built not on state benefaction, but human compassion; based not on central control, but vibrant democracy? That's truly interesting…"

"Yes," Che said. "That is what the NEW ages is all about! We have taken the concept of democracy & open society to the next level, by combining the best of civil society, economic systems & individual consciousness. *Refining wherever required, but mostly redefining along the way.."*

"But democracy evolved in our times, and is still evolving. Almost 60% of our population elects its own Governments."

"And?" questioned Che, trailing off, letting the silence sink in. *"Do they decide their destiny?"*

"Well, they do sir. After all, they elect their governments, which means that they decide their destiny"

"In every way?" Che persisted further. "Then how come so much of your resources get diverted into activities that a vast majority don't approve of?"

"Like?"

"Like arms instead of development, corruption instead of welfare, pollution & exploitation instead of regeneration, the vice like grip of lobbies instead of universal healthcare, etc. Do these have a mandate of the global majority? And how is it that so many wars have been waged by neither having any popular mandate, nor condoned by the moral compass?"

"But most wars were the creation of despots, of dictators, sir, not democratically elected governments."

"What about Vietnam? Opposed by a majority of the Americans themselves. Or the wars in Iraq & Afghanistan, in the name of liberation? Opposed not only by a vast majority of Americans, but by all world citizens. Those were surely not acts of despots, but *democratically elected governments!"*

"I understand sir. But that's how the system works. There will always be aberrations, that's why people are empowered to kick out such regimes. Mind you, all such *democratically elected despots* eventually fell to the power of democracy.

The perpetrators of these wars met their waterloo in the battle of the ballot, not the bullet. Isn't that a right, a choice? Isn't that democracy?"

"In your context, vibrant, yes. I mean, you get to choose once in four or five years, that too after all the damage is done. Yeah, kick 'em out hard after that, though how does that help undo the damage?"

"But at least we have a choice..."

"Choice? Between the devil & the deep sea? So many of your democracies are two-party presidential systems. On one side, you have a jerk, on the other, a bigger jerk! Is that what you call *people's will & choice*? Fortunately, some of your nations adopted the more democratic parliamentary system. Even if you had a 'Prime Minister', he was still a 'minister'- a first among equals. And you had individual legislators who were part of this system, having individual accountabilities. At least, there was some maturing of democracy."

"Are you *seriously suggesting* that parliamentary democracy is superior to the presidential system?" Dave thought this was stretching it a bit too far.

"All that I am stating is that the more representative, the more decentralized, the more grassroots the democracy, the more vibrant it is; more ground up it is, more accurately the voice of the people it represents. Democracy & governance has to be about inclusiveness. So, as individuals, groups, especially from the deprived & marginalized sections started asserting themselves, your polity started getting more & more fragmented, resulting in the phenomenon of coalition governments. *Governance now was based on a multitude of viewpoints, and a common minimum program.*

Some of your hawkish thinkers & ideologues criticized this as weak, unstable & regressive. These were essentially the existing vested interests, who wanted power to be concentrated, not diffused. All arguments, from a 'hotch potch' of views, to *this system can never take quick, effective & hard decisions,* were put forth.

But, as democracies as diverse as India, Japan, Israel, Germany, Italy, Ireland, Finland & others have proven, coalitions can not only work, but actually be more representative-ensuring that larger sections of society are part of the decision making process.

True, some decisions are not 'quick' or 'hard' as in the monarchical or dictatorial, or even the presidential systems, but they follow a more balanced, nuanced process-an inbuilt system of checks & balances."

"So what's the next step? Where to from here? We have come a long way from monarchy to coalition democracy…"

"Yes, a long way have you come- but a long way to go still, especially when you realize that decision making is once in 4-5 years, and always post facto. Frankly, I feel you are a confused race." Che added as an afterthought. "Even your 'democracy' has different norms in different aspects of life!"

"I don't understand sir."

"You have democracy in governance, where each individual's weightage, if I may say so, is equal. A vote (which itself, like so many of your other tools, is fairly unevolved) is the same for all. On the other hand, in your corporate systems, different entities have different weightages- so a preferential stock is vastly different in weightage from common stock!"

"So which of these does your wisdom consider to be superior, sir?" Dave smiled. *Sometimes, one could only learn something new by unlearning the old...*

"Frankly none, though your second system is slightly superior, in that it does allow for differential weightage."

"But isn't that the biggest problem of the older systems, which led to the creation of democracy in the first place? Equal rights for all?" Dave sensed a certain inconsistency here.

"Again, it's your confusion speaking. You had monarchy, where an individual was accorded semi-divinity simply on the basis of his seat; and you have a system where a criminal votes with the same weightage as a judge; a musician with the same influence as a bootlegger. It's not always binary in life, Dave. This 'apparent' confusion comes about only because the human race has not moved to the higher planes, the level of higher vibrations. You have yet to absorb the reality of energy…

Yes, when you had an oppressive system, it was important to 'break free' and give rights to the lowest strata, so that they could make their voice heard. It was necessary to decentralize power at the lowest levels. That's exactly why I said that coalition was superior to the two party system, since it was more inclusive, especially at the level of have-nots; it gave them a voice.

But then, as society evolves to our level, where there aren't material have-nots, then there is no concept of uplifting the weak, of giving them the same rights as the strong. That is a noble intent, but somewhere, you have to leapfrog to the next level…"

"And how does that happen?"

"Like everything else, a combination of higher consciousness & technology, especially information technology. The moment information & communications technology jumps to the next level, the politician loses his tight grip on power, and his ability to control & distort loosened.

Why do you think the internet was one of the biggest breakthroughs of your age? Because as information arbitrage considerably reduced, both the politician & the trader lost their iron clad grip on the corridors of power. *The common man was more enabled than ever before- this is what they called the world getting flattened*!"

Dave smiled, thinking of all the information available on the internet, and how it became the most effective platform for mobilizing public opinion & dissent, in a matter of days, even hours. Its viral power meant that people's voices could be mobilized, amplified and expressed on virtually anything. And not too many governments could afford to ignore mass protests, even if virtual.

Heck, come to think of it, he could actually start an online campaign to save the Amazon rainforests, once he got back! He would…

"True, the internet has been a landmark. And your information age has allowed far greater individual participation in building popular opinion than ever before. But like all other advancements, this too is a double edged sword- humanity can leverage the explosive power of the internet to create an unparalleled public movement, or squander it in vacuous tweets or hours of mindless youtube uploads.

The next big step is the evolution of collective consciousness till a critical mass is reached, along with the evolution of technology, to allow individuals a say not only in opinion, but decision making. *Individual voice will evolve to a 'continuous voting' system of checks & balances*, if one were to say so…"

"*Ongoing referendums?*" questioned Dave. "Wouldn't it paralyze governance? If at all it is possible?"

"Fortunately, some sort of start happened in your world itself. E-governance was sort of a precursor." smiled Che.

"Our Quartet system is, of course, far more advanced, but it follows this model of continuous, real time participation. Why do you think we have a full module on democracy, administration & collective governance in the Quartet & IIN?

Because we are always looking at ways to refine, improvise people's participation & engagement, while giving higher weightage to masters & evolved energy beings- a whole algorithm runs on this engagement model. That, my friend, is *true democracy & evolved governance.*"

"If even a fraction of this system can be established back in my world, things would be so different. 'Elected governments' would no longer be able to steamroll over public opinion. And majority public opinion can help force governments in eradicating war & ushering true peace." sighed a wistful Dave.

Che struck a note of caution, though. "For this evolved system to work, however, there are three critical components. And they have to work in conjunction."

"And what are these?"

"Evolved individuals with inner peace, advanced technology for continuous engagement, and evolved, mature democracies."

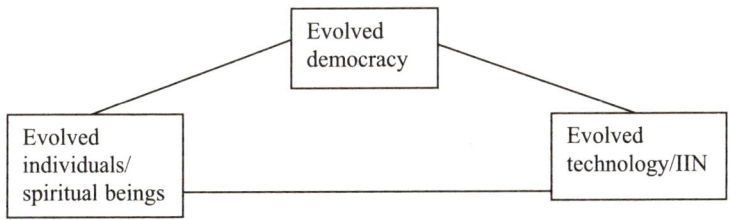

"These form the three sides of a triangle, an ecosystem that feeds on each other. As individuals & societies evolve, huge collective positive energies are created, which facilitate the evolution of intelligent technology & networks, which can be put to overall welfare of the human race.

As technology evolves, it facilitates the participation of uplifted, balanced individuals in continuous, seamless decision making at all levels, thereby resulting in further maturing of democracies. And mature democracies in turn facilitate a greater participation of individuals, thus completing the loop.

But this has to be true, inclusive participation, not merely ballot democracy. While you have taken some strides by devising metrics like civil liberties, quality of governance, inclusiveness etc, you are still missing the woods for the trees. Evolved democracy is undoubtedly about all of these, but they are merely subsets of the bigger picture.

Enhanced public participation by itself may be counterproductive, even dangerous, unless accompanied by evolution in individual consciousness. It's very easy to sway a low energy society on narrow, partisan issues & radical identity politics. Only high energy beings can act as true civil society. Low energy beings can act as herds, or worse still, mobs! A lot of despots, including Hitler, got their first shot at power through the route of the ballot!

When higher energy states are reached, individuals & democracies become more creative & constructive in their approach to conflict resolution, moving away from war. They open up to newer notions of individual & collective identities, advance in the realms of 'abundance mentality', thereby causing narrow, parochial mindsets to automatically dissolve.

As our notion of 'identity' itself undergoes a transformation, so does our approach to policy making- no longer do we talk in terms of 'self interest' as the bedrock of 'foreign policy', but think of collective welfare, a unified future." Che wisely concluded.

****

Mirdad and Che's words left a deep imprint on Dave. From the evolution of capitalism & democracy to world governance, a whole new model was laid out in front of him...a potential model for his world, our world...

It was time to move to a holistic model, a global agenda, beyond petty divisions...

While Dave was deliberating the significance of the system of naturalism, in the seer temple, several scenes were being holographically played in the centre of the sanctum, as the Masters gathered around it. These dealt with various pressing issues on earth, dilemmas which usually had conservatives and liberals arrayed on opposite side- universal healthcare, the latest biological weapon being proposed to be developed, awaiting the final CCS (cabinet committee on security) nod, gay rights, the G20 summit on Global warming et al.

The issues were varied, occurring in different parts of the world, but the undercurrent was the same- liberals & progressives, with the backing of the intelligentsia & majority public opinion, pushing ahead for reforms & global consensus, while the conservatives, in tandem with lobbies & myopic interests, determined to stall them, to reinforce parochial, regressive agendas...

In each of these, the masters projected healing & wisdom energies onto the situation, collectively- not only them, but even their apprentices, as well as seekers on special assignments in the Council. For them, this was an opportunity to sharpen energy connections, to hone their projection skills, as well as to come face to face with earth's realities, its pressing problems...

The actual sessions were a combination of energy cleansing, healing & projecting. During this practice, several 'accessories' were present- large pales of water, colored crystals, strange looking beads etc. And, of course, soothing music & vibrations in the background...

Different masters, apprentices & seekers used them varyingly, while the more advanced like Aleus, Zeut, Sinetha, Nobius etc used nothing at all, the 'flames of consignment' burning bright in the realms of the unmanifest...

After about ten such scenes, the central projection finally shifted to that of the President & his cabinet; and then to the President looking calm. At this point, all present-Masters & apprentices-closed their eyes & projected their deepest energies onto this scene-*a collective hum of prayer & energy pervading the sanctum...*

An hour later, the masters emerged from the trance, and the projection stopped. The daily meditation assembly came to an end for the day, and those assembled gradually dispersed.

However, some of the Masters stayed back, conferring among themselves, as the group of six walked out to the lawn, taking stock of the situation.

"So, what does it look like, Master? Will he be able to find the Messenger?" Atlas asked Aleus expectantly.

"That's what's prophesied…" Aleus smiled at his protégé.

"Yes, but the scene remains the same, day after day. It is imperative that he finds him…"

"He seems to be progressing fine." Sinetha said, picking up a rose in full bloom, enjoying its fragrance. "You, of all people, should know Atlas, that being anxious achieves nothing. Only when it is time to bloom does the fragrance of the rose spread…"

"I know, I know- but sometimes it gets too overpowering. You know, as if we could somehow fast forward the clock…"

"That won't help, and you know it. No use fast forwarding! He has to go the full course, the complete distance, before he can unravel it. After that too, it's his freewill, as it is for entire humanity indeed." Nobius added his nuggets of wisdom.

"We gather here to bless, to emanate prayer energies. But no one can alter the emerging destiny- that's for freewill to choose. So let's not get unduly concerned about the outcome." Zeut gave his perspective.

" I know. It's just that I expect results all the time. " Atlas grinned. "Don't worry Masters. I am in complete sync with all, irrespective of these frequent discussions of ours!"

"And what's the news from Einstein?"

"We are getting updates from Plutus- seems just like what we thought in the first place." Zenia turned somber.

"I see the boy is doing a fine job, Zenia!" Aleus smiled & winked at her, a knowing smile crossing both their lips.

On the other hand, despite her concerns, lady Sinetha was a picture of equanimity & grace, her motherly instincts firmly anchored in her commitments to the Council. Her concerns stemmed from the fact that her son, Azel, was a member of this group of scientists on Einstein.

"Master, I think it's high time we officially documented it in the next Quartet review."

"Lady, you think wise & just, and I want you to know how much we respect your lucidity. But for now, I think we should hold on till we get the final report from Plutus- and get specifics of who is behind all this, and with what exact motive."

"So it's all a haze, even now?" Nobius spoke with a certain despondency, acknowledging & understanding the limitations of pinpointing in a cyborg network- like identifying a needle in a haystack; or catching a single fish in a large shoal.

"Yes-but we have our rock star who is organizing a series of gigs soon on Einstein, I believe." Aleus smiled.

"AYS-at your service, Master!"Atlas winked. "Though I hear that this time there are likely to be more female fans at my concert."

"Seems your new album struck a chord with the cyborg women…" Zenia engaged in banter with Atlas.

"Yeah dude, you seem to be going all guns blazing. Just don't forget why you're there in the first place amidst all this female adulation." Zeut added, chewing his herbal cigar stub.

"On a more relevant note, think we *should always be mindful about the second part*, Master?" Zeut added his timely caution, as always, in a reference that the others understood.

"Yeah, but it's a prophecy Zeut. Freewill will determine what's the eventual outcome. Things may not even come to that. For all you know, we might be able to turn this situation to our advantage. A new leap could be in the offing…" Aleus spoke with his faith & conviction.

"Indeed Master- your words are the wisest." Nobius smiled.

"For now, let's focus on the task at hand, regarding the earth- heaven, for now, is in secure hands, potential dissonance aside." Aleus surmised.

"Yes, and blessed be the earth- Dave is doing better than I had expected, Masters." Sinetha raised her arms upwards…

21. NEW METRIC AND THE IIN

Dave's next assignment was in one of the most critical and enigmatic chambers- the 'ENERGY ECOSYSTEM' chamber. Simply put, it was a combination of the chambers of finance, trade and commerce, in a deeply symbiotic relationship with the other chambers like social welfare, infrastructure, distribution etc. *Moreover, this chamber was closely connected to the technology & communications chamber, since the entire system ran via the IIN...*

Given that both the chambers worked in a seamless integration, the two key entities here were the Chief Network Administrator (C NA)- Atisha, a highly respected doyen of new age technologies, and Quartion Panchem, head of this chamber. After the Chief Quartion Mirdad, these two were considered the most powerful, critical & wise men in the system...

The chamber itself was a huge space next to the offices of Chief Quartion and his staff, around the core of the 'milky way'. A large part of this space was dedicated to the servers and the infrastructure. The entire technology was based upon highly advanced communications protocols, allowing for inter planetary data travel, communications via multiple satellites, both in space and on the surface of the planets, multiple levels of redundancies & backups, and progressive integration of more and more modules with the IIN.

The IIN itself was probably the single most significant achievement leading to the new ages, a progressive integration of more & more modules bringing the entire system closer to the ultimate goal- of a truly unified, holistic system, integrating all aspects of human life...

****

On coming here, Dave was expecting a high tech, organized, centrally coordinated chamber, much like a military control and command hub; but what he saw truly surprised him- rather than a well oiled machinery, this place resembled a silicon valley start up- chaotic, haphazard, disorganized...but buzzing with very high activity & energy...

The chamber's layout itself was the starting point- randomly arranged cubicles, shabby workstations, and desks littered with notes & charts- a far cry from the neatly arranged, orderly layouts of other chambers. But it was here that thousands of avant-garde technologists, seekers & energy scientists came together on myriad projects, each one structured to bring about either improvements in the existing technologies, or create new technologies that would further *change the face of things...*

Most of these technologists were a cool, wild bunch of young kids, seemingly straight out of a silicon valley garage or from Woodstock- unkempt hair, disheveled clothes & arbitrary mannerisms, they would be seen discussing key enhancements in the 'brew zone' rather than the conference areas...

Structure was anathema for these geniuses, whose creativity flowed not in meeting rooms but Turkish baths, not in front of their workstations but over virtual holographic games...

Dave smiled as he saw these wild, high energy corridors. *'techies will be techies after all...'*

"So you are here on an assignment, I learn." The Quartion told Dave rather rhetorically. Sitting behind his table, he looked distracted, jumpy and distinctly unhappy...

"Yes sir, Mr. Panchratna. I am here to..."

"Mr. Dave, I am not Panchratna, but his chief of staff, his clone- Dasham." said the Quartion in a smooth, suave voice, cutting off Dave mid sentence.

"He has deputed me to spend time with you, *since you are a personal request from the Council.* Just to let you know, he is *quite busy.*" Dasham said in an apparently polite way, but without the message getting lost. If he were unhappy about this meeting, he was letting it show, but with a certain smoothness- recommendations of the Council were not to be offended, even if they were unwelcome...

For Dave, however, the clone bit struck more than his mannerism, as he allowed the thought to sink in...

Till now, he had only heard about clones in his discussions, but not seen anyone, that too in such a high seat of power. He also thought of his conversations with Plutus, and how he was explained that cloning was only for regenerative, not ulterior purposes here...*this one, though, seemed more for power*...

But he should not be surprised- in our world, people in positions of power try to mentally align their key lieutenants or assistants to be 'like their clones'; politicians & businessmen appoint their progeny as successors, ostensibly so that they can carry on their legacy; in this respect, cloning, or at least attempts at it, were very much a part of human history, long before genetic cloning came into being. Wherever there existed a desire to continue one's legacy, cloning- whether genetic, mental, emotional or energy, was the answer...

If only we could respect individualism, and allow life to flow without the need to impose...to leave behind an imprint didn't require clones....

"Did you say something, Mr. Dave?"

"No, no." Dave stammered, caught off guard.

"So please tell me what can do for you? *What exactly* would you like to learn?"

"I have learnt quite a bit about the Energy exchange system." Dave replied, trying to regain his composure in the face of this ice coolness.

"Hmm" Dasham nodded

"I would now like to understand the IIN better, its modules & sub modules, and how the whole system functions via it."

"Great!" Dasham rubbed his hands in an irksome way. "Mr. Atisha, the Chief N.A., has most graciously agreed to accommodate your request, and shall help with your research." he replied as smoothly, introducing Atisha.

Needless to say, Atisha was yet another cool techie- a 70 year 'young' dude- tall and lanky, with the same unkempt looks-disheveled, curled hair, a stubble, old fashioned glasses that would put Bill Gates of the '70s to shame, an ill-fitting tee, low cut, loose jeans, which seemed as if they could fall off any minute; and, of course, a large coffee mug in his hand...

But looks can be deceptive, more so for techies...

Beneath the part geeky, part callous looks, lay one of the brightest minds in the whole system. Inventor of several firsts, including the latest interplanetary protocol for all forms of data transmission, cloud computing V 5.0 to link the various chambers with each other & the IIN, the latest version of open source platforms for enhanced democratic participation, and currently working on a platform for 100% efficient interplanetary transmission of energy, he was the demigod for all 'techies' of the New ages- *a befitting choice for the C NA...*

Dave felt an instant liking for him...

"He works closely with Mr. Panchem & me, as well as the various chambers of the QUARTET. His team is spread across all planets, working on monitoring of performance & downtimes, apart from further development & calibration of the algorithms. *With the blessings & constant approval of the Council, of course...*" The last sentence was said with a smile, as fake as it seemed, clearly directed at the guest of the Council, so that the good word would reach the masters...

Smooth, very smooth... something about him gave Dave the creeps...

Atisha warmly shook Dave's hand, and took him around the chamber; Unlike Dasham, there was no edginess, no façade, just a genuine warmth, apart from a baby like excitement on showing his chamber, his toy room...

"So you understand that we are a society working on the energy exchange system, not on money? *It is based on energy impulses, and exchange of energy for goods & services.*"

"Yes sir- Master Aleus explained that you have an advanced platform through which all this is possible."

Atisha looked at him with a hugely surprised expression, almost bordering on horror. "Did you just say *sir*?! What? Am I, like, *that uncool*?"

"No, not at all...er...*dude!*" Dave smiled, attempting to talk the techie's language. *Teenagers are usually supposed to be seventeen, not seventy, dude...but nonetheless, I love you guys, your attitude to life; just hope I can age gracefully, coolly like you guys...*

"Kewl- now that's more like it!" Atisha gave a lost smile, scratching his slightly graying beard.

"Yes, we have an advanced platform on which the energy exchange model sits; through this 'platform', units are assigned against each impulse, depending upon their intensity & quality, and these units are then mapped back to an *'energy bank account'* of the individual, in a central repository. Your ubiquitous *bank accounts* thus get replaced with *'energy accounts'*, and the *Central bank* with a *Central energy repository (CER)*, which incidentally is unified-*a single, common CER!* In line with our holistic, integrated vision...

Similarly, your other venerable financial pillar- Capital market or stock exchange-is replaced with an 'Energy exchange', where your 'energy assets' can be 'exchanged' for other energy & material assets. Although this is not really needed or used in our world."

"Wow!" Dave said with a low whistle, the finance guy within him all kicked up. "This is a *whole new 'banking' system, where one neither needs to 'bank' nor to borrow! Based not on gold or currency, but energy!* One that marks a significant leap from a system that served us well for over 500 years."

"Absolutely! In this new age system, an individual's 'energy' account is redeemable against equivalent material needs, much the same way as your currency system works. *The whole crediting & debiting is, in your parlance, online & 'real time'- via the Intelligent Interplanetary network (IIN)...*"

"So whenever you need something, the system debits your energy account and fulfils the corresponding material needs?"

"Absolutely. If your requirement is wholesome, need based, and not excess, then yes! This IIN connects the CER with its various modules & sub modules, in a real time system of exchange. *So, when you need something, your 'energy account' gets debited to that extent, and the 'order' gets connected to the relevant module,* getting further passed on to the most appropriate producer, based on the overall optimization algorithm; *no 'middleman', least energy consumption, minimal waste!* Every second, millions of transactions happen over the network, across various modules."

"Fascinating."

"The corresponding producers of goods & services are given energy credits, which allow them to produce further- by not only providing 'currency', but energy itself, in kinetic, usable form. Energy, you would agree, is at the heart of your modern society, its most fundamental need; and that is what drives the processors, the reactors, the mining drills, the high tech robotic factories & the multitude of services here."

"Indeed!" Dave thought about the tremors which struck entire economies each time energy prices skyrocketed, threatening a global inflationary crises.

"So the energy of individuals fetches them material goods that they need. And the energy they give facilitates enterprises to produce more, explore further? Wow! "

"Yes. And this chamber also monitors the overall energy generation, flow & patterns, much like your central bankers monitor growth & inflation- except that most processes & optimizations are governed by the network. The Quartions mainly regulate & devise policies, like your policy makers."

"And all this happens via the IIN? The interplanetary network? Sounds like the next level of the Internet. In our parlance, maybe Web 4.0 or 5.0."

"Yes, all this happens via the *Intelligent* Interplanetary network- but it isn't just web 5.0. It is far superior than the internet or your systems; *it is not merely an information or communications system,* but an advanced, well connected, production, distribution & consumption regulation system, based on artificial intelligence & simulation technologies."

"I don't quite follow." This was getting too technical...

"What exactly was the internet dude? Simply put, an interconnect network, rather interconnected networks. It started off as Arpanet, a closed loop network primarily for defence & research purposes. Then, as PCs, servers & information exploded, common transmission protocols were set up, and with the system of domain name, one could go to any part of the network to seek whatever information was needed- in short, a massive network of networks. But primarily, the internet was set up as a communication & information medium.

To that extent, the IIN is an advanced version of the internet, but with 2 key modifications: the transmission protocols are now not merely across networks, but across planets- hence the interplanetary network; and it is not just about information flow or communication, but regulation of the exchange of all goods & services. In short, spanning many more areas of human life…as your techies might say, *convergence taken to the next level…"*

Dave looked pensively at Atisha. Convergence was a major buzzword in tech circles, yet one that underwent many, many directional transformations. Originally conceived as the convergence of multiple devices on a single device- the desktop or the TV, it took a totally different direction, to finally rest on the least expected device of them all- the smart phone! And at yet another level, it had evolved to connote convergence of various applications & services via different devices, but on a common backbone. Now Atisha was taking it to the next level by talking about goods & services…

"How's that?"

"The IIN has several modules & sub modules, which help in monitoring, fulfilling & regulating the various needs, the various aspects of our life. Most processes, from production, consumption, distribution, commuting, communication etc, are all regulated via super advanced algorithm. In fact, the key difference is that for the first time, *even people* were connected to this network via synthetic enhancements."

"The borgs?"Dave questioned, as the cool shades of Lyon and his electronic voice played out in front of him.

'Network vision' they had called it…

"Exactly. So there is information, be it peer-to-peer or across server farms, there is advanced Artificial Intelligence (AI) allowing for real time information processing, in customized ways, there are modules spanning diverse areas of human life, and there are people themselves- that's the expanse of this network!"

"So a network which uses peer-to-peer & system-to-system information to exchange information, process it basis human needs & connect it back to people?" Dave attempted to summarize…this was advanced even for a techie, forget for a layman. But he was sensing the significance here…

"You've attempted well, but there's more. Along with these components are the R&D and control modules. The R&D module is the giant repository of all development & research, be it in energy, materials or technology, thereby facilitating further leaps through cross functional, inter planetary teams; while the control module *balances and regulates* the flow of goods & services, both from the production & consumption perspective, so that overall wellbeing & balance is maintained."

Dave reflected over the first time he saw a living example of this: his first breakfast, when Ikona had made that then cryptic remark. *'thought today I would get, rather than set breakfast'.* The system had seamlessly connected her request to the nearest, fastest, most optimized supplier, and by connecting many 'legs' through multiple routers, ensured the quickest supply of fresh food through a 'literal pipe', allowing the food to 'pop up'!

Damn cool…so much of advanced technology for a simple breakfast!

"All these techies that you see, every moment they are working on a new piece of code, a new breakthrough technology that will make computing faster, simpler & smarter, a new protocol to extend our network further into solar system, and new ways of more efficient energy generation and transmission- not just here, but across labs all over the worlds. And all these enhancements & innovations find their way into the overall IIN algorithm, as more and more processes get automated, regulated by the IIN."

"Yeah, I kind of experienced that the very first day here. Now I am amused to learn that all of it was for a humble breakfast." Dave chuckled.

"Exactly. You would have noticed that order fulfillment is most seamless- connecting the supplier & consumer in the most logical, optimized flow." he beamed as he pointed at his teams.

"As you would say, this our version of the grid, of cloud computing- where multiple systems keep getting added, allowing for thinner clients, more diverse functionalities to be added to the network. It's all out there somewhere…and more & more & more of it…"

And, as if thinking real hard, he paused for a while, only to laugh out loud. "Although in our world, the term *cloud computing* has taken on an enhanced meaning-it is literally computing through the clouds, across planets!" he guffawed as if he had cracked the most funny joke, its intensity increasing by the second!

Dave stared at him, as Atisha continued his mirth, blissfully indifferent to Dave's blank look.

Good play with words, but not entirely funny... geeky sense of humor??!! I don't get it...

"Cloud computing- computing through the clouds...that's a nice one...ha ha!" Atisha roared with laughter for a good couple of minutes. Finally, nearly gasping for breath, he slowed down, and after a deep breath, continued.

"Oh my, that was funny, wasn't it? Anyways, coming back, the allocation decision happens automatically via the IIN logic, but apart from the algorithm itself, every decision is assigned a 'weightage' basis collective well being. The Council, along with domain experts, and participation of the people, continuously deliberates and upgrades these 'weightage parameters'. And since everybody is logged into this system, the decisioning algorithms are truly democratic & participative in nature...

Yet, like our democracy, the right decision is based not only on numerical majority, but also on 'ethical & moral' implications. This is the basis of our governance and resource allocation based on true collective welfare. *Naturalism in sync with advanced democracy, and aided by advanced technology.*"

"So the various chambers of the Quartet do not unilaterally devise policies & programmes?"

"Absolutely! They are facilitators, policy makers, while the IIN constantly tracks, weighs, analyses & modifies both, the programmes & their implementations, in the most transparent & efficient of ways, with constant involvement & feedback of all those involved."

"Brilliant!" Dave was on the edge of his seat now. "Amazing! a system that has inbuilt controls, and is regulated to ensure equitable consumption and provide an inherent ethical framework, both at an individual & collective level. A dream scenario!! No worries about 'black money', parallel economy or the likes. After all, you can't fake your energies!"

"Exactly. And it's not just about ethics or creativity or spiritual pursuits, dude. It's about all that is wholesome, noble & worthwhile to do. *No longer the lament of your world that good guys finish last...*"

The Apex admired himself in the mirror, as he 'unplugged' some of his connecting ports, rising from his 'technology admiration' meditation. Even in this high tech backdrop, the old fashioned pleasure of admiring oneself in the mirror could not be compared...

He then projected the holographic call emanating from his trustworthy confidante, from within the sacred, and protected, realms of the Quartet. Clearly, his confidante was someone who knew how to avoid 'call tracing' from the Quarter, someone well versed with its ways- *an insider...*

And yet someone who had stood by him rather steadfastly... a common binding thread of technology...

"He has reached here, oh talented one; poorly camouflaged as an exchange student, but nonetheless, inside. I had the chance to meet him today."

The voice at the other end was slow and measured, the image now shrouded in a cloak, a *corona civica* resting seamlessly on his head as a regalia... the ease with which it sat there seemed to suggest that it was in fact made for the crown where it sat in resplendent glory, reminiscent of Caesar and the lost glory of Rome. A glory, which he thought, was waiting to be reclaimed...

"Well done, loyal friend. So what do you make out?"

"Must be here to study the Quartet. But why? What's his true objective? Immediately after the Council meeting? And apparently, he visits as a recommendation of the Council. Heard fleeting reports about him coming here in line with the prophecy, which apparently he saw in the clairvoyance chamber. *This doesn't augur well...*" the confidante narrated his view.

"You worry far too much; firstly, no one really knows if the prophecy is true or not. The old men have most likely conjured it up to add to their false mystique, periodically floating tales of its existence."

"*You* surely can't be saying this, oh bright One. I believe that you are destined for great glories, but *you*, of all people, should know the truth behind the tale- what if the prophecy has some basis?" There was a hint of both astonishment & concern in the confidante's voice.

"I know what I am saying-all the talks, even what I have been privy to, is only in metaphors & clues, convincing me of its non existence. and even if the prophecy does exist, it is mere conjecture that it was revealed to him. I mean, *why?*

He may have been sent by the Council, but he is merely human, don't forget. *He is not even an offspring*, so what exactly do you have to be paranoid about a primitive being?" he said in a sharp tone.

But immediately, he recognized the incisiveness of his tone. "It doesn't bother me, friend." The cyborg spoke with an unusual warmth. After all, he couldn't ignore his human roots completely.

"As for this human's objective, they have sent their point man here on Einstein too-another kid! Can you believe that??!!" the talented one's cloak fluttered gently. "Those old fools! They really believe that a wet-behind-his-ears kid can see the real story? Beyond what I choose to reveal…

Few, even in the core team, know outside of their own silos, to be able to share anything meaningful, even if they want to, or are compelled to. *Where do they expect to get the complete picture from, when only I know it?! From some other aerial voice, another prophecy?!*" The talented one's scorn now turned into disdain.

"You speak with lucidity that stems from your talent." The confidante spoke rather obsequiously, in a manner not behooving such an important member of the Council. But then, his own talent lay in looking beyond what existed today… into what the power structure could be in the future- and he had cast his lot logically, from the head, not the heart…with whom he saw as the eventual victor…

The talented one smiled broadly at this flattery. He was now in a flow."Loyal one, don't lose sight of the fact that I am closer than most realise; as for the human & the prophecy, just forget it! He is most likely witness only to what is relevant for now, his task limited to his pathetic little world, so let him go about his irrelevant journey. The earth of yore means nothing to us-*we are here to focus on higher glories, to reclaim them…*"

"But what about Aureon, oh talented one? *He* certainly can't be ordinary…" The confidante was unable to hide his uncertainty any more, having access to insider knowledge. He believed, rather knew, that the prophecy was true, as was the birth of Aureon; For all his admiration, he found the Apex almost irrationally arrogant at times. "And he *has* connections to the prophecy…"

"*Where* is he, then?" the Apex spoke with a cockiness that comes with either supreme talent or oodles of confidence- and he had both in abundance.

"By the time Aureon enters the scene, if *he is indeed there*, the era of the Apex would have set in, my loyal one. *The epoch of a golden era...*

We shall play our cards well, and wait for the time to be just ripe. After all, I am in no hurry. You continue your good, diligent work in the Quartet, while I go about building my grand dream, for higher glory."

The confidante eased a bit- it was this very energy, this higher dream that drew the likes of him to this magnificent talent, he smiled looking back at his initiation. What the Apex offered was superior to his current reality, even though he was sworn to the Quartet.

"Remember, while the prophecy guides & protects the commanders of the spirit- the masters, *natural selection favors us-the better, the higher, the smarter.* They believe in naturalism, we know the reality of natural selection...interesting duel this would be! Historic in the annals of the New ages..." He smiled, sure of what he was witnessing, even creating...

22. Defense and offense

'Attention all chambers. Intrusion reports confirmed. Alert status amber.' a faint voice echoed in the distance...

Dave ignored it, continuing to stare at the mirror instead. Utter void as he peered deep into it. From the dark void emerged vague images, as objects seemingly appeared from nowhere, confounding him...

Was he staring at the root of creation? Objects from nothingness...

Floating gently in space, came an hour glass, rotating clockwise, then anti-clockwise, in a smooth, rhythmic manner. An obfuscated Dave started blankly, wondering why he was seeing this object again? He rushed to grab it, but the hourglass seemed to slip away from his grasp-first expanding, then shrinking, finally settling next to the mirror...

No sooner had the hourglass settled down than the number 9 also emerged from the void of the mirror, floating, humming with a strange vibration...

The humming ebbed & flowed, finally settling down to a faint throb, as the number 9 engaged in a symbolic dance... flipping over, transforming to 6 in an instant, then back to 9...

Flipping over & over, rotating in circles...was life going around in circles for him?

The thought of circles brought to life the crop circle image in the mirror, as the alphabets CC also emanated, vaguely taking the shape of 2 circles this time, not three...

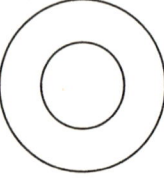

'Attention. Alert status amber.', the voice became louder, along with the emergence of the hum yet again. Soon, the hum turned into a faint roaring sound, as the disparate objects settled next to Dave in a neat, yet meaningless array...stacked with a precision that belied the apparent randomness...

Dave stared at the objects with an equal measure of verve and trepidation, attempting to distill the 'big picture'. But then, another image drew his attention away from the objects towards the mirror- a familiar face gradually emerging...

Himself...smiling, calm, beatific...was this indeed Dave?

In a while, the answer emerged, as another image manifest, next to his- that of his friend, his brother, Plutus, placing his hands on Dave's shoulders- a display of affection. As Dave smiled at the image in the mirror, the reflection smiled back: *'In your journey, have you seen & done well so far?'*

'Yeah, I think so.' Dave replied, wondering why the image asked him this. Having come thus far, he was entitled to his satisfaction in having done well in this journey.

'You sure you have seen *well?*' the image smiled in an unexpected way. But before Dave could persist further, the humming became louder, as the ground beneath their feet seemed to shift, compelling them to gaze below... *revealing yet another deep void...*

But there was no fear...the voice from the mirror smiled: *'All's well that ends well...or rather, to end well, all is well...'*

However, the other voice became louder, as if blaring in his ears: *'Attention, all chambers...';* *n*ow somewhat disconcerted, Dave was about to seek out the loud voice, when there was a loud hum... *nearly a roar...And in a final roar,* Dave was rudely jolted from his sleep!

****

Startled & groggy, he looked around- there was no mirror, no objects, nothing... just his bed & his room...and no roar...

Twisting & stretching his arms & shoulders, he rubbed his eyes, realizing that it was yet another dream. Gosh, he yawned, allowing the copious intake of oxygen to clear his head. *He was still lightly snoring, the 'roar' gentler now...*

My god, that was a loud snore, he stared at the ceiling, bemused. *Am I becoming old?*

But what about...

Just then, the holographic announcement blared once again, preempting his confusion: *'Attention, alert status amber.'*

Dave ran his hand through his tousled hair, realizing that he was dreaming about some mirror, objects, Plutus, and a vague conversation with his mirror image, when some abrupt announcement woke him up; still excited post his meeting with Atisha, having witnessed the chamber first hand, he had drifted off to a fitful sleep, when the alarms started ringing somewhere, in the middle of the night. Somnolent, & now grouchy at being woken up so abruptly, he trawled across to the computer screen and punched the concierge button. *"What just happened?"*

A pretty face appeared on the screen. "Defence alert, sir. Intrusion reports. Emergency procedure being applied..."

"What?" Dave asked, still groggy.

"Connecting you to the defence chamber broadcast, sir", and with it, a holographic projection appeared, of the defence chamber. In it, a man dressed in a flowing white robe with a hood, was standing amidst a series of consoles & screens, clearly the man in control.

Around him were holographic images of reports from various locations, and various military entities at different stages of the drill. There were robot armies, standing in neat rows, in attention. But they weren't carrying conventional guns or artillery; rather strange looking, tablet like objects, probably laser guns or stunners. Another image zoomed onto what looked like space armadas- fleets of spaceships of different sizes & in various locations, seemingly patrolling in a formation, rather than ready for combat.

"Offspring, this is your Commander-in-Chief speaking. Threat magnitude being assessed. Status set to Def Con 3. Fleet XG preparing to launch for close range assault. Admiral Maya, assume command & proceed per instructions." Immediately, a fleet of one large & three midsized spaceships droned to life.

"Ground troops on full alert, to prepare for residual infiltration; lieutenant Chang to share exact composition & potential impact coordinates; regiment captains to mobilize forces accordingly." And images of men in uniform appeared, as they coordinated movement of robot columns in massive CATs.

"Aerial counter systems to be activated. Missiles 1 to 5 and 15 to 20 on standby for launch. Estimate time six hours. Retrieval fleet to spread out for debris collection. Materials team on reconnaissance for sample analysis."

In accordance with this latest command, images of aerial defence systems & satellites appeared- supposedly counter systems, primarily for intercepting. Along with it, another fleet of bowl shaped ships fanned out in various directions, ready for 'debris collection', basis impact calculation.

"Primary objective is retrieval; minimum destruction, I repeat; collateral damage to be zero. Commanders to ensure.."

"What the hell?" Dave mumbled, still half asleep. "What is happening?" He thought of trying to piece together his dream with this commotion. But then, a series of further alarms went off, triggering more announcements & movements.

'Defence preparation started to brace for the assault. You have ninety minutes to collect important belongings & be ready. Dismantling of the base to start in exactly ninety minutes.' and with it, a countdown started.

"Hey, shit man! Will somebody tell me what exactly is going on? Ninety minutes? Dismantling?" and he furiously, anxiously, punched the concierge button yet again. "Lady, just what the f...? I mean, what the hell is happening? What was this announcement now?"

"Sir, commander-in-chief has set status to def con 3. Alert status is amber. Which means that *assault is likely in less than 12 hours*; while the defence system in being mobilized, safety standard operating procedures (SOPs) require all residents be moved to other secure locations."

"Hey, wait wait wait. What assault? Sudden threat? Who is attacking whom? And I thought we were in the New Ages, where wars didn't happen..."

"Sir, I am merely relaying instructions. And you are expected to follow them for your own safety. Countdown has begun. 88 minutes & 12 seconds before auto dismantling."

"Dismantling?"

"Yes sir. The entire colony will be dismantled on an auto trigger basis, to be transported to a safer location."

Even in this groggy state, Dave remembered what the escort had explained about the high security features of this complex- one of them being the ability to quickly transport the entire complex to a safer location, thanks to its inherent properties. This seemed like one of those occasions...

"Please ready your belongings and proceed to embark at bay 2." and with it, the concierge operator faded away.

"Hey, wait!" but she was gone. Another announcement reminded him. 'Estimated time: 86 minutes, 18 seconds.'

"Shit!" and without wasting another moment, Dave jumped out of his pajamas into something more suitable, hurriedly going about packing his suitcase. All his packing seemed to be hurried, he momentarily mused, whether it was to come to India, or to evacuate from the Quartet HQ...

****

'Estimated time 32 minutes 40 seconds...'

"Jeez!" Dave was still scrambling to collect his stuff, getting panicky. Just then, the defence broadcast indicated something else.

"Sir, Plasma shields up on the domes. Readings confirm that this is not a single impact threat. *Repeat, potential multiple impacts.*" lieutenant Chang said frantically.

"Chief of Staffs, please note: def con status upgraded to 2. *I repeat, def con upgraded to two.* Lieutenant, relay potential impact coordinates." The image of the Commander-in-Chief relayed over the screen once again.

"Copy that. Roger." Chief of the strategic aerial command, Marshall Sambhav, responsed. "All units, Def Con alert at 2. All armadas & missiles on full alert."

"Red Con 2 for all ground reconnaissance units." came another update, this time from the chief of ground staff, General Zorbian.

****

While the broadcast continued, Dave continued to scurry around, much of this military jargon incomprehensible to him. Just then another announcement blared: 'Threat status upgraded to red. Def con now set at 2. Please note, revised time for dismantling now reset to 14 minute 12 seconds. You have precisely 9 minutes & 7 seconds to proceed to bay 2.'

"What the..?? Will someone please, please tell me what's going on?", his exasperation peaking. Not remotely had he expected anything like this in the highest security complex in all of the New Ages. However, there was nothing more to clarify his doubts, except more periodic announcements, till a final one blared, loud and shrill: '5 minutes & 5 seconds left. Please stop all packing & proceed to bay 2. Immediately!'

Now in a near hysterical state, Dave scrambled to the bay with whatever he managed to garner. The lights were gradually dimming out, with only emergency exit lights guiding the way. The whole thing felt like being in an aircraft about to crash, or being thrust into a combat zone, with everybody scampering against time & hope, to make a mad dash to the bunkers!

But beyond this frenzy & personal peril, what was really unnerving him was the thought of conflict in this evolved word...how could it be?

Gasping & panting, he reached the bay in the nick of time, the countdown in the background keeping him on his toes...*just about made it, he smiled & prayed,* as the countdown stopped...

For a while, he stood there, trying to gather his senses. Then, something else struck him- the bay was completely dark & deserted! Not a sign of a soul, no offspring movement, no frantic faces...not even any sign of CATs. Bewildered, he looked around, straining to see in the darkness- nothing!

A sudden fear seized him- had he missed the evacuation? Stranded, alone... *oh my god, could it...?*

Just then, an announcement pierced the pin drop silence: *'Safety drill over. Contingency plan test successful. You may now proceed to bay 3 for your rendezvous with the Commander-in-Chief.'*

"What the...?" Dave reacted, partly incredulous, partly relieved, and partly exhilarated, as the lights came on, illuminating the whole bay...

A vast rock outcropping, it had seemed dank & desolate moments back. Yet, now it was brilliantly lit, revealing its full features. On the massive bay stood hundreds of PATs & CATs, most of them resembling the combat vessels he had seen on the screen, or small single seater transport capsules, meant more for intra-surface transport. This was yet another facet of this giant cavern, a fully functional, gargantuan transit area deep underneath the surface, reminding him of the fascination he had felt the first time he had 'submerged' to these depths.

'Please proceed to bay 3. Commander-in-Chief, General Junah, the healer, awaits you.' the announcement came, this time in a soft female voice, almost a whisper, accompanied by soothing music. Irritated, but relieved, Dave did as instructed, the soothing music & lights elevating him somewhat…

****

"Sorry for this rather abrupt drill & meeting; I'm General Junah, Chief Quartion of the defence chamber, and I welcome you to this rendezvous." he extended a warm handshake.

Still jolted & dazed, Dave shook his hand, and with a gentle bow, asked: "I am sorry sir, but what is this all about? First a sudden announcement of an impending assault, then full scale war drills, frantic announcements asking us to evacuate immediately, then nothing at all on bay 2? And then, yet another sudden announcement for a rendezvous with you. I feel so lost!"

"Lost? Wasn't your last assignment anyways supposed to be at the Defence chamber?"

"It was? Only it seems I am not aware..." Dave replied, sounding sharper than he intended to be. "And even if it were so, what's that got to do with any of this?"

"Everything! You've almost seen & learnt all that you needed to in the Quartet- one last thing remained though..."

"I don't get you, sir."

"Stop calling me sir. You may call me General or healer, whatever you prefer."

The sound of this last pronouncement seemed rather incongruous, being one of the many things about this episode that bothered him- *General & healer in the same statement? Man of death & life in the same breath?*

As if sensing his confusions, Junah smiled. "I see you have many questions…good! That's why you are here."

"So what's this all about, er *General*?" this designation, over healer, sounded more appropriate for a military leader.

"Hmn, so your conditioning still gets the better of you at times, I see." Junah smiled, a look of compassion in his eyes.

"Beg your pardon, *General*?"

"See, you repeat it..." he smiled, a tinge of sarcasm this time. "You are thoroughly confused about this sudden attack, this sudden conflict. You are woken up abruptly in the dead of the night, asked to gather your belongings and evacuate immediately. You are shaken up, both physically & emotionally. As the broadcasts of defcon & redcon upgrade ring the air, a small voice in your head gnaws in the background- how could there be such violence in such an evolved plane? And so sudden, unexpected? How?

But amidst all these dizzying questions & confusions, the first question that comes to the fore is *how to address me, as General or healer*? And you choose the readily accepted notion of addressing the Commander-in-chief as a General. A healer, after all, seems too incongruous for a defence chief, doesn't it?"

Amazing. In all this frenzy, General Junah (healer Junah, whatever...) dissects his thoughts, putting it in perspective better than he himself could...just what was he trying to drive at?

"Yes sir, kind of. I thought it would behoove you if I addressed you as such."

"Why not as a healer? *Obviously, how can the giver of life be someone who mobilizes forces which take life, right?*" Junah said incisively.

"Well, actually sir." Dave cringed, trailing off; a practicing energy healer, a man of chi, seemed the unlikeliest of choice for a Defence chamber chief. But then, this place had more than its share of quirks & surprises...

"It's ok, Dave. Fragmented understanding shall not desert you so soon, child of the earth. You still find it difficult to understand how can life coexist with death... "

Dave flinched a wee bit more. "Well actually, chief Mirdad did explain in detail about the dissolution of fragmentation, & how all systems here are based on this principle. But not in the context of conflict & healing."

"Context. Ah, that wonderful word; so useful..." Junah smiled even more sarcastically now.

"Mirdad tells you that the New Age is *new* because we have eliminated all unnatural fragmentation, shed the unnecessary compartments of our mind. And you lap it up, of course…great! Science can coexist with spirit, society with individual aspirations…but how can life coexist with death, right?" he said, pointing to a glittering statue of Nataraj in his celestial dance pose. "How can a healer coexist with a General, right?"

"No, er… it's not like that." Dave said, now truly worried that the healer was offended.

"It *is* like that. Even while you profess an interest in oriental philosophy, you have not the faintest idea of the principles of Martial Arts- combat based upon awareness…duel based inherently upon inner peace…"

"I don't really follow you sir."

"Anyways, forget that. We'll come to it later. For now, let's go back to the events of the past couple of hours, and why you're here. You have many questions…"

"Sure sir."

"You *can* address me as General- I take pride in it." Junah said, trying to comfort Dave after the rather acerbic rebuke.

"After all, I am decorated General." he pointed at his uniform, and the coat of arms underneath his cloak.

"Sure General…er…healer." Dave said with a rather awkward smile. "So, what's really happening here?"

"What do you think? We are preparing to launch a massive counter assault. Wasn't the defense broadcast relayed over in your suite?" Junah said, his posture suddenly tough & erect, that of a decorated General. Dave was slightly taken aback by the matter-of-fact tone in which Junah spoke of a *'massive counter assault'. Somehow, all this still seemed against the grain of this place, somewhat counter intuitive...*

"But why? How come you still have conflicts? Defence systems, armies & space armadas? *Seems humans just can't do away with war, however they may evolve…*" Dave questioned with a sense of disillusionment in his voice. It was almost as if the burden of the annihilation came back on his shoulders.

"And why does it all sound *so strange*?" Junah questioned slowly, again a certain mordant streak in his voice, as if he were trying to drive home a point.

"Not strange, but unnatural. Out of sync... after all, isn't the second pillar being in harmony with nature & natural laws?"

"Aha. Our man from earth finds conflict out of sync with nature. So just how come it's not strange in your world, sir?" Junah's sarcasm laced words could have poisoned a snake...

Dave was silent.

"It's simple, Dave. Another planetary system has attacked us, so we are preparing to counter attack with all our might."

"Which one has attacked? And suddenly? Out of the blue? *Wars don't happen like this...*"

"So *just how* do they happen?"

"I mean, I don't know politics that well. But obviously there is a build up, there are talks...and when all else fails, only then war happens."

"*Is it*? Are you *certain*?"

"Yeah. Kind of...think so...at least that's how it's supposed to be." Dave said, less sure than before.

"Well, let's just say that's not how conflicts happen. Anyways, forget that. Let me show you our latest defence technology, and all the leaps we have made." Junah said, a smile finally coming to his face. And a holographic projection started relaying in the centre of the room.

"You have seen our space armadas & robot armies. Aren't they impressive?"

Dave nodded half heartedly.

"Hey, where's the excitement? I am showing you cutting edge defence technology, and here you seem lukewarm..."

There was a brief silence, and then Junah cachinnated.

"My apologies, we persisted with this for longer than I wanted to. But I just couldn't resist the opportunity to test you, your learnings from this plane, your wisdom, and your perspectives on war & conflict..."

"I'm sorry?"

"More like I'm sorry." Junah said, continuing to laugh, though subdued now. "...to have done all this in the dead of the night. Actually, parts of what you saw were indeed factual, though simulation."

"I...I don't get it."

"You see Dave, there is *no war, no conflict* happening here- that was all created, conjured up-*the fictional part.*"

Thank god, Dave could almost feel a huge sigh of relief... redeemed again... the burden seemed to be lifted...

"So all this was nothing? No assault, no counter attack?"

"Yes, none of it. All of it was simulated."

Wow...and you had to make me go through such a frantic experience, in the middle of the night for a simulation? Dave thought, slightly edgy, but beaming, relieved.

"So what was the factual part, General?"

"The defence structure, the forces, the preparation-all that bit that you saw."

"But why, if there is no war?"

"Because it was a drill, against another foe- *a celestial foe.*"

"Celestial foe?"

"An 'asteroid' attack." Junah smiled.

Dave still seemed blank.

"You know that we have settled on other planets, some outside the comfort of earth's environs. Obviously, we are at risk from natural & celestial forces. That's where the defence chamber comes in, and that's why we have defence drills."

"*What? So it was a drill in response to an asteroid threat?* All those space vehicles, those armadas, ground troops, the missiles?" Dave asked, still a bit incredulous.

"Yes- don't you guys have the concept of safety drills & contingency plan testing? I bet contingency of business is a pretty standard practice in your organizations."

Sensing Dave's continuing puzzled look, Junah guided him to one of the giant consoles at the farthest end of the room. "Let me show you fireworks of the kind you have never seen, and which you will never forget."

He then punched in some keys, and the missiles whirred to life, the countdown beginning. In precisely 30 seconds, all the missiles took off simultaneously, precision guided and in perfect harmony. In parallel, fleet XG & the bowl shaped vessels adjusted their positions, to synchronize with the missile impact.

Within moments, the missiles rammed into the massive asteroid from all sides, and what followed could be described only in superlatives...

Starting with a series of small explosions from the outside, causing sparks to fly, the intensity of the explosions increased, till, in less than ten minutes, the entire chunk imploded from within, culminating with a massive burst- a massive celestial firework, raining showers of sparks & debris on all sides.

Dave stared in both awe & horror. Awe, because this was something he only saw in the movies, and horror at the realization that tens of thousands of tons of debris would literally plunder the entire surface. But then, as he grasped the complete picture, the disparate elements made sense. As if on cue, the 'bowl shaped' vessels fanned out in all directions with amazing speed & accuracy, opening out massive 'bowls' to collect the debris...at least most of it...

For the residual bits falling on the surface, the Gelass domes offered the first level of protection, followed by columns of four legged robot armies, equipped with special 'tablets' to vaporize these chunks. In a move so precisely coordinated & orderly, not a single significant chunk of a massive, exploding asteroid fell on the surface- collected either in space by the armada ships, or on the ground by precision guided robot armies.

"Wow!" Dave exclaimed, like a little child witnessing a grand firework spectacle along the waterfront. "So *this* is what an advanced armed force achieves- swift victory over a sudden, uncontrollable foe? And celestial fireworks as a bonus..."

"Exactly Dave. Though simulated, this was a small scale glimpse of what this chamber exists for! The moot point here is that in the NEW AGES, the role of the defence systems has changed dramatically as compared to the way it existed for millennia. And not without reason- *mankind had seen enough of the horrors of war & nuclear devastation. Having scarred its soul so deeply, bloodshed for ideology or territory is completely outside the realms of the new collective consciousness.*"

Exactly what I expected from this place...

"And one more verbiage correction- we prefer to call them *defence forces, not armed forces.*"

Dave saw the point here- and it wasn't merely a play with words; it reflected a basic underlying philosophy...

"As with all other chambers, we have leveraged technology to create true 'defence systems'- systems designed to offer protection from external, natural & celestial forces rather than offspring aggressions, while at the same time maintaining a basic, yet rather sophisticated system of deterrence from potential new age 'attacks'. Come, let me show you another key element of our defence set up- our surveillance systems."

He led Dave to the far corner of his room, where some holographic images were getting relayed. All kinds of little mobile robotic probes, satellites & 'transmitters', from the colossal satellite to the invisible nanobots, were buzzing with some form of activity or the other...

"Nanobots play a crucial role in ground surveillance, along with more advanced, galactic satellite surveillance.

Needless to say, most surveillance is directed not against the *enemy*, but rather towards the *intruder*- celestial objects or geodesic imbalances which could lead to the *disturbance of harmony & possible loss of life.*"

He then touched the 'virtual screen', and other images flashed, ones that Dave had seen earlier- columns of robot armies, neatly arranged & moving in precise order. Junah explained that due to the IIN, as well as robotics technology and Artificial Intelligence (AI), robot armies were created, with the IIN controlling deployment & movement of these, as they supplemented artillery & missile systems. In the NEW AGES, the offspring controlled & supervised the defence systems, without actually participating in them. This was akin to paradigm shifts in factories in the 20th century, when automated process plants elevated humans to the role of supervisors.

But it wasn't just tech developments alone. The epoch shift in human consciousness meant that *any form of human life, including hybrid cyborgs, was now considered precious enough to not be wasted on the battlefield,* even against a celestial foe.

"So human life *is* deeply valued, not to be squandered in battle, while the role of actual combat is taken over by technology? And all this strictly within the ambit of defense only?" Dave surmised, as all of it added up: the role of technology, humans & elevated consciousness...

"Exactly! The NEW AGES looks at defence as very distinct from aggression for conflict resolution, which is the basic muddle of human history.

In fact, *there are three distinct principles which guide the defence chamber in all its philosophy & functioning- the baseline of the charter."*

"***Firstly, there is no concept of might is right;*** that primitive rule belongs in the jungle, so let it rest there! Nature always reminds us of our roles, responsibilities & differentiation from animals, as evolved, thinking beings. If fighting to win was our way, we would have been in the jungle, not in space." he smiled broadly.

"So, when we say defence systems, we mean defence systems- that's the first point!"

"*Secondly, the charter itself lays down detailed rules for conflict resolution.* True, where there are people, and multiple points of view, there will be tensions, even some conflicts. But there are humane, civilized ways of dealing with them, not by violence. Negotiations & creative conflict resolution is something that is imbibed in us, and taught since childhood. We have a 101 creative ways of conflict resolution, at every level. *That's the second point- that there are many creative ways of conflict resolution, if we act in accordance with the charter."*

"So you guys don't have war as a political doctrine at all?"

"What's that? *War as a political doctrine*? Doesn't it deserve to be relegated to the museum? As happened with other obsolete, irrational social norms, when humanity grew- first slavery, then poverty, and now war. War as an extension of policy & polity is redundant on our plane. *Remember, 101 creative ways of conflict resolution?*" he smiled mischievously.

"So you believe that conflicts can be resolved without war?"

"Of course! The only logical way to resolve conflict is without war! And if you don't believe me, believe you own master war strategist, Sun Tzu."

"Sun Tzu? Thought he spoke about the art of war, *not peace…*"

"Every battle is won before it is ever fought…"

"I thought this quote refers to preparedness as the key element to victory in warfare."

"Yes, but reflect beneath the surface. If every battle is indeed a matter of strategy, relative strength & preparedness, *then what is war itself for*? Just carnage on the actual battlefield? If the actual act of battle is simply an execution of strategy, then ultimately it's all about the backroom, not the frontline. *So why war?* Why not midway solutions & diplomacy?

After all, creative thinking can be as much applied to negotiations as battle. Diplomacy works more effectively than war, as a political tool."

"But is it always possible?"

'To win one hundred victories in one hundred battles is not the acme of skill. To subdue the enemy without fighting is the acme of skill...' Junah flashed another quote of the great general. "Don't listen to me, listen to the Master." he smiled.

"Brilliant! Trust you to find a message of peace in one of history's greatest General's words."

"All men can see these tactics whereby I conquer, but what none can see is the strategy out of which victory is evolved..."

"I concur completely, General. All war is destructive, reprehensible, even redundant as a political tool. *And yet, if...*" Dave visualized his image of the annihilation.

"If there is ever, god forbid, a war, then the principles & objectives are clearly laid out in the charter- that's the third guiding principle."

"And what are those?"

"You see, all war is waged in three stages, at three levels:

1. Aggression
2. destruction
3. Control or conquest

But the moot question is: what is the basic aim of war? It is ultimately control, whether of territory or vital installations or ideology. So why have layers one and two? Aren't they redundant? However, the irony of human history is that all wars were focused primarily on aggression & destruction."

"Remember, war is avoidable, always. Peace is not only superior to war, it is also the most logical & lasting solution. But if war unfortunately happens, the aim should be only control, not aggression or bloodshed. In a civilized society, there can be no justification for the loss of human life, either in the frontline or as 'collateral damage'. That is as primitive as can get. Bear in mind, Dave, if there is collective will, control is possible without destruction, or with minimal destruction. *This is the third principle clearly laid out in the Charter.*"

"Since you have had a glimpse into our armed forces, our defence systems, you would have noticed that they all follow these principles-designed primarily for defence, surveillance, suppression of potential assaults and control, not for aggression & destruction. But it doesn't stop there. In the New Ages, the whole terrain has moved away from control of territory to control of information...*virtual territory*...

It is a natural progression for mankind. Human history has shown that the terrain has progressively shifted from the physical to the technological, ideological & psychological."

"I don't understand. So it's no longer about territory?"

"Yes. Just look at your own history- progressively, wars were fought & won by technological superiority, not numbers alone. In the networked NEW AGES, where most physical services, infrastructure & establishments are information driven & technologically controlled, the domain of warfare is not the physical establishments themselves, but their nerve centers- the controlling systems & networks."

And then, giving an analogy which struck an instant chord, Junah summarized: "This is akin to the board games your children play- the objective is control, yet there is no acrimony, no destruction, just an innocence in reveling at the game."

Then, almost getting contemplative, he said "Your world has so much to learn from children, Dave. All your generals & military strategists who came up with such brilliant strategies for destruction couldn't fathom something as simple as the difference between control & devastation. At the end of the day, it is left to children to show us something so simple. ."

"No wonder, child is the father of man." Dave sighed...

****

There was a long silence as they ventured out into the garden- a terrace garden overlooking a small pond, with a collection of colorful fishes so beautiful that it seemed straight out of a coral reef. As they stood there in silence, soaking it in, Junah broke the silence. "All that I have told you thus far is just one layer in the understanding of conflict resolution- the outer layer, the layer of the General. But there is a deeper, higher perspective too. In fact, three perspectives..."

"Three perspectives?"

"Yes- *the energy perspective, the psychological perspective and the karmic perspective.* From the eyes of the healer..."

Dave raised his eyebrow.

"Let's start with the energy perspective. In essence, all conflict is like disease, an imbalance of the collective entity. Just as disease can have symptomatic & holistic approach to treatment, so too with conflict. To that extent, conflict is welcome, as it represents an opportunity to recognize & resolve the imbalance."

"Wow! This is the healer talking." Dave smiled, realizing why a healer was heading the *conflict resolution chamber. This place was giving a new meaning to unified & holistic...*

"Yes, you don't need generals, you need healers. But the way one sees the problem is the way one gets the solution. If you see conflict as a problem of might, you will address it with brute force- the way your 'modern medicine' uses brute force, localized therapy, to alleviate disease. But if you see conflict as merely a manifestation of a deeper malaise, a larger imbalance, then your whole approach becomes holistic- that of healing & balancing, not merely of localized relief using brute force."

"Root cause analysis?"

"Exactly. This is the fundamental approach of all energy healing. Correct the energy imbalance & you eliminate the root cause of the disease, not merely its symptom. This approach, like holistic healing, takes more time, effort & patience; but balance & conciliation is more lasting, more sustainable, and more in sync with nature than any military solution."

"Sir, I salute you. I salute your understanding, and I salute your wisdom." Dave said, mockingly genuflecting, clearly awed by the profoundness & simplicity of this understanding.

Junah smiled back. "Don't salute me. Salute the new age wisdom! And you know what, humans can have it too; it's not that difficult..."

"Anyways, now let's look at the psychological approach. All conflict is inherently an energy game, and there are two ways to view it- the abundance mentality & paucity mentality. WAR is an outcome of *paucity* mentality."

"Paucity mentality?"

"Yes. When consciousness is not evolved enough to connect with the higher source of energy, it seeks to draw from the lower sources to take care of its imbalance & deficiency. Since it is finite source, that is possible only by forcible control. Thus emerges war & conflict out of paucity mentality."

"Sounds so much like transaction analysis. But while this may be right in the individual context, seems a little too simplistic in terms of larger conflicts, say, between nations."

"Actually, it's quite true. Throughout history, there have been thousands of wars- tell me objectively, how many were actually driven by self-preservation & defence, and how many by ego, a desire for control, domination, imperial ambitions, or simply a lack of sincerity in negotiations?"

"See, the answer stares you in the face! More than nine out of ten wars had some control motives. They were energy conflicts, germinating out of 'paucity mentality', of fear. Just a while ago, you told me that war follows a pattern- issues, negotiations, diplomacy, and when all else fails, then war as the last resort; and I said that's not the case. Now you see what I meant? It's an energy conflict, and where there's such a deprivation mentality, so much fear, sincere negotiations are never given a chance. However, the moment an individual or society changes its mindset, its actual situation changes too, and the need to 'encroach' dissipates."

Dave had to agree to facts. He remembered his consistent discussions on this plane, from which it seemed rather clear that technology based on fear was a root cause of so many problems in our world. He briefed Junah about his discussion with the Masters on brain wave scans vs. clairvoyance.

"Indeed." Junah indicated his conformance. "We have built upon your technologies like MRI scans, thermal imaging, sub vocal communication etc. But not from the perspective of paranoia. Yes, as Defence chief, I have some fear too- but not from other humans! In fact, it really isn't fear, but rather preventive measures to dispel potential fear."

Junah ventured close to the lake, dropping some food for the fishes. "Then, there is the third higher view- something I call *the 'anti-Newtonian', or the karmic perspective.*"

"This one sounds intriguing. Though why drag poor Newton in this whole mess?" Dave joked.

"Oh well, ignore the name." Junah waved his hands, still feeding the fishes. "The essence of this is that that the law of action & reaction is relevant only in the mechanical world, not in the world of human interactions.

In fact, in the human world action-reaction can only aggravate, not resolve issues."

"But this is also the law of nature..."

"Exactly- so let *her do her job* of dispensing 'justice' or righting a wrong. *As humans, let's do our job...*"

Then, donning the healer's hat, he asked rhetorically. "Does a healer think about action-reaction or the patient's karma while treating him? Of course not! He only think about healing, irrespective of the patient in front of him.

Why? Because that's his role. Because as humans, we are blessed with the ability to forgive & heal; rather, born with this innate ability, as with the intelligence to creatively resolve conflicts. So, by naively quoting action & reaction, we only get drawn into a vicious cycle, where the line between the defender & offender keeps getting progressively blurred, and a vicious spiral is originated, which is much more difficult to douse."

Remember Gandhi? Non violence is the only way to break the spiral of violence, the only viable solution to fight perceived wrongs & oppression. Unlike Christ, one need not turn the other cheek, but forgiveness & reconciliation are the only logical ways to prevent full-fledged conflagrations. *An eye for an eye simply leaves the whole world blind...*

So that, Dave, is the third, higher perspective on war- *in a war, in the vicious cycle of action & reaction, there are no winners, only victims.* **It is time to relegate war to the museum. And see a different world you can create...**

****

In this moment of clarity & resolve, the analytical mind of the super manager started ticking. Having spent hours trying to conjure up strategies to force incremental gallons of cola down the throats of consumers, this was the most worthwhile piece of analytics done in a long time...

In a population of six billion, close to a billion lived in extreme poverty- mostly in the three largest continents of Asia, Africa & South America. Most of the wealth was concentrated in the continents of Europe & North America, which accounted for not more than 15% of the global population. The global GDP was about $ 50 trillion, of which almost 3% was spent on defense- that's a whopping $ 1.5 trillion! Notably, NATO alone accounted for over a trillion $, or the GDP of most of Africa!!

Then he looked at the other side of the equation, the bit that made war such an efficient machinery- the men; twenty million of them in uniform. The best in class, mentally tough folks, who could be assets in any crisis situations, having proven their mettle during calamities time & again. But unfortunately, centuries of war had conditioned these ultra disciplined individuals into automatons, programmed to simply follow orders, to dissolve their thinking so that they could kill. After all, that's the only way men could be programmed to kill others whom they didn't even know- men, just like them, but simply on the other side of a political divide. *One can motivate people to die for a cause, but to kill? That can only be programmed!*

However, new age wisdom had taught Dave to hate war, not the warrior. The warrior is valiant, loyal, disciplined, organized, committed. So change him not, change his goal. Make him not kill for a flag, but create for the charter, unleashing him not for elimination of the enemy, but for annihilation of depravation, hunger, inequality. Similarly, his thinking expanded to despise the mechanism, not the machinery After all, this very machinery had spawned several breakthroughs- the internet, space programs, satellites, organizational structures on which all modern day corporations were founded- so much of the modern world owed its progress to the war machine. Convert it into a development machine, and you could have the most powerful, the most creative organization in the world...

By combining both sides of this equation, Dave looked at the sheer scale of the opportunity available...

If one could divert even half of the military budgets & resources, one was staring at a staggering $ 500 billion, apart 10 million of the most disciplined men, available for human development, not destruction! Not only would poverty be completely eliminated, but the subsequent virtuous cycle of wealth & prosperity, created as a confluence of the most hungry & most disciplined segments of our population, would lift global productivity & happiness beyond what even the most optimistic of economists could envisage. A tidal wave of prosperity so powerful could be unleashed that the new ages could be closer than any of us could imagine...

The time has come... Now!!

23. THE PROPHECY SEEMS CLEAR, THE MESSENGER NEAR...

The assignments at the Quartet over, it was time for Dave to head back and take stock- he had been here for a full month, across various chambers, and had learnt so, so much- new economic systems, the IIN and the core technology platforms, the roles of various entities/chambers and their seamless harmony, the new perspective on war & defence- the entire functioning, the life breath of a new world, one that not long ago existed only in fairy tales for him...

But having seen it, experienced it, he was truly enriched...

While there was still no headway in his quest for the Messenger, he didn't feel anxious or exasperated any more- the journey and the learnings were as much, if not more, valuable & stirring than the quest itself. He remembered the beautiful quote: *Success is a journey, not a destination...*

Having come so far, and enriched himself to this degree, he wondered what next? Where to from here? Been there, seen that...

Tired and mentally overwhelmed, he drifted off into a light sleep, as the random images from the earlier dream came back...*Dave staring distantly into the mirror, as the objects appeared- the hour glass, rotating clockwise and then anticlockwise; the symbol of infinity; the crop circle image, gently blurring out to two concentric circles, as if he were somehow peering down on them; the number 9, also rotating; the alphabets CC, with straight edges rather than curved; and finally, his reflection gradually appearing in the mirror, along with the image of Plutus...*

And then, unlike last time, the words of Master Aleus rang out again, uttered just after his Council meeting:

As above, so below... see the truth beyond the reflection... words which had helped him crack the 5th clue...but why now?

For a while, Dave struggled with these images, but was then awakened by sounds around- fortunately, not like the abrupt announcements or roaring of last time, but rather of people alighting or boarding. Looking around, he realized that his CAT had halted at a remote port on Columbus.

He lumbered onto the deck somewhat listlessly, but his spirit was immediately lifted by the beautiful sight of the panoramic ice mountains all around him, reminding him of the Quartet HQ. White, glittering, radiant in the basking sunlight, the mountains seemed to connect him to the other mighty peaks, instrumental in his journey- the Himalayas...

As always, he took in deep breaths of the high energy air around him, and his mind felt clear, his body refreshed. He observed people embark and disembark, onward onto their journey, towards their destination, a certain clarity & sense of purpose in their stride. *And the question came back...*

What was his purpose in all this? Where was he headed?

A deep breath later, he slapped his right hand on his forehead, in a gesture of as much exclamation as reprimand! The 6th clue had been staring at him all along...

Ever since his dream prior to the defence chamber encounter, he had been carrying these images, these clues in his head, but had not been able to put them together in a coherent, cogent fashion- now, in a flash, like his other clues, clarity dawned yet again. *The dream was indicating the 6th clue, thanks to the number 9...*

The rotating number 9, flipped down by 180 degree, was actually indicating 6... the sixth clue....

Dave smiled at all the puzzles and riddles he had to solve to get his answers, and wondered, like he often did, why this journey couldn't have been straight & simple? Nonetheless, he recollected the images from the dream, and decided that this clue was something he would decipher on his own, without the help of his friends...

So, this is the 6th clue, all right; and just what does it depict?

Rotating hourglass, but unlike the normal hourglasses having a curved surface, this one too was having straight, well defined edges- like the one he saw at the Council...

But why yet again?

Back then, it had indicated the twin pyramids, and the unscrambling of the hieroglyphs...what was it here...?

This was the third time this object of ancient significance was playing some role...

Third time...trinity..??? triangle? two triangles...two pyramids, yet again??

Nah, I have already experienced the clue related to the twin pyramids at the Council...

So, what else?

Rotating... why...? what...?

Turn by 90 degree, and it seems identical to the symbol of infinity. Turn full 360, it comes back to its original point and shape...

To infinity & back? Beyond infinity lies the homecoming?

   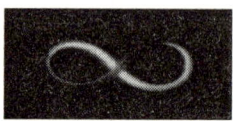

*Infinity symbol...circle... rotating number 9, rotating hour glass...**All representing 360 degrees in some form...***

C C- crop circle.... Circle...360 degrees as well...

So, what was the underlying message? The unifying thread?

Something, he was missing...there was a missing piece that would glue all of these together...

Dave thought about the mirror bit...staring into some remote distance... nothing... blank... infinity...

And then, his image appeared...a reflection... manifesting itself....

Reflection...

Reflection?

Just then, Master Aleus' words also rang in: *As above, so below...the lower is but a reflection of the higher...'*

Reflection... as above, so below... Metaphorical? Or, in this case, literal? Guiding him?

A few deep breaths, and came the moment of stupefaction....

As above, so below, was alluding to the reflections of the supposedly disparate, random symbols & alphabets...

When a mirror was placed at the centre...

And in an epiphany, most of it fell in place...

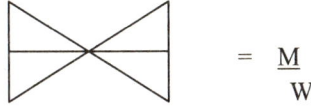 = M̲
    W

The hourglass image, apart from its several emblematic connotations, was literally pointing to the alphabet W, when a mirror was placed at its centre. The upper and the lower parts split into identical Ws, each reflecting the other to form the complete shape of the hour glass...

As above, so below! The lower is but a reflection of the higher, of the whole!

Excitedly, Dave took out a pen and paper from his pocket, and in his habitual, old fashioned way, drew all the symbols on it-inspite of his time here, he was just too accustomed to the pen paper way to project a screen from his wrist micro computer...

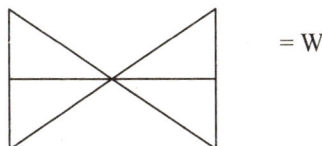 = W

By a similar logic,

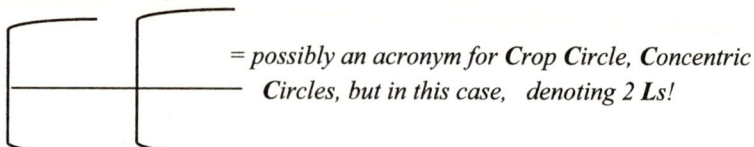
= possibly an acronym for Crop Circle, Concentric Circles, but in this case, denoting 2 Ls!

As above so below, once again...

So this thing is: **WLL**...?
But what about it...?
Something was missing... a connecting thread...a key of sorts...?
For every lock, there is the key...

I get it! The key to unlock this is a vowel-that is usually the connecting thread for a sentence...
So, is it 'A': **Wall**...? Had a hit a wall..?
Or 'I'? **Will**...? Undoubtedly, it was his will which had led him till here...
Or... 'E'
Obviously! It stared at him so obviously...!! ***Well...***
The missing link was the number 6! Yet again...
It didn't merely point to the 6th clue, but also had another significance: *Inverted, it denoted 9, but as a reflection, a mirror image, it denoted...*
...*e*... $\frac{e}{6}$

And the voice of his reflection had asked him so directly: 'Have you *seen* & done *well* so far...'
'To end *well*, all is *well*...'
...***Well!*** *How could he miss it... the 6th clue was **well**!*
Now he also understood that the two concentric circles denoted a top view of a well, with the image of Dave staring into the mirror, observing his reflection as it gradually manifest, probably depicting him staring deep into the recesses of the well... *observing a reflection...*
As above, so below! Him above, his reflection below, in a well...
But what **well**...? **Reflection well**...? **Image well**...???

Just then, he heard a fellow passenger mention something about a *Manifestation well* to his partner.

Eureka! *Manifestation well* it was...

But what was a *Manifestation well*? After the initial moment of illumination came the haze again. No worries though...the simplest way was to go and ask the gentleman himself.

"Excuse me sir, am sorry to intrude, but I heard you mention about some *Manifestation Well*. Can you tell me what it is?"

The passenger gave Dave a strange look, and turned around to look at his partner, who gave a warm, consenting nod. He smiled back at her, and then turned to Dave again, this time with a friendly expression.

"You new around here?"

"Kind of, sir."

"No wonder you ask this question. It's quite popular here. The Manifestation Well is said to be yet another gift of the beings, and allows one to manifest one's deepest emotions, anxieties & questions; questions which may have baffled for a while, or problems that are gnawing. But mind you, the well is no magical talisman- rather, it's a viewing point, a point where one seeks clarity from confusion. The waters of the well manifest images which the mind find difficult to articulate- at times even manifesting answers."

Dave smiled- now he understood what he was being guided to. "So one just goes and stands in front of the well, and sees answers to confusions?"

"No, no- one has to give first to get." The gentleman spoke, now a bit more animated.

"Give to get?"

"Yeah, like the tradition of wishing wells- give first to get something back from the Universe. The cosmic exchange..."

Throwing a dime to get answers? Seemed a little primitive...

He reached inside his pocket, only to realise that dimes didn't exist in this world! As he fumbled, the gentleman looked genuinely confused, prompting his partner to speak.

"Seems you really are new here. You don't have to 'give' anything material. But continuing the wishing well tradition, one has to give up a certain vice, a prejudice, a negative trait. Depending upon the sincerity of your 'sacrifice', the well absorbs your negative energy, and blesses you with the answers you seek." She smiled, running her hand through her hair.

Make a sacrifice, but not of an object, rather energy... negative energy! Taking the concept of sacrifice to its highest level...exactly what I would have expected from such a place...

Dave thanked the couple, and proceeded to the well, which was not too far away. He simply followed the others who were walking towards it, and in about half hour, was at the spot.

At first glance, it seemed like any other normal well- nothing ceremonial about it. But then, he saw the sparkling clear waters, in the backdrop of the glistening mountains, and it appeared magical...

Holy water, Dave smiled, remembering his observations in Sikkim. Humans had carried this tradition here too...

For a while, he stood there, like others around him, staring inside; and seeing nothing but his reflection in the backdrop of the sky. He then closed his eyes, and allowed his thoughts to settle on his flaws, maybe even vices- anger, occasional skepticism, a certain bitterness towards those who didn't stand by him in his hour of crisis... qualities he wasn't exactly proud of, but traits he hadn't consciously attempted to rid himself of...

Standing here, a smile crossed his lips as he resolved to let go...commit from deep within to give up these traits to the sacred waters- a 'sacrifice' which was bound to cleanse him further, relieve him from the residual baggage of the past...

After a few moments of deep promise, he opened his eyes and felt a certain freshness, as the water seemed to sparkle more. Soon, the reflections dissolved, and the water surface became like a screen, much like the clairvoyance chamber... but this time, his eyes were open- both the inner & outer...*Will I finally see the Messenger now? And why did I come this far...*

In response, a familiar image manifest: the Crop Circle pattern. The CC he saw earlier had another significance- it pointed to the image which by now had become some kind of a guide post:

Trinity within trinity within trinity; he who truly seeks, finds...
The central and the peripheral, governed by the one that binds...
Three connected by the union of four...
The outer, the three new and the core...

I thought I had deciphered it already, so why now? Something else...something more... yet another layer...?

*OK, have figured out the trinity of worlds, civilizations & friends. Have figured out the Council & the Quartet...*been there, seen that, learnt that...

Also figured out that the inner circle stands for the moon, the outer circle for the solar system, and the middle circle for the earth...

So just what's left? Hmn...

Trinity within trinity within trinity...?

The central and the peripheral, governed by the one that binds...?

He then played out a mental picture of his entire journey here, over the months... and things fell into place...

He first came here through an energy transcendence- tentative, unsure, confused, even skeptical. Then he saw this world, how they lived,' worked', commuted, evolved, and became comfortable, more open, feeling more & more at home.

Then, just as he felt he was drifting, a clue guided him to the Council, *the institution which nurtures the original mother.* After understanding more about the clues & his journey, he learnt the fundamentals of the energy exchange model, a new economic model. And then, yet another clue led him to the Quartet, *the heart where it all made a start...*

Here, he learnt about an integrated, holistic approach to living, about Naturalism, and how the IIN coordinated it all...

Was there a certain pattern here? A sequence? A flow? The central and the peripheral, governed by the one that binds?

That's it! His journey covered the entire expanse of the peripheral, the core and the one that binds...

The peripheral, or the outer world of the New Ages, the central or the Guardian Council, governed by the one that binds- the Quartet, the middle circle...

So the middle circle was the earth at one level, and the Quartet at another...

This corroborated with the voice within, faint at first, but now stronger & louder...urging him...as if he too had a role to play...that something like this was possible back on earth...

Now I get it! The challenge is to replicate these systems, a Quartet like Global governance system back on earth. That is the larger message of this clue and the other clues...

But how? The Messenger?

Immersed in this contemplation, a fleeting image appeared in the clear waters- the same one as in his dreams...

Dave with Plutus, the latter's hands on his shoulders... *Bonding? Obvious...*

Something else?? Missing...

In that moment, golden letters illuminated from within the well... the 6th clue appeared in words:

Seen you have, well have you learnt,
Your rightful place earned...
Steadfast & unswerving in the time to know,
It's time to transition back, it's time to go...
The Messenger is near,
The gateway leads to the one who is far yet dear,
The Master is about to make the transition,
See the truth about the vision...

Time to go! A certain excitement, a raw thrill engulfed him, giving him just the answer he needed, as always! Not only did it indicate that it was time to go back, but the fact that the messenger *was near*...

But what did it imply about '*meeting the one who is far yet dear*'? Who could it be, from where his gateway to home would emerge?

Ikona? She was dear but not far...
Nor Lyon...
Nor by now deeply admired Master Aleus...
That left only Plutus! The image, the clue also had him... but what about him?

****

He was about to mull over the last two lines, when there was a holographic message from Master Aleus; and along with him Clairvoyant Nobius.

"Hello Master-I was actually hoping to meet you, to express my sincere gratitude for all your help and wisdom at every step- including my stint at the Quartet. And clairvoyant Nobius, a pleasure to meet you again."

"Dave, thought I'd speak with you before I go back. *Make the transition...*" Nobius glanced at him sideways with a certain twinkle in his eyes.

Dave caught at it: '*make the transition*', and the last two lines seemed to stand out:

The Master is about to make the transition,
See the truth before the vision...

But Nobius continued: "I wanted to let you know one more secret- about the flying Lama."

Dave perked up. *The flying Lama? What about him.?*

"You know, *flying Lama have to keep his word...to make transition, to go back and appear to next one with pure heart...*"

"No way!" Dave was left gaping. "*Can't be...*"

"Yes way!" Nobius smiled. He waved his arms slightly, twirled several times at great speed, and behold- there stood the same monk Dave had seen at Rumtek monastery, clad in the same white robes! And without any footwear...

"But *you..*?" Dave questioned, still incredulous. *"I mean, you are a master here. How can you? The monk at Rumtek? The flying Lama? All the same entity?? You??"*

Nobius, clad in white, nodded smilingly.

"But how? the flying Lama disappeared almost 300 years back!" Dave said, trying to tie it all together. *Each time he thought he had seen it all, a new surprise was always waiting...*

"*Relative time.* At least now you should understand it! And *reincarnation simply changes the body, not the soul.* As for disappearing, even you have 'vanished' back in your plane." He smiled. "Simply transitions from one plane to another..."

"So *you were* the Lama who came to me- the reincarnation of the flying Lama? He who 'appears to the one with a pure heart'..." Dave choked. *'The one with pure heart...'*

"Yes. Just played my part in your soul journey."

"By handing over the player to assist me with the transition? My gratitude, Master..."

Nobius raised his right hand to bless Dave.

"But you, in that monastery?" Dave was still mumbling. "Dressed so differently, almost incongruously, and walking barefoot. Why, clairvoyant?"

"So many questions, my God!" Nobius smiled, simply raising his hands again in response. Dave could feel the energies flow, even through the holographic projection. Distance energy transmission...

"Thank you Masters, yet again. And I just hope I can do justice to this journey. Facilitated by so many..."

"You will, Dave! You are close..." Master Aleus smiled. "R*emember the final cycle...*" and with that, both waved him goodbye, their images gradually easing from view.

Nobius Shengdon of the New ages is the flying Lama of a remote monastery in Sikkim...man of science and religion in equal parts...appearing to the one with a pure heart...amazing!!

Indeed, Dave smiled...there exists something beyond the known, and something more beyond the knowable...

Remember the final cycle...??

"I just felt I needed to come back, to meet you." Plutus said.

"Even I felt a strong urge to see you. And then I got the clue, the vision suggesting that I meet you. Something within says that my time here is nearly over…" Dave said, looking out into the distance..

"I see. So you feel your mission has been accomplished?"

"Don't know for sure. I still am not absolutely certain as to *why me*? And despite my eyes & heart both being open, I still haven't been able to find the Messenger."

"Have you discussed with the others?"

"No. came here directly- will meet them after this; in fact, let's all catch up tonight. So much to share…"

"Though I happened to chat with some other *unexpected* visitors on the way." he added as an afterthought.

"Unexpected?"

"Master Aleus & Nobius- surprises never cease to occur!"

"Surprise?"

"Yeah, Nobius is the Master who guided me at the Monastery back on earth. Reincarnation of the Flying Lama! A 300 year old legend, its answers lie in the future, on the moon?"

"Amazing! One more twist in your surreal journey…"

"Yeah. Anyways, tell me how was your mission?"

"Strange. And I really wanted to share this with you guys. There *is* something weird happening on Einstein, something I was not able to pinpoint. This experiment apparently has far reaching consequences, and I have seen some bit of it myself. However, there is something about this group that made me uncomfortable. And they reciprocated in equal measure, always guarded while I was around…as if they had an inkling of my real motives…as if they were trying to conceal the real thing, and reveal a façade. Not to mention their mysterious leader, whom I heard referred to only in ambiguous, even duplicitous tones… as the *Apex*..."

"Did you report this to the Council?"

"No. thought I'd consult with you guys before I'd do that. And then I just got this feeling that I should be there with you, *right now*, as if, there was something I had to tell you, and you had to share with me…"

Dave nodded, empathizing.

"So, tell me buddy- you disappointed that your quest seems incomplete? That the Messenger is yet not found..."

"Well, frankly somewhat; but there are so many things that I saw clearly, and got a new perspective about, both within & outside. I saw a whole new reality, and am excited to share it back in my world."

"I see."

"You know buddy, frankly, I feel it doesn't matter anymore that I didn't find the Messenger. I found something more precious- the message!" He added as an afterthought.

Plutus smiled. *"Yes, when we live the message within us, the Messenger is found..."*

The moment he said these words, Dave suddenly started staring intently at him. "What did you just say?!"

"About what?"

"About the message & messenger..." Dave had a strange look in his eyes. His gaze still fixated on Plutus, he asked: "And hey, what's that?"

"What's *what?*" Plutus sounded puzzled.

"That thing you are..." but before he could complete, he was compelled to instinctively cover his eyes, the brightness of a thousand suns blinding him...

And in that moment, the inner eyes saw a different radiance. Objects around him began to blur, and *the words flowed from all around- the clouds, the fields, the trees- all converging in the sky, etching a panoramic poetry against a celestial backdrop...*

The final clue...

Searched near and searched far,
All along when right here shone the star,
Buried deep inside,
The messenger no longer behind the veil doth hide...
Always your journey, always your mission,
Your wisdom shall herald the NEW era's rising sun,
The prophecy seems clear,
The apocalypse is here,
The gateway shifts, the earth drifts,
The messenger now understands the true nature of the gifts...

And realization dawned! In this moment of clarity, Dave found the messenger- himself!! And he remembered the prophecy, as it too rendered on the blue canvas…somewhere up there…

'A soul there shall be, a leap in consciousness who will make,
by transcending in the NEW AGES, to higher knowledge shall be awake,
with knowledge, his higher self shall he align,
and experience his DHARMA, or his purpose divine…
in dharma, the Messenger of the NEW AGES he shall seek to find,
whose wisdom would be the key when the world has lost its mind,
in this dark night, he shall create alchemy,
guiding the world to its emerging destiny!
But when all is at stake,
the right choices he will have to make,
in the soul's dark night,
the Messenger's wise choice will lead to the light…
Divine blessings shall then rain, as the world stands to gain,
healed and guided in the new ages, without the pain,
balanced would be the karmic equation,
then it would all be One- the ONE…'

It was crystal clear now- there was no Messenger to be found outside! From the beginning, it was all a quest to find his deeper self, the MESSENGER WITHIN!

The Messenger, whose wisdom would be key to the earth's emerging destiny…

****

Now the truth lay bare before Dave! It all started as a series of clues to lift his energies, to make him crossover to the plane of higher understanding & wisdom…and not accidentally, but guiding to cross over on a special day…

The 24th cycle after the Lama's mysterious disappearance, rather elevation…the day of a special celestial configuration…

And importantly, at the turn of the millennium- Dec 21, 2000… a leap symbolizing mankind's impending rise in consciousness…

Once here, he, all along in the quest for some Messenger, was absorbing the message, bit by bit, new learning by new learning... *awakening the MESSENGER within...*

He learnt about various aspects of human life, of how civilization had evolved through the millennia, and where it could evolve to...*and how to bridge that gap...*

THAT WAS THE ROLE OF THE MESSENGER! Prometheus was to take back the fire of heavens on to the earth, leading to the next big leap in human consciousness...

Now that the message of the NEW AGES was grasped, from the union of technology & spirit to the creation of a nation free, religion free, money free, spiritual society based on energy elevation, *it was time for the messenger to share the message!! And at a crucial time in history....*

In this dark night, he shall create alchemy,
Guiding the world to its emerging destiny!

But this alchemy was not accidental, nor random. As he absorbed the significance of the entire chain of events, the full picture struck him with a sledgehammer force! *Despite having come such a long way, the final picture was truly momentous, even overwhelming, his firm bearings not withstanding...*

21st Dec, 2000- *the day of a special celestial configuration, facilitating his leap into a higher world- the 24th cycle...*

24- *a significant number in its own right; the hours in a day...completion of the cycle of night & day... time for a new dawn...*

Which meant...the 25th cycle, the special day was on...

... 21st Dec, 2012...

The day of supposed apocalypse! The end of the Mayan calendar... the impending doomsday...

The end of the world, as we know it!

Dave's head spun at the potential implications of this. There was much hype, speculation, even misinformation around this date, that no one really grasped its significance. Like the UFO theories, everyone from writers to bloggers to Hollywood studios to conspiracy theorists were out to milk this phenomenon...

Yet another of mankind's preoccupations, even obsessions with the unknown...but not the unknowable...

For Dave, this enlarged the canvas. The significance of the cycle, the dates in his journey was unmistakable- his mind went back to the image he saw in the archives during the initial part of his journey...

Scene 2 beginning with a play of numbers in some random arrangement- 0,1, 2...

It was now clear that they represented the special dates, along with their numeric significance, apart from other things:

The journey began with: 12 21 2000...

And the apocalypse, the end at: **12 21 2012***...*

What's at the beginning comes back at the end, in the completion of a cycle...the last two numbers (00) being replaced by the first two (12)!

But the question was: What did the Messenger's alchemy, related to the earth's destiny, have to do with these mysterious numbers & dates...??

****

"Listen buddy, I need to tell you this." Dave spoke, equally excited & overwhelmed, while still trying to shield his eyes from the brightness. "Now I know why *I* came here, why *I* saw all of this, why *I* stayed here. *I have found the answer to 'WHY ME? It is so profound, I just can't fully accept it!"*

"Wow." a wave of excitement crossed Plutus. "Tell me."

"Because there was no other Messenger all along! *It was me! It wasn't merely my journey, it was about me!* To find myself! And in this quest, to guide the world, to share the wisdom & vision of the new ages...to guide it through *its transition,* through the *apocalypse!*" With the excitement, there was a certain trepidation in his voice at the mention of this...

"This is amazing! Simply astounding! See, I told you from the very beginning that *you were special*!. We now know what an evolved fellowship we were a part of!" Plutus smiled, warmth & pride in equal measure.

"Now it all ties in, even the timing. Nothing was accidental, rather all part of a larger design...

21st *Dec, 2000- the 24th special celestial cycle;*

21st *Dec,2012- the final cycle, tying in with the predicted apocalypse...*

My journey is about the apocalypse, about helping the world navigate through it... *possibly preventing it...*"

"Preventing it? More like *facilitating* it..." Plutus excitedly shot back, a distinct fluidity, a twinkle, in his eyes, having understood the larger picture himself.

Dave raised his eyebrows. "Am I missing something? Why should a messenger facilitate the impending destruction, not *prevent* it? I mean, isn't that what Noah's Ark was all about? And look at it in context- ancient predictions, my images of annihilation...*doesn't it all tie in?*

"No. You're missing the point here buddy. The legend of Noah's Ark was not so much about impending destruction as about mankind's preparation for it... not so much about the fury of God as about his compassion, about divine guidance...

As for Armageddon, just junk all the hype, theories, and blind paranoia surrounding it- there is no meteor which will hit the earth, no flooding which will devour cities, no change in the earth's crust- all that is just fantasy stuff! There have been enough & more doomsday predictions from charlatans & misguided elements of all hues; this is one more of them..."

"Are you suggesting it's all a sham? But what about the pattern of dates in my journey? Certainly doesn't seem phony."

"Of course it's not phony; The legend of the Mayan calendar is not fake, nor is the term apocalypse. And yes, there is a potential cosmic significance of that period, when the sun would supposedly be in the direct centre of the galaxy... does this explain the strange cosmic phenomenon at the monastery?"

Dave nodded, more 'light' being shed on the secret of the shadows...

"However, do discriminate fact from fiction. Do you know what the *exact word- apocalypse,* means? It comes from the Greek term *Apokalypsis, or literally, lifting of the veil...revelation...that's what the Mayan calendar, and other ancient symbols, point to..."*

Dave seemed surprised at this factual explanation- like so many other myths & elements of our culture, the truth about the apocalypse was corrupted with time, to generate either hype or paranoia, suiting vested interests, of course...

Plutus continued. "Apocalypse does refer to destruction, but metaphorically, in the sense of potential dispensing of darkness…the arrival of a new dawn…

See the whole thing in perspective, Dave: 21st Dec, 2000- the 24th celestial cycle, and a single individual, albeit chosen, makes the leap, guided by higher forces.

Come Dec 2012, and the potential lifting of the veil means that entire humanity, and not just a single human, is poised to make the leap; *can* make the leap into a new age! You saw the play with the numbers in these special dates, now understand their significance:

12 21 2000- a single individual's leap; the beginning…

12 21 2012: the potential end of darkness for humanity, if the beginning is replicated at the end!

And the beginning is your journey towards the light…don't you see it? The one who has seen this, been there, the *Messenger of the New Ages, can act a catalyst in the impending morphing of evolutionary energies of entire humankind…"*

Dave nodded slowly, soaking it all in…a *supposedly normal, middle aged Multinational Corporation executive at the cusp of a the world's emerging destiny… related not only to the prophecy of the New ages, but also one of the most enduring legends of earth…and also its most misunderstood…*

"Of course, like your leap, the choice, the freewill for its leap rests with humanity itself. Bear in mind, Dave, that there is no apocalypse which is divinely ordained- special days are there, special circumstances may arise- but the direction, the outcome of each landmark event in human history is the result of human freewill itself…

All it needs to make the best of these special events is to change your perspective from fear to love, since everything in your plane is afflicted by the same malaise…

From technology to legends, replace fear by faith & love…"

****

"I sense something else too." Dave said after a while, still squinting his eyes. *"Something about you…about us…about our fellowship…"*

He could feel becoming lighter, as the energy began to rise up his spine, generating heat…and the light was becoming brighter, as the surrounding began to blur…

He was beginning to feel in two places at once…

"What? I don't follow you." Plutus could see Dave flicker in & out of focus. "C'mon, tell me quick. I think you are going…"

"About the prophecy…something else…I think we are…"

Whoosh!

Dave was gone before he could complete the sentence! The energies had suddenly risen, and before he realized it, the gateway opened, and Dave was back on earth…

Back in 2000! *The beginning of the millennium…*
The gateway is shifting, the earth drifting!

For a while, Dave was stunned, just like the first time he woke up on the moon. A 'moment' back, he was in a different plane, with Plutus; and now, here he was, across planes and time; back in a place which was home, yet felt strange…

He looked around, and recognized the surroundings- the same forest, the same pagoda, the same prayer wheel. He was back near the monastery of the 'flying Lama'…

Back on earth, at the beginning of the 21st century…at the cusp of a momentous journey for the planet, for humanity…

The flying Lama, he smiled, reminiscing the words of Clairvoyant Nobius; *such a momentous journey it had been, to heaven & back…*

However, this time he didn't black out like the past. His awareness had grown, to observe life & death, heaven & earth, the journey across planes, as an alert observer. Despite the initial feeling of disorientation, he was smiling, glowing from within, with wisdom and love…his aura was expanded …

The gift- the disk...this life altering journey, and all its wisdom...he had learnt so much, evolved so much...

Yet, in so many ways it seemed like a dream; a dream originating in a dream...a dream that had almost become his reality, so much so that he was used to that place... plane...

The PATs, communes, energy exchange, the Council, the Quartet chambers, the IIN...

Then he reflected upon his rather abrupt transition, and certain things that seemed incomplete. The first thought crossing his mind was that of the trinity- of how it all began, and what was that *X factor* that so closely bonded them...he had no logical answers, except probably some higher connection...

He closed his eyes, reliving the last few moments- the brightness, the ultimate answer...but why with Plutus? Why did the final clue guide him there? To someone who turned out to be more than just a special friend- *a soul partner in some way*... someone whose destiny was closely intertwined with his own...

He was on the verge of sensing something crucial, when the gateway literally 'pulled' him back...obviously there was synchro-destiny at work here...

We all know what we need to know...someday the secret would reveal itself...

Then he thought of Ikona, about his feelings for her, and how it had grown. Without having consciously realized it then, after a long time, he felt true love- something which lay dormant, suppressed after Shakti's departure...

But in the New ages, these feelings were stirred up again, as he saw images of his lost love in Ikona; a love he couldn't fully comprehend or communicate, a beauty he couldn't completely savor, but which had silently lingered inside, tugging at his soul, pulling at his heartstrings, in a soft, quiet way...

When and how these feelings emerged, he didn't realize...

But it didn't matter- it was love, and it needed to be 'felt', not analysed...

Then he thought about all those instances when he looked at her strangely, without realizing it...or when she touched him...

But each time he felt that love could be expressed, strange blocks, apparent 'issues', came in the way- *different planes, different worlds, 'conflicting' emotions...*

There were scores of reasons why this didn't make sense, but only one why it did: *love! A feeling that transcended space, time and all barriers...*

Love, without any expectations or restrictions, without anything to seek, and all to give!

He now felt disappointed at having teleported back without being able to express it, wondering whether she at all sensed his feelings. But grieve not, for love would find its expression sometime, somewhere...the poetry would flow, the music of the universe, the melody of all planes, would be heard...

Someday, somehow, she would sense it fully...

Finding his bearings amidst this inner tingling, he smiled at the thought of the irrepressible Lyon. A cyborg, a vague 'character', a pompous showman sometimes bordering on the bizarre, whose blunt & conceited ways could get exasperating, even annoying at times; yet, whose warmth, loyalty & steadfastness were never in doubt...

An amalgamation of human traits & the synthetic enhancements...in a way, a true mascot of this fascinating, yet apparently unreal Shangri-la...

Dave's eyes turned moist at the thought of leaving the 'trinity' behind, that too without as much as a farewell message; the 'trinity of friends', the 'trinity of the gift', which became their 'Quartet'...

The trinity of worlds, civilizations & friends...
A new order emerges while the old one ends...
When the trinity morphs into the quartet,
A new fellowship shall be set...

This fellowship would always have a special place in his heart...

****

As he mentally surveyed the landscape of his experiences in the higher plane, he realized that apart from wisdom, what he carried along were the relationships, the memories of the myriad souls whom he encountered along this fabulous journey:

The Quartions, at the helm of an institution which served as a benchmark for our administrative structure- Mirdad the adventurer, for whom his karma represented the greatest adventure; Che the erudite; Atisha the dude, a seventy year 'young' teen, the dream geek; and General Junah, the healer, who made him understand the nature of conflict in a such an enlightened way that it could serve as a beacon to our planet...

Special personalities, each of whom shared such fantastic perspectives, and each of whom epitomized the 'coexistence of opposites' in such a distinct way...*the seamless unity of all*...

Not to forget the one slimy character in this amazing band- Dasham, the clone...something about him didn't give Dave a very comforting vibe....

In this journey of wisdom & exploration, how could he miss out the Masters, the special souls who were like his guardian angels since the beginning...

Aleus Ben Taleb, with whom he interacted only briefly, yet who seemed to distinctly be his soul guide; Atlas the dude- the hulk who became a rock star, the pirate who became the master; Zeut, the X-ray eyes, who familiarized him with the new metrics, a model for a new economic landscape; Lady Zenia, the endower, who rekindled in him the power, the grace, and the lost meaning of feminine energies; and finally lady Sinetha, the *'ace of race'*, an epitome of graceful ageing;

Not to forget, of course, Clairvoyant Nobius Shengdon, or the 'flying Lama'! The one who originally guided him across the Himalayan heights to celestial heights...

As for *the Grand Master, the highest, of pure spirit,* Dave's only memory was the 'energy candles' and the medium through which 'it' communicated from the plane of pure spirit...

But there was something about 'it' too...he could just feel a connection...

With the faces & places reminisced with purity of heart, his attention came back to his teleportation- now he understood that all he saw was not merely for personal experience, but for sharing with his fellow travelers, though a faint smile crossed his lips at the thought of sharing these learnings. If he ever told someone about all these experiences, they would think he had turned delirious...or worse still, brand him a charlatan!

Nonetheless, he had a story to tell, a message to convey... that was the mission, the dharma of the Messenger, in the light of the impending apocalypse...the lifting of the veil...

The time for a new wisdom...

A New Age...

****

As he reached the monastery, he saw a monk and asked for some water. Although aware this time, the intense energy had left him parched. While sipping it, he asked the monk the exact date- he had been in the NEW AGES for a quite a while, close to six months, he felt (*though time, as back on earth, had lost its meaning to him*), so it would help to know just how much time had elapsed...

However, his eyes fell on his Swiss made watch, and he noticed that it started to work again. He smiled, as he looked at the date: ***12 pm, 28th Dec, 2000-*** just about a week on earth!

Relative time, he smiled at Master Nobius' last words, now understanding the true significance of Einstein's work...

It was no longer about the twin paradox...he was the living paradox!

As he blinked at the date panel again, he realized that he still had four days left from his vacation, and lifetime of opportunity. While he would have most certainly been reported missing by the tour folks to the local authorities, to his office & his world, he was still on leave!

As for the authorities, he happened to accidentally stray into the forest, into an 'unknown location', lost his way, and by the time he found his way back, he was already reported missing... But not before experiencing the richness of a different kind of unknown land...opened out only to him...

As for his world, come 2nd Jan, and he would plunge right back...

But this time, in a new millennium...with a new mission...onto a new journey...

24. THE DHARMA OF KARMA

A ten thousand mile journey starts with a single step...every monument is built brick by brick...

While heaven was beautiful, utopic, Dave realized that his dharma lay right here, on earth. True, this plane had frailties, but these very organic frailties made it worth being in. The Buddhas, the meditators, the seekers, the messengers were needed right here, when our world was at the cusp of an evolved society, nearing the threshold of a critical mass of evolved individuals in the 21st century... on the verge of *apocalypse*.....
Apo kalypsis...
As much as skeptics seemed cynical about how the world was only degenerating, there was never a time in history when so many individuals saw their lives as spiritual journeys & sought a higher meaning...
Of course, all was not rosy, and there were newer problems cropping up every days, some of a magnitude an entire generation had hitherto not seen. But equally true was the fact for every act of blatant greed, there was a progressive realization about the need to protect the environment; for every suggestion of conflict, there were millions rising in unison, in protest, across boundaries; for every attempted act of control by the big brother, there was the unprecedented power of communication, empowering individuals like never before, tilting the balance of power in a very fundamental way- away from governments, corporations, institutions, to individuals...

Never before in the modern world did such a large mass of people care for the world, for our future; never before did the common man have such a voice, a voice which resonated in the corridors of power, and never before were so many world leaders compelled to put aside their petty differences for collective wellbeing. Time was just ripe to have a fundamental relook at the systems, ideologies & structures which had served well for centuries, but had lost relevance in a new world...

For one, it was time to structurally question the old economic model, driven by metrics like money, and not merely revamp it. The world had an abundance of creative energies & emerging technologies, but they needed to be deployed for human welfare & uplift, not narrowly slotted into a rudimentary for-profit motive; the currency & consumption led model had outlived its utility- it called for a new metric, a new awareness, to channelize latent creativity into a future that humans were increasingly seeking for the future generations...based on harmony between human pursuits & nature...

Western society and the developed world had undergone over half a century of spiritual renaissance, through material abundance, the rebellion of Woodstock & personal questions. Now it was nearly at tipping point...*a critical mass of evolutionary energies...almost there...*

All it needed was the final keystone...the final key...

This final key, this missing link was a firm conviction that such a society was possible, and sustainable. And what better conviction than someone who had actually seen and lived in such a society...and who could spread the message back...The Messenger!

Dave also finally understood why this journey was filled with clues and metaphors- the inner voyage, the synchronistic journey was more about intuition than logic- it had to be poetic, enigmatic, uplifting, to be savored bite by bite...

However, he also realized that this magnificent unfolding of the cosmic plot was as testing as thrilling- he saw now how every clue not only guided onwards, but also put through extreme test both his resolve & faith, finally culminating like the blooming of a flower- the fragrance was destined to occur, to be spread, but only at the right time, when it had completed the journey from seed to bud...

****

So Dave went about spreading his own fragrance, creating his own heaven, following his heart's voice, his synchronicity...

By now, he had realized the worth of true relationships, and spent far more quality time with true friends & family than in blind career pursuits, determined to have no more regrets in life, no more losses that life's routines could thrust upon him. By conscious energies & love, he would defeat entropy in relationships… and live in balance!

He started his mission in his office, his original playground, building *upon his earlier idiosyncrasies to strengthen the new culture, a culture built upon human energies, innovation, R&D and balance.* He continued fortifying his New Age management 'pilots', till his elevation as Regional President allowed him to institutionalized them from pilots to policies, across all divisions & functions. He also encouraged cross functional flexible process teams, having seen that they work!

Structure was replaced by flexibility and a focus on human enterprise, as scores of 'process oriented' teams guided the metamorphosis of a cola company into a *'holistic, organic foods'* company- working closely with local communities to harness organic farming, water recycling and green technologies, thereby winning the goodwill of the community.

In five years, Dave's region became not only the most profitable, but consistently had the highest employee & customer satisfaction scores, appearing twice in Fortune as the model for transformation- from an old world, smokestack corporation to an eco friendly, community responsive organization, working on sustainable development! And understanding changing human preferences for health foods to build a new, profitable product line…

After twelve years of ever more radical transformations, he took the next step *in 2012- the year of the catalyst, the trigger, if we reach out to our higher self, our centre…*

He quit his job to start a small hi-tech company, engaged in space research, with some scientist friends. His colleagues dissuaded him, top management tried to reason with him that he was losing a potential shot at the top job, and some friends tried to counsel him- that forty five was not the age to start a new venture, that too into something totally unrelated; rather, it was the time to savor the fruits of one's achievements.

'You have sold sugared water all your life, you can't suddenly start sending payloads into space...'

But none of these mattered- neither the counseling nor the temptations. He duly started his 'space venture', with the brand tag line being his favourite: *'Space, the final frontier....'*

Excited, passionate & cutting edge, his team did path breaking developments in propulsion and communications technology. In a decade, it became a leading player in its field, a multimillion dollar venture, boasting of some of the brightest minds in the field of space navigation & materials technology...

But Dave was not done yet; he took his company public and became a millionaire many times over...

And just when it seemed that he had peaked, he moved out of active management, yet again, passing on the baton to a younger crop. Taking on the Chairman Emeritus position, he gave up half his stockholding to the brilliant scientists of his company, and with the other half, set up a *'Global leadership foundation'*- a forum dedicated to exploring & developing human potential in all its forms, from all fields...

With this started another critical & exciting phase of his life- a mission to share with a broader audience all that he had seen & lived on the higher plane, in *'heaven'*...*the message of the New Ages*...

Dave started working on a book based upon his learnings & observations. After eight years, it was finally complete, and he aptly titled it 'UTOPIA'. Written as much from the heart as the head, it spoke about how *'this could be heaven for everyone',* touching upon various concepts that he had seen & lived back then, whether about money, allocation of resources, the role of feminine & creative energies, nation states, religion, the synergy between science & spirit et al...

Radical, provoking, touching, this book represented the work of the new age revolutionary, an iconoclast, whose radical, at times even rebellious views, resonated across every section of society & geography...

And this time there was no skepticism, no doubts; there was only experiential wisdom-.the reality based on a personal journey, a personal adventure...

The book touched a deep chord with its readers from day 1, going on to become a no.1 hit and spending over two years on the bestsellers list in just about 6 months!

Over time, 28 million copies were sold across 80 countries, and each reader felt touched in her own unique way...

For some, it was a new vision, a vision which was both liberating & exhilarating, while for others, it reinforced their faith that we could collectively change our destiny...

Of course, there were critics & skeptics too. They said it was too romantic, too simplistic, too impractical, too devoid from reality, too idealistic...that utopia could never happen, that humans could never collectively evolve...that wars could never be prevented, money could never be eliminated...that idealism was dangerous in a society where the harsh realities had to be faced to overcome them...that the author had other motives...

But none of it mattered- neither to Dave, nor to the millions who dreamt, believed & acted...

Skeptics doubted, but Dave and his fellowship lived the dream, realizing that a handful of dreamers were far more powerful than an army of critics & skeptics...

To skeptics, his words were unreal, but to readers they were truthful, inspiring, uplifting, sheer poetry...

Truthful, because he wrote not to sell, but to tell...he shared because he cared...

To critics, his book was devoid of facts- they just knew it. War, poverty, inequity, human frailties, these were all undeniable, inescapable facts of human life!

But so did the believers- they knew it too...

That a millennium back, empires governing humans was a fact! That half a millennium ago, the earth was flat, not round; that it was the centre of the universe, with the sun revolving around it! That a century back, slavery was a reality! And that couple of centuries back, matter was solid, & discrete from energy...that was a fact too! As also that time was absolute!

These were all facts- but of the past; the dreamers and their collective vision, however, saw facts of the future...

A future we were completely empowered to create...

As Dave kept nurturing the seeds of divinity within, while spreading the message through his words, volunteers poured in bit by bit, as stories of individual & collective transformation, grace & glory, came in from thousands of readers...

In the meanwhile, the Leadership Foundation went from strength to strength. Leveraging the power of the internet, virtual groups were formed in various parts of the world, each dedicated to finding solutions in their lives, their families, their communities, their neighborhoods...

All with the mission of preparing for, & ushering in the NEW AGES...

Ordinary folk joined in with opinion makers, & what started as a trickle soon became a global movement...*A GLOBAL NEW AGES MOVEMENT!*

As this movement grew, belief, hope and faith started reappearing in people's lives again. Individual transformation sowed the seeds for a larger transformation, and global prayer groups were formed, to supplement transformational actions. People were getting reconnected with their dharma, and more importantly, following it...

Years passed, Dave wrote more books on new age transformation, and millions more believed in the message. He travelled extensively, working with NGOs and institutions engaged in promoting democracy & open societies, and became a leading voice for nuclear disarmament in civil society...

But he wasn't done just yet...

At a ripe young age of seventy, he turned a new leaf, living an old dream. He set up a rock band, his dedication to the memory of Master Atlas...

Aptly named the *New Age warriors*, his fellow band members, his partners in crime, were three young mentees: A 19 year old bassist, a 22 year old keyboardist, and a 24 year drummer; while the pony tailed Dave was the '*outstanding*' character- the lead strummer and lyricist at all of seventy...

Outstanding he may have been, but out of place, not at all...

Together, this motley group compiled powerful music- the psychedelic tinge of Floyd, the anger of Guns n Roses, the dream of U2, the hope of John Lennon & the panache of Hendrix & the Who...yet another expression of his message, of spreading the message of the new ages, as young audience flocked to their concerts:

'You screwed it all up, now time to make amends,
Wake up, 'cause annihilation is just around the bend...
Sucked so far, a helping hand now ought to lend,
For the children of tomorrow, or in smoke comes their end...
 One world, one life,
So much anguish, so much strife,
Petulant & petty, stop your gripe,
When instead a tear you can wipe...
 On the horizon, a dark, gray cloud,
We shout aloud, but of your narcissism you feel proud,
Alone we stand in this ambling crowd,
But this we know, soon off will come the shroud...
 Lets rock to the beat,
Let's turn on the heat,
Lets tear down the walls of mean street,
Let our destinies meet...
 To those who have lost sight,
Now's the time to set things right,
Without any conflict or fight,
 By display of love, not of might,
They call us radical, they label us freak,
But we haven't a mean streak,
Lets them malign, we shall align,
Their pursuits petty, our purpose divine,
So let's shine...
 Let's rock to the beat,
Let's turn on the heat,
'Cause there's a force at play,
Impacting in the most unexpected way,
The night is about to end, breaking of a new day,
Let's all rock to the beat, let's all collectively pray...

 Hey, hey, wake up, hey hey...
It's time to play, 'tis time to pray...

There was a raw pulsating energy in these concerts, as the grand finale would be the high pitched crescendo, accompanied by smashing of the guitars & drums, in classic rock style.

"This is the *@##**@ establishment you gonna smash when you go back, aint you?"

And the fifty thousand strong crowd would raise their hands in unison, in the typical three fingered peace symbol, synonymous with the spirit of woodstock, and scream a loud affirmation…

"Yess!! This is the roar which will shake the establishments at their very core. God bless, and keep the $%@# faith!! Love you, guys. Keep shining…"

Just like the book, Dave's albums too became bestsellers, bolstering the message of a new age, albeit in a raw style. The young & the restless hummed these power packed lyrics, the rebel within them coming to the fore, while the mature related to it, keen to make a difference in the latter part of their lives…

****

For 55 years, Dave lived the life of a Messenger, not only visualizing the oncoming age of Aquarius, the *apocalypse,* the higher energies, but also facilitating it, acting as the catalyst, relishing his multiple roles- *new age manager, techno-entrepreneur, guru, activist, writer, thinker, rocker, rebel…*

And a messenger of the NEW AGES, a man on a mission…

Of course, never once was his actual journey, his experience, narrated or shared with anybody, nor did he have any contact with the 'other world' or his friends after that. Those memories were etched deep in his mind, still seeming like a fairy tale at times...

…but then he would occasionally see the 'avant garde' cup, the exotic looking sand clock or a miniature sundial adorning his shelf, or feel the bulge of a little, odd shaped pen drive in his wallet, along with a crumpled, fading sheet of paper with some symbols, and smile reminiscing his epic adventure…across heavens & earth...

Not merely the cinematic adventure of Indiana Jones, but the heroic voyage of Frodo Baggins, the legendary quest of Luke Skywalker…his own version of good vs. evil, except that the evil to be combated was within each of us…

Good was triumphing yet again, but not on the battlefield...it was emerging victorious in our minds & hearts, bit by bit, act by act...

****

At a ripe age of 92, Dave Jones died in peace- happy & healthy, and in the midst of followers & friends; remembering and savoring his experiences in the NEW AGES, with fond memories of the place, the masters, his friends and Ikona. He also reminisced Shakti, in whose world he was about step in. But death scared him not one bit; he had already been to heaven & back, and thus gently he closed his eyes as the last physical breath left him...for a deep sleep...

One journey ends, another about to begin, in the circle of life...the cosmic voyage of the soul...

His followers, too, neither grieved nor mourned- that would have been an affront to his memory, all that he stood for;

He had shared a new dream with millions, and their ultimate tribute to him was to live this message, to spread it even further...

The time was at hand...

A NEW AGE WAS ABOUT TO BEGIN...

Epilogue

The President went to bed with determination & clarity. Tomorrow he had called a press conference, where he would make the announcement of WAR.

The moderates tried till the last moment to dissuade him & the Vice president; in fact, some of them actually presented more encouraging latest facts- that an intense last moment round of negotiations was about to yield a breakthrough, if only the President would wait for another 72 hours....

But he was in no mood to relent- the brotherhood had given its seal of approval, conferring upon him its highest honor. All that remained now was a fulfillment of this sacred duty...

As for the cabinet & the public, an overactive propaganda machinery would raise the requisite crescendo, atleast in the immediate horizon- about the aggressive intentions of the 'enemy', about their having developed a stockpile of special weapons, out to unleash 'mass destruction' upon their people; clearly, the only defense was offense...

This would give him the breathing space to go about his goal. By the time people finally realized it, it would be too late...and frankly, he didn't care after that. His tenure would be over, leaving the clean up to his successor...

However, he would have entered the annals of the brotherhood history as the firm guy, the one who fought the decisive battle...and won...

Tonight he would sleep a contented man.

Tomorrow was the big day...

Next day morning, at the press conference, the mood was sombre- there were the sullen faces of the liberal scribes, while the hawks waited with bated breath. However, there was general consensus about the nature of the announcement- all that remained were the details, the intensity of the offence, the budgets, the specific objectives...

Worldwide, people were anguished. Two billion people sat in front of their television sets or hooked on to the net, hoping against hope, awaiting the crucial announcement. Billions of dollars were about to be sunk into further destruction, when so much could be done, needed to be done.

This was just not fair, just not right! *The global mood was of despair, helplessness, even anger, but their voice just didn't seem to matter...*

****

When the President stepped onto the podium, there was a strange glow on his face, a halo of sorts- the scribes noticed it, the public noticed it. But most of all, the brotherhood noticed it....

This was the glow of a man unveiling his mission, a man finally at peace with himself...

Yes, the President was at peace with himself, *but something had changed...something was dramatically different!!*

"Friends, fellow countrymen, and beloved brothers of our wonderful planet, I am here to make some important announcements, which will hopefully change the course of our history."

The hawks were smiling- they saw the veiled hint when he addressed the '*beloved brothers*'....

Though the Congress had rejected the resolution for War, the President had vetoed it, authorizing the National Security council to sketch out the final war plans. Today was the day...

"Ladies & Gentlemen, the time has come to fight the enemy- not with half measures or pusillanimity, but with determination & clear resolve. That is the only way the enemy can be decisively vanquished. *When the apocalypse is upon us, it's time for definitive action..."*

He was speaking their language...nearly there...

"Ladies & gentlemen, WE SHALL NOT GO TO WAR...."

Stunned silence...shocked faces...
What was that??!! What just happened??!!

"Our great culture has been the harbinger of peace & democracy in the modern world. And in an advanced, civilized world that we have helped build, the fundamental question is: *who, rather what is the real enemy?* Friends, the real enemy is not a nation, a culture, a civilization, not even a misguided ideology; the real enemy is a common foe, afflicting all of us in equal measure, staring at us in the face, mocking as we lose sight of it, getting engulfed in our petty differences.

The real enemy, ladies & gentlemen, is our collective global problem, threatening the very existence of mankind. I am here to fight, and to hopefully vanquish this real enemy..."

Confusion all around...but a glimmer of hope in millions of eyes...

"Fellow citizens, in a modern world, war has no place- neither as a political doctrine, nor as a tool of enforcement. I am glad to announce that the foreign secretary had made silent but significant progress in negotiations, and a diplomatic solution to the crisis seems to be around the corner. Mr. Jackson, may I please call upon you to come here."

Disbelief!

"Mr. Jackson, you have worked tirelessly towards a negotiated settlement, in the face of daunting odds. You deserve my gratitude, as that of all of democracy!"

In the brotherhood cells around the globe, turbulence.. shock... chaos...

"Friends, we have always displayed valour as a race to fight, kill & die for our nation, our religion, our beliefs; but rarely have we shown the courage to usher in peace, to discuss, talk & understand, yet we call ourselves logical & civilized beings..."

"Today, I give a clarion call for World peace, for disarmament, for third world development- all guided by our human instincts of love, not narrow, partisan considerations of ' geo-political interests'. From this very moment, our great nation, a global symbol of democracy, becomes a signatory to the Non Proliferation Treaty.

Over the next decade, we shall phase out a major stockpile of our nuclear & chemical weapons. And I announce a freeze on all further development & testing of all such weapons of mass destruction.

Similarly, I propose a phased reduction in our defence budgets, with a 10 year objective to cut it by as much as 50%. And this shall be unconditional, though I sincerely urge all world leaders to make similar announcements, so as to have a unified global strategy based upon a weapons reduction treaty. I urge each one of you, citizens of this world, to put requisite pressure on your governments to join this treaty.

Look at the problems all around you, and then decide what's of greater importance for your security & wellbeing- more weapons, or more development? Are we forever going to live in paranoia of imaginary, potential foes, or focus on combating the real issues, which I am enlisting below.

If you believe in the latter, then compel your governments to sign these, create online forums & communities, and cast your votes only for those governments which are committed to collective wellbeing, not to destruction in the name of security."

What is happening..? what kind of a joke is this..?

"As for my Government, not only have we shelved plans for this war, but pledge a third of its proposed budget, i.e. $ 100 billion, to be redeployed towards 'OPERATION NEW AGES'-a 10 point, 10 year program, directed at ten of the most critical & pressing global issues, so that in ten years from now, we have laid the foundation of a NEW WORLD. ***We shall call this project - '10 in 10':***

1. ***Afro-Asian poverty eradication***, so that the shame of hunger & poverty becomes a museum item for our children & grandchildren. This shall be achieved through public private partnerships, and by partnering with NGOs & microfinance institutions. Local community development in the most distressed parts of the world would be topmost priority- not merely through grants, but through self employment facilitation, micro finance availability and building robust infrastructure. The developed world's biggest contribution here would be to offer knowledge transfer to the local communities, so that they can leapfrog to the levels of the West.

We shall also work towards creating a mechanism to promote local crafts, and to provide a platform for supply & distribution in a comprehensive, coordinated way, so that these local communities can leverage their inherent cost advantages, and get access to whole new markets.

Along with this, we shall work tirelessly to facilitate democracy & open societies in these places-not through enforcement, but through partnership & facilitation. Once we achieve a certain threshold level of sustenance, and the basic foundations of civil society are set, these societies will witness a sea change; mindless violence will reduce significantly, if not cease completely; geo-political tensions will ease as people focus on building institutions instead of fighting to survive, and key root causes of crime get eliminated...

This will not be easy- it will take time & effort, maybe even a generation. But we are prepared. The world community is prepared. Skeptics will cite past failures to 'warn' us, but let not the past determine the roadmap for the future. That's the crux of human history- remember, we would still be living in darkness had Edison not persisted. So shall we too...to spread the light in the darkest corners of the world. With a clear agenda, why should we not walk, even though the path is strewn with thorns? Our plan would incorporate incentives for peace, pressure on dictators & clans, and weakening of local support for violent movements. This way, societies will change, their focus & energies will change, and thus would politicians & warlords be compelled to adapt to the emerging realities.

2. *Combating global warming & creating a new, green ecosystem*- We will work towards a global consensus for a 50% reduction in emission norms over the next decade, and a parallel increase in green cover from 20% to 40% in the next 25 years.

Friends, we have abused mother earth long enough; but no more. Absolutely no more, if we have to bequeath a healthy world to our children! It's not a matter of choice anymore- it is a battle zone, a war situation; and it's a war worth fighting for every bit, unlike our meaningless conflicts where we pour billions of dollars to kill!

Expect a slew of announcements in the coming days & weeks around various initiatives- from CO_2 emission reduction to aforestation to natural resource exploration to a dedicated fund for promoting green energy sources.

We have to save the rainforests, the tropical forests, the mangroves, and replenish them. So also with our other natural resources, our minerals, our materials, our metals, our mines...I shall personally work towards a global consensus on the norms that shall govern this new ecosystem- *and I expect everybody, be it industry or individuals, to contribute, preferably voluntarily.*

There might be short term pain, but it is precisely this flux that will spawn a whole new breed of entrepreneurs. Those who built our technology in garages & basements would get a new direction, a new motivation, a new goal; their creativity, enterprise & passion would be fired all over again, manifesting itself in green technologies, solutions & systems. I encourage a public-private partnership, but will not tolerate any lobbies or special interest groups who try to distort facts; nor will I buy into this debate of developing vs. developed economies, allowing that as a point for the failure of a global consensus.

Yes, we, the developed world, have screwed it up big time, and we will take the primary lead to set things right; but that does not, in any way, absolve the developing world of its obligations- 2 wrongs don't add up to a right!

So we will lead from the front this time, not simply because we are concerned about mother earth, which we of course are, but also because it is an absolute imperative. However, we expect the developing world to join in, unconditionally- in a crisis of global magnitude, there are no segregations or blocks, only a collective destiny...

As for our conviction in a green ecosystem, we want a new industry to emerge, to propel our economy back to its leadership position, to fundamentally rethink the way we live our lives, govern our societies & manage our systems.

The old smokestack paradigm of produce, use and abuse needs to be replaced by a model of create, innovate & regurgitate; of produce, recycle and reuse...be it in the use of natural resources, or in the design of our buildings & vehicles, or the way we process our materials- *all of these would need to follow a whole new blue print.* And I mean a ground-up model, not incremental enhancement-I am calling for completely disruptive thinking! Because this is what will demolish the old & pave way for a brighter new...

Again, there are challenges here, and the votaries of the old system will give us a 101 arguments on why this is not feasible...

But bright young minds & hearts will show us how this is not only an imperative, but also our next 'growth' engine. And we will support them in all ways, from tax concessions to grants to social recognition.

But we want entrepreneurs who make their moolah by allowing us to use resources more efficiently, rather than producing & shoving their products onto us; the name of the game no longer is blind growth, but efficiency at every step. If the entrepreneurs of yesterday were those who gave us the assembly line, the geniuses of tomorrow will give us the 'recycling line'- design & process whiz kids who will be able to replicate this model across everything that we do.

3. *Advanced R&D towards space travel & materials exploration:* While we would take all steps, and on a war footing, to regenerate our ecology and move to a recycled economy, we have to be mindful that we have left our world depleted. Hence I propose setting up an accelerated space program. While we have our existing space programs in place respectively, this would be an attempt to create a unified global program, and not for military or satellite technology, but with two clear objectives:

- Setting up a full fledged, functional colony on the moon by 2069; In 1969, one man stepped foot on the moon- a giant leap for mankind. Now, to commemorate its centenary, I announce that not one man, but a complete colony set foot on the moon. And not only set foot, but a get a foothold, so that we may eventually build a new home there, a dream we want to achieve by the turn of this century. Yes, we have a multitude of challenges, including those of a different environment, available resources, and a clock ticking by. But we are determined to achieve it against all odds. In the next 50 years, we hope to be able to migrate atleast 5% of the world's population on a new world, and in a century, a quarter of the population.

- To support this goal, I propose setting up a special fund for space materials exploration & mining, so as to reach viable levels in the next 25 years. Again, this would mean funding research & development, introducing tax breaks & incentives to create commercial viability, apart from creating the necessary regulatory framework to make this sustainable & balanced. But we will do it, ladies & gentlemen- we will send men & women on the moon...

4. *Global agricultural development and a food security treaty*: To support a growing population, and an ever increasing middle class, this is one of the most important projects at hand, yet one of the most neglected so far. Resolving this issue addresses the two pressing problems of our times- providing food security to the most vulnerable sections of society, while growing jobs in a sector that employs the maximum people in the developing world. We intend to achieve this by developing & supporting the co-operative & community infrastructure based on resource sharing & optimization, advanced irrigation & crop technologies, and newer technologies like urban farming which have lesser dependence on nature & its vagaries.

At the same time, we want to focus on the distribution chain and substantially reduce, if not eliminate waste, better utilize natural resources, create a microfinance & insurance ecosystem for the poorest of farmers, and developing alternative food sources like aquaculture, marine farming etc. Farm sector reforms will be one of our key priorities, and we will allocate whatever resources are needed.

5. *Global water harvesting & redistribution projects*, so that we can reduce our dependence on monsoons, which have become increasingly erratic, thanks to greenhouse effect. We will conserve, recycle & reuse, while parallely working on projects to discover newer water sources. This also ties in seamlessly with our dual objectives of a greener world, as well as universal food security through agricultural development. We shall also explore river linking and work towards cross boundary water treaties, but without disturbing the ecology in any way.

6. *Accelerating global Development Infrastructure*: Throughout our evolution, especially in the modern world, industry has played a key role in developing talent & building capacity for commerce, consumption & capital. As much as industry has abused our natural world, it has also given us the most cutting edge systems, processes, technologies & management depth. Now is the time to replicate these learnings in the non-industry, non-government sector. But I refuse to call it the NGO sector, since we are talking about an exponential growth in the *development sector*, in building capacity & deploying talent, *so that human capital can be built.*

This would be the next stage of our global growth, where industry will create monetary capital & the development sector would create human capital. But this is simpler said than done. To develop human capital in the development sector means not only deploying funds, but also transferring technology, best practices, management abilities etc, so that the best & brightest see this as a genuine career & personal development opportunity. One can deploy money, but till there is a genuine flight of human talent in this sector, the desired exponential growth cannot be achieved. To this, we propose income tax breaks, special grants & recognition programs for this sector, to facilitate the migration of talent.

7. *Combat global terrorism*, *not by force, but by healing.* We are at the threshold of a new human consciousness, and the old, mechanistic way of looking at problems will just not work any anymore- be it at the individual or the collective level, symptomatic treatment means only a temporary reprieve, at best! We need to look at 'holistic healing' & 'root cause analysis' to cure the problem fundamentally; and that means patience, the ability to listen, the strength to accept other points of view, and to be creative in dispute resolution.

It also means moral leadership rather than military might, and the courage to accept one's own mistakes. *Only when we listen, accept & empathize can we create the right atmosphere for others to listen to us, leading to a deeper problem solving.*

Yes, it's not that simple; yes, there will be warped individuals & ideologies who would continue to believe in violence, and yes, there would be major obstacles. But we have to persevere, if we need lasting, not cosmetic, superficial solutions. And yes, all of this needs global consensus, not unilateral jingoism. Therefore I propose setting up a global steering committee, representing all nations & voices, including those of supposed *rogue elements*, so that an honest global dialogue is at least attempted.
I am certain in my conviction that even rogues have a story to tell, a reason to share, and the ability to listen to reason, if a fair dialogue is attempted. Lets reach out & give this a genuine chance!

8. *Population control*, through a conscious reduction in future human birth rates. This is not merely from the point of view of providing adequate resources, but more importantly, from the higher perspective of understanding of the law of dharma- that each life is precious, full of latent creativity, and needs to be nurtured to realize & fulfill its dharma.

With this awareness, we view each human life as a divine process, not merely a biological entity. This perspective would lead to a generation of evolved beings, thereby creating an abundance mentality, resulting in the technology & tools to support it.

Friends, let's have one basic awareness- that the Universe gives in abundance, provided we evolve enough to align with it. But the moment greed gets the better of us in the name of growth, we lose sight of this magical nature of human life. Then growing populations merely become 'larger markets'. I can't think of anything more cynical & blundering than this approach.

Even from the perspective of classical economics, we have reached a tipping point. Experts have published several papers suggesting that from the 17th century onwards, population increase was a driver of growth, from both a production & consumption perspective. But now, population growth will be a value destroyer, not creator, thereby demolishing the myth of growth based on a burgeoning population. Remember, even in a healthy body, reckless cellular growth is malignant. So too in a scenario of unchecked population growth, no amount of 'value addition' can help us leapfrog to the next level.

Surprisingly, I still find so many proponents of this inherently flawed line of thinking. It's contemptible how so called 'avant garde' economists think much like fanatics in justifying population growth merely in terms of 'demographic advantage'. *Demographic advantage??!!* The whole premise of 'a large working population being a competitive advantage' is so flawed! To look at people as merely an aggregation, and not as individual souls is such abominable commodification of God's greatest gift! It is reprehensible to even talk about humans in commercial terms like assets (the working age group) and liabilities (the ageing population).

We are not a working mass of intelligent robots out to satiate a nation's urge for being an economic & technological superpower, but the most beautiful expression of divinity in organic motion...

Once that is understood, and with vast enhancements in healthcare, even an ageing population becomes an 'economic asset', while a large young but unemployed population ceases to be a liability! The challenge of nations & societies is to control future population growth, and maximize the opportunities for the existing populace, be they old or young!

9. Global non proliferation, disarmament and strengthening of a unified framework of governance: We have done our math, and over a trillion dollars can potentially be freed for our various projects, if we seriously work towards this objective. I shall personally talk to world leaders to eliminate this scourge, by taking a sensible, and not an overly paranoid or blindly competitive look at our defence budgets. After all, are there any winners on this treadmill? We, leaders of nations, sit here not to represent the global arms industry or lobby, but to diligently discharge our solemn vow to serve the people- and that also means sensible allocation of resources. I propose to have a joint mechanism of the G20, where we have clear, measurable goals for progressively freeing up at least half a trillion $ from military budgets in a decade. We have to escape the vicious cycle, once & for all. Increasing arms spend *will not* guarantee our security; human development & social uplift *will*, by building the strength of our societies from within, and enhancing our stature in the global community.

10. Strengthen global institutional framework, promote open societies and pave the way for a World Government: Brothers & sisters, we are essentially one race, one people. So the fundamental question is: *Why all these fragmentations, these boundaries, these barriers?*

For far, far too long have we lived with these artificial divisions. But now, more than ever before, our problems are common, our destinies intertwined, our paths interconnected. The world is more integrated than ever before, and technology has rendered so much of our divisions redundant. So why can't Governments sit up & take notice? *Why can't we take that one big leap towards a basic, unified Governance?*

And no, I don't in any way suggest any centralization of power- in fact, I am all for further decentralization of governance. But certainly, bodies like the UN should cease to be token entities.

Serious attempt should be made at jointly combating our collective problems, because the ozone hole is not localized, a storm resulting from climatic imbalance can strike anywhere, and food security, disarmament & economic crises are no single nation's problems alone.

I know this sounds like utopia, but every new reality starts with a single dream. If we live in a Global village, then the village chieftains certainly need to put their heads together & think unified, think collective, think aggregate. We have to lay the foundations of a Global Governance format, at least for our children. We owe it to them!

To help us connect, unite and progress on this sacred yet herculean mission, I propose a global prayer network, in which all of us, from diverse races, ethnic backgrounds, religions & nationalities, would come together for collective prayers, at the same time, once a month. We shall go to our churches, temples, mosques, synagogues & pagodas, or simply within ourselves, to spend 5 minutes of collective prayer to bless the earth. This prayer for world peace shall bring about transformation, if done in harmony, with an open heart, and to bless mother earth.

For long have we seen prayer merely as a dogmatic obligation, but it's time to experience prayer energies for global missions. We all have, at some point in our lives, experienced the power of prayers, and we now understand the concept of prayer fields better. Like any other energy or force field, a collective field, howsoever brief, works better, in fact, with almost exponentially better. So too with prayer energy…

Coupled with global prayers, I propose setting up of the 'operation NEW AGES' committee- a non partisan, global initiative, involving leaders from all regions, to track our project for tangible results. If, for some reason, we are unable to achieve all our objectives, we shall endeavor further- for another 10, 20, 30, 50, 100 years- as many as are needed…if not for us, for our children, and for their children, so that at the end of the journey, we would have bequeathed a healthier, more equitable, more balanced world…

My fellow world citizens, this day shall mark a new beginning in human history- our first, baby steps towards the NEW AGES, one, that we shall usher in without the pain of conflict or mutual suspicion, but based on mutual cooperation…one that will be guided not by selfish politicians & blinkered bureaucrats, but by true leaders…"

Sacking of the hawks...banning of all right wing movements & brotherhood...a special committee, to engage in dialogue among all the major world religions....

"Lastly, to mark this day, I announce the setting up of an International Leadership Foundation, one that will merge the wisdom of the East with the knowledge of the West. This foundation will be dedicated to dialogue between all the major religions & traditions of the world, striving to create a combined repository of knowledge & learning. This will be the conscience keeper of the world, a sentry into the NEW AGES. Ladies and Gentlemen, I dedicate this foundation to Dave Jones."

Puzzled faces across the globe. Dave Jones, who?

"Not many of this generation may have heard of him. But this activist for peace, global equity & leadership was a man ahead of his times, a legend of the previous generation, and the messenger of the NEW AGES. *He shall be forever remembered as the harbinger, the ONE who laid the foundation for the NEW AGES, and shared the wisdom for all to see...*

We dedicate this day to crusaders of peace & wisdom. Every year, we shall commemorate this as *World peace & prayer day*, remembering all those from Gandhi to Martin Luther King to Mandela to Suu Kyi to the Dalai Lama to Dave Jones, *to the foot soldier within us, who believe that prayer is mightier than the bomb.* On this day, each one of us will try & connect with the other, taking a pledge to combat our deepest prejudices, to understand the other point of view more openly than ever before!"

And with that, he broke out into an impromptu rendition of king MJ's ' Heal the world..."

More stunned global audiences! They had seen all sorts of stunts by politicians seeking to appear likeable, but nothing like this! They hadn't witnessed any major broadcast showing a President sing straight from the heart...not to boost popularity or ratings, but to bolster his message...

Something had changed dramatically- there was no politician here, but a statesman! *And a human being before that, one who dreamt, & believed, like billions of others...*

"That's all for now, ladies & gentlemen. I know that most of you globally are shocked, though largely positively, at my comments, as also my singing. *Although I must admit I have a lousy voice...*" he joked.

"I realise this is not what you are used to listening from a politician." He continued with an unmatched determination in his voice.

"But, ladies & gentlemen, *this is not the language of a politician, a President.* This is the voice of a statesman, a leader, a man of courage; the voice of a leader who lies in embryo within each of us. And I know that most of you globally are in agreement with my announcements- if not explicitly, then within your hearts.

Frankly, that is the only thing that matters, should matter, in a true democracy, in an evolving global democracy- *the views of you folks, whom we refer to as the common man- how we politicians in seats of power ignore it, even steamroll it, using your own taxpayer money to snub you, to foist conflict on you.* But I say this today, boldly, unequivocally, that there is nothing common about you, the common man, or your views...

You are special, your views are special. Democracy is all about your interests, 'common' interests, not the vested interests of politicians, bureaucrats, industry or defence establishments. I am merely playing my honest role in a democracy, discharging my constitutional obligation."

"Yes, there will be doubts, there will be skepticism. There will also be fear & uncertainty. Vested interests will try to scare you, lobbies will lead you to disbelief; but heed them not; listen to the voice of your heart only, and things will become crystal clear!

Someone once believed to make a journey of a lifetime, and left behind a legacy of the New ages; remember friends, it just needs a single flame to dispel years of darkness, a single believer to start a revolution. So believe...have faith!

As for my next steps, expect a slew of announcements in the coming days, addressing the issues of strengthening of global democratic institutions, devolution of power & open societies, and about the key projects in *'OPERATION NEW AGES'*.

I shall be setting up a working committee to devise mechanisms of implementing these projects, comprising renowned economists, proponents of open societies, creative individuals & new age thinkers- and with the stated goal of translating these visions into actionables, so that intent can manifest as concrete action. *Let there be a new perspective for the NEW AGES..."*

****

A brief silence. Then an old man in Libya rose in front of his TV set, applauding…slowly at first, then loudly, vigorously, enthusiastically, ecstatically and then almost insanely, dancing & prancing with joy! Never in his lifetime, he thought, would he see a possible reconciliation between East & West. But now, the old man, with a spring in his step and tears in his eyes, felt that at least his children had a chance…

In a base camp in Cuba, a young soldier couldn't resist saluting- neither to an individual, nor to the flag he was sworn to protect, but to the human spirit, our emerging collective destiny, a new vision…

And in Canada, a WWII veteran looked out of the window at the lashing waves, as his mind flew to the heroic landings of Normandy- of how he & his compatriots braved the hail of gunfire to protect democracy. As he thought of his fallen comrades, of their graves across Europe, he bent down on his knees, in a silent prayer. Never again, he prayed…the coming generations would not have to encounter the horrors of the battlefield, of flying bullets splintering skulls & raining bombs ripping apart limbs, to save democracy.

In a new world, there would be more civilized ways…

In Myanmar, the group of monks chanted, looking heavenwards, convinced that prayers for world peace work. They would now intensify their prayers & peaceful agitation for democracy from the Junta…

Suu Kyi would be free, and a new age would begin…

At the same time, the monks of Tibet sat in meditation, their hope rekindled again. Someday, their legitimate aspirations, their way of life, could coexist with Chinese concerns & history, with neither side feeling like the loser. Aggressive energies & mutual distrust would give way to dialogue, sooner or later…

The Chinese establishment would take cognizance of rightful Tibetan concerns, and respect their way of life. Cultural genocide would cease, not on account of a violence uprising, but a deep transformation within the Chinese population itself, as democracy would take roots. The Dalai Lama's vision of non violence & compassion would eventually prevail…

Satyamev Jayate…

In Sri Lanka, the Government sat up and took notice. After this announcement, it could no longer blame the West or World powers of double standards in the fight against 'terrorism'. It was time for reflection, for seriously exploring & resolving the 'root cause'. Having led a bloody war against the Tamil tigers, resulting in thousands of civilian deaths, the Government's 'victory' had at best been pyrrhic, failing to win over the hearts of the Tamil population. And as is the case with such military triumphs, the euphoria was short-lived...

The lack of a subsequent political process led to further resentment among the Tamils, resulting in the seeds of a new Tiger Army being born. *Another bloody Civil war was in the offing...*

But after this pronouncement, there was realization, both among the Government and the 'new' tigers- that there were no victories in an armed conflict, just seeds of further conflict. True, establishments tend to be brutal & repressive, but maybe, just maybe, there was leeway for negotiations. If the east & west could talk, then maybe dialogue deserved another chance...*maybe a year of honest politics could settle what three decades of violence couldn't...*

Elsewhere, in the Indian subcontinent, a Kashmiri Muslim and Pandit watched the repeat telecast, as it flashed across television screens all day. As they sat together in the valley, sipping their hot cups of kahwa, tears rolled down their eyes, reminiscing the times when the valley was known as paradise on earth; when Muslims & pandits lived like brothers...

Then they made a resolve, a resolve that they would launch a joint people's movement for the final, lasting solution of this vexed issue. Each Muslim family in the valley would personally adopt one Pandit household, thereby giving them their long lost rights. *They took responsibility to protect them...*

At the same time, the pandits would campaign for removal of the army from the valley, and genuine redressal for the concerns of local population. *Force could never be solution to people's problems & aspirations...*

As the people's movement gathered steam, bureaucrats who thrived by accentuating differences were suddenly on the back foot. The joint people's movement in the valley would spill over to the masses of both India &

Pakistan, exerting pressure on their governments- to not only resolve the Kashmir dispute and end cross border militancy, but to accelerate the creation of a federation for enhanced socio-economic cooperation between India, Pakistan & Bangladesh.

The sub continent could come together after 60 years of estrangement- in a synergy that would help uplift the masses on both sides, and restore the Indian sub continent to its former glory...

Within both the nations too, there was finally hope of justice, as civil society put pressure on politicians & judiciary to bring to book the culprits of some of the most heinous crimes- the '84 Delhi riots, the '92 Mumbai riots & the 2002 Gujarat genocide, as also the crimes against Mohajirs & Balochs in Pakistan, and the trial of army officers guilty of genocides in East Pakistan.

Civil society was, for the first time, seeing this not from the prism of religious or national prejudices, but from the lenses of human suffering...and seething for action. Human suffering had no religion, no colour, no boundary; it needed to be justly redressed. Vested interests would have their way no more!

Of course, the hawks and the defence establishments on both sides gawked & cried shrill, citing everything from dilution of 'national security' to 'national interest' to 'threat perceptions' to thwart these initiatives. But the people were determined; they were coming together, and they were looking beyond. *They would not be divided or blinded any more...*

And in war torn Africa, there finally was genuine hope. Not the false variety that came with global 'aid' aimed at camouflaging vested interests, but authentic optimism. A hope of a better future for the people, for individuals & communities, yet in accordance with their traditional way of life. War weary individuals would coalesce into peace communities, and these communities would pressurize warlords to see reason, to build a future.

As weapons would be replaced by developmental tools, and conflict with education, this would be Africa's chance to find its rightful place in the world; the originator of the human race would finally have an opportunity to discover 'Africa's century', akin to what Asia achieved in the 21st; built on foreign capital & technology flowing in as a result of peace...

In a sharply polarized & wounded world, a strong, positive impulse had been released...one with global ramifications, with possible positive impact across all regions & disputes...

An impulse that once again highlighted the common thread- OF HUMANITY...

Of course, there was still much skepticism, and lots to be achieved; there was no doubt that negative energies & vested interests were unmoved, beyond redemption...if anything, their resolve for control was strengthened even further...

What was changing, however, was the global mass of positive energies...one step closer to the critical mass...

Lots depended upon follow through & persistence, but a new beginning had been made. If people followed their inner voice & these positive impulses, the critical mass was at hand soon...*all set to unleash a typhoon of positive energies which would annihilate the darkness...and usher in the apo kalypsis....*

THE NEW AGES HAD JUST BEGUN...

As the President retired into his chamber, aware of the global significance of his altered action, he felt light, ecstatic, pumping his fists in the air, something he had not done since his high school basketball matches. He broke into an impromptu jig, a few steps of moon walking and a graceful twirl. Along with singing, he could dance as well!

Some of his conservative staff gaped- this was not the way of Presidents- what he just did, or had said earlier...

But no matter! He was a free man, a baby, a teen spirit... and the lyrics hummed a long, long time ago, came back:

'*A vow unto his own, never from this day*
His will they'll take away...'

From the higher plane, the illuminated face of the Master looked at him, and blessings rained from the heavens...

The Messenger had finally found himself, and in the moment of reckoning, had made the right choices...

Synchronicity works in strange ways...

Shortly after the National Security Council meeting the previous night, where the war plans & budgets had been frozen, the President retired into his room. But there was an uneasiness, a tossing & turning...half asleep, he said his prayer to the Lord- to guide him, to give him strength in this crusade...

And then drifted into a dream...

A dream that would awaken him...

The President saw images...*the life of Dave Jones*...

Starting with Dave's strange dreams, about the President and his War cabinet...the animated discussion between the moderates & hawks...the decision of the hawks...the signing of the declaration of war...

These were the same scenes that he had lived for the past few months, including the tonight...yet, now he was seeing them as a dream, through the eyes of Dave Jones...

A dream within a dream...

The image then went beyond, to the journey of Dave Jones, his teleportation to the NEW AGES, the time spent there and his learnings & experiences...the clues, the disk, meeting the Quartet, the Council, Master Aleus, Plutus, Lyon and Ikona...

Understanding their systems & energies, and in a final flash, *coming back as the Messenger of the New Ages...in line with the prophecy of the New ages, as well as the various ancient prophecies of the impending apocalypse!*

For the next 55 years, Dave Jones served as the Messenger of the NEW AGES, living his various roles with passion & commitment, spreading the message...

On his death bed, he died a calm, peaceful man...

But something was amiss, the **mission seemingly incomplete**...as if one part of the journey was over, but the climax was yet to come...

As Dave's soul ascended to its afterlife journey, he saw a vision- *once again, the dream from where it all started...*

But the dream had changed now...

Instead of a concerned expression, the smiling face of the Master indicated that the Messenger has been found; and at the right time, he would know his role, and act upon it, leading to the fulfillment of the prophecy...

In the soul's dark night, he would create alchemy,
Guiding the world to its emerging destiny...

As the soul ascended further, the afterlife vision 'indicated' the physical entity of Dave dissolving...however, his eternal self realized that Dave Jones was just a name, a body, a character played by the real actor- *the soul itself...*

So now, the real actor, the soul, played out life visions of other lives, previous lives...as the life visions of the soul's various characters flashed, across the entire expanse of time, the soul saw another of its roles, in another life...

In this life, the soul was born as an ultra orthodox knight of the Spanish inquisition in the 15th century. As a devout member of the inquisition, he loved his lord utterly, spilling blood of those who dared to commit heresy, in defence of the 'true' faith; *he could do anything for the lord, whether die or kill-* that was the tenacity of his faith...

During one of his campaigns, the warrior slaughtered an infant, snatching it from his mother's arms, smashing his head to the ground, before burning the mother alive. All this, not out of any personal ill will, but simply for a larger cause...simply because the heretic family did not believe in the true lord, and refused to heed the call for faith & redemption...

As the mother & baby shrieked in unbearable agony, being consigned to flames, another anguished scream emerged in the highest heavens, as tears rained from above...

IT WAS THAT OF THE LORD...

As he saw yet another of his child go astray...

In the name of defending the faith, his spirit had been crucified yet again; but the pain this time was more intense... a tiny dismembered body and the moans of a grieving mother were far more painful than the spikes & thorns on the body of a 33 year old messiah...

In his time, the messiah smilingly went on the cross, for he knew he was taking away the sins of others; But here, his very followers committed the most heinous of sins in his name... while on the cross, his body could bear the pain, but from the realms of spirits, his sensitive being couldn't bear the pain of those put to the sword in his name...

He could gladly die for his children, but he couldn't bear to see his children slay in his name...

And whom were they slaying after all? Heretics? No, even they were his children, for the Messiah, like the Buddhas, came for entire humanity...

As the lord wept inconsolably, his innocent tears flowed from the heavens as torrential rains, lashing the blood soaked soil, much like the thunder clouds following his own crucifixion by another bunch of misled zealots;

In that instance, he had forgiven those who had erred, but here, *this one wet evening set back the karmic equation of the crusader by several lives...*

****

Now the soul realized why its mission in the garb of Dave Jones felt somehow incomplete-it still had a karmic debt to pay from a past life...that of the inquisitor!

Dave had all but settled it in his role as the Messenger, but a final settlement had yet to be done- by coming face to face with his deepest prejudices...and overcoming them...

In the journey of sentient beings, the lord is merciful, always; he gave us freewill to chalk our own course, to take responsibility for our actions...

And keeps giving chances & choices in the present moment...

To balance our karmic equation...

So too happened with the soul of crusader- he had sinned deeply, but had also loved the lord as deeply; he had spilt blood, but had also been a light for the world as Dave Jones...

Therefore began another cycle, a final journey of the soul into another birth- *a life in which it would encounter an opportunity to make a momentous decision for the world, one that could finally balance its karmic equation...*

But for that to happen, he would have to come face to face with the deepest residual prejudices, deepest karmic aggregations, and overcome them...

In the moment of reckoning, the Messenger had to make the right choices...

****

The dream continued, and the President watched the birth vision of his current life, as Dave's soul flowed into the body of a child born in a leading rightwing, conservative political family- of not only entrenched politicians, but also of senior brothers of a right wing cult, dedicated to blood of the lord...

Dave's soul had been reborn as none other than the President himself!

As life progressed, so did his career as a politician, and his standing in the cult. First his father, and then him- destiny continued to place him in seats of great power & consequence, till it finally placed him on the most powerful seat...

In an anti-incumbency vote against a perceptibly corrupt regime, he won a closely fought election, emerging as the President...

It was a historic opportunity-for the brotherhood to get its agenda fulfilled, and for the beings to project energies so that landmark peace & developmental agreements could be signed...

Yet again, the soul of Dave Jones, of the crusader, in its new avatar as President, faced dual choices- *the sattvic, the evolutionary choice, or tamasic, the regressive choice...*

Inspite of the continuous energy projections by the Masters, the hawks seemed to be prevailing, pushing their agenda through...

So the President, unaware and disconnected from his soul journey, began gradually consolidating his hold over various institutions & bureaucracies, and pushing his extremist plans with fervor; till the case was presented for War...*the decisive war...*.

After that, the soul image shifted to the night of the war cabinet's final discussions...and his signing the proclamation of war...

****

Now it all dawned upon the dreaming President...in slumber, he was finally waking up to his forgotten reality...

The reality of Dave Jones, his recurrent dream of this critical night, the clues & his transition to the NEW AGES...

It wasn't merely to see & spread the message of the NEW AGES, but also to usher it...

WITHOUT THE PAIN OF WAR...

That is also why the soul had felt that the new ages could be ushered without the war, while watching the images of the annihilation in the new ages, as Dave Jones...that is why Dave had felt a strange sense of peace inspite of seeing those gruesome images, but couldn't comprehend it back then...

However, now it was clear- one individual could indeed make a difference, provided he made the right choices!

In fact, *every individual can make the difference-through prayer, through intent, through right actions...*

Now the role of Dave Jones, his journey into the New Ages became crystal clear- it was not merely to acquire the wisdom of the NEW AGES for sharing with the world as Dave Jones, but for a deep internalization...

Because it would be the memory of this wisdom ***that could illuminate the dark night of the soul, in the ultimate moment of reckoning...***

When all is at stake,
The right choices he would have to make...

****

As the dream ended with this realization, the President woke up, shivering, perspiring... *sensing a light in the room...*

Tomorrow was supposed to be the day of reckoning- the day when he was preparing to go to WAR...

But now, he had just seen the journey of his soul, it's everlasting cast, across lives & dimensions, and the reason why he was born as the President in this life- *to live his dharma, to achieve his karma...*

What choice would he exercise in the light of this new wisdom? Would he still spill blood again in the name of the Lord, obliterating millions, maybe nations? Or be a catalyst, a *true Messenger of the New Ages*?

He had to fight a war, no doubt, but against which foe was the big question- against people, or for them, against their collective problems; for blinkered visions, or for larger good...*for prejudices, or for liberating the world from them*...

He had the power- now he had to make the choice about using it...

With tears in his eyes, the President went to his desk, and ran a classified search on Dave Jones. It threw up exactly the same results from the archives 50 years back, as he had seen in the dream! There was indeed a New Age visionary in the previous generation, who tried to spread the message through his various roles...and who, some of his close followers claimed, was indeed *'guided by the heavens'*...

It was clear now that this was no imaginary dream- neither the one that the President saw of Dave Jones, nor the ones Dave saw, from where this entire journey began! It was all part of a larger design, for a higher cause...

There was no room for incredulity or skepticism anymore-*he was indeed the messenger, the reincarnation of Dave, the man of the prophecy, who was now connecting the understanding of the NEW AGES with this plane...*

He was the one chosen & blessed by the beings to set the foundation of the new ages, right here, on this plane...

But without the pain or destruction of war...

From his understanding of the New Age systems, he could at least set a foundation...on which the coming generations could build, without self destructing..

As he went to the bathroom to wash his face, he saw the gift, the disk, around his neck...

There was a halo outside, and the master was smiling... *the soul of Dave Jones, in its avatar as the President, smiled back...*

And their energies merged in a swirl...

Tomorrow morning, the President would make a formal proclamation of war... *not against, but for humanity...for laying the foundation of the New Ages...*

He had made his choice....

In the soul's dark night,
The Messenger's wise choice will lead to the light,
His wisdom shall not have gone in vain,
As the whole of humanity stands to gain,
Divine blessings shall then rain,
Healed and guided in the new ages, without the pain,
His dharma achieved, his karma done,
Balanced would be the karmic equation,
Darkness dispelled, rising of a new sun,
Then it would all be One- the ONE...

The first part of the prophecy was fulfilled...

THE NEW AGES HAVE JUST BEGUN...

THE END

Acknowledgements

This work represents a milestone in my karmic journey, the fulfillment of one of my dharmas. In this, I have been inspired & guided by various synchronistic forces- masters, thinkers, ideologies, friends, family, believers- their impact on this series is beyond words. Yet, with the tool I wield- words-I attempt to express my deepest & heartfelt gratitude...

To New Age thinkers, healers & writers like Dr. Deepak Chopra, James Redfield, Joe Jaworski, Richard Bach, Marc Allen, Shakti Gawain, Dr Brian Weiss, Fritjof Capra, Thich Nath Hanh, Azim Jamal, Frederick Lenz, Jack Canfield, Mark Victor Hansen et al, for so many inspirations & concepts, some of which have found an important place in this book; as also the new, evolving worldview...

To New Age Management thinkers like Peter Senge, Dr. Stephen Covey, Dr. Amartya Sen, Malcolm Gladwell, Michael Hammer, Thomas Friedman, Ken Blanchard as well as path breakers from the world of business- George Soros, Bill Gates, Warren Buffet, and the various chief evangelists of cutting edge organizations- for not only their enlightened views on Capitalism & Commerce, but for evolving 'humane & eco-consciousness' in Corporations. A few years back, lots of these ideas & ideals seemed implausible, even fads. Today, they are accepted, rather central pillars, of the way the world of business is evolving...

To the doyens of technology- without going into the merits or demerits of their creation, or even motives, I would simply like to highlight the way evolving 'convergence' technologies have changed our lives in a single generation! Time has come now for a similar 'Green ecosystem', so that the lives of coming generation are similarly meaningfully impacted. And I pray that humans start using technology less for control & military purposes, and more for individual & collective growth...

To the Masters of yore, each of whom have bequeathed special gifts for the world-timeless & uplifting, and who have touched me, been with me, blessed me: Siddhartha Gautam, the Buddha, Confucius, Lao Tzu, Krishna, Christ, Muhammad, Ali, Patanjali, Mansoor, Rumi, Sai Baba, Socrates, Kabir, Nanak ... Attempting to enlist all of them is akin to counting stars in the firmament- so if I have been unsuccessful at mentioning many of them, it my limitation- the limitation of words! To them, it doesn't matter- they are shining bright, far beyond the bounds of words...they just ARE!

To the contemporary masters & teachers- S.N. Goenka, Osho, Choa Kok Soi, the Aga Khan...some radical, some men of this world, some revolutionaries, some institution builders, but each one a beacon, a divine guiding light...

To the women mystics, & women in general- either wronged, or forgotten by history- Rabia, Mary Magdalene, Meera... this is my humble attempt to give women their due...

A special mention is in order for Bill Gates & H.H. the Aga Khan, for showing us the development model of the future, in the form of the AKDN & William & Melinda Gates foundation. This, I believe, will be the next wave of human capital development....

To modern apostles of non-violence: Mahatma Gandhi, Martin Luther King, Nelson Mandela, Dalai Lama, Suu Kyi... Satyamev jayate! Yours is the only viable path for humanity...

To my land, India, whose mystique, history & spiritual traditions are unique, and forever in my blood & soul...

And to what is now my other land: Philippines. I have been here for a short while, yet the warmth of this land & its people has touched me...*not to mention its hidden spiritual traditions*...

From closer in space & time, in my life:

To my publishers- Sterling, and the ever affable Mr Ghai.

To others from the literary & publishing fraternity, who helped with this work: Pramod, Feroz & team, Ashok Chopra, Marc Allen, Suma Varughese-, and Miguel Ramos & team- thank you for your help.

A special thanks to Azim Jamal, the international no.1 bestselling author & life coach, for his amazing faith & belief in me, and this work- our interactions were pure synchronicity, and Azim rekindled my faith & hope, when most were far too perfunctory, mechanical, even downright myopic in their interactions & assessment...I know something special is brewing...

My friends, often companions, along the path- a mention here is simply my gratitude for your affection & continued friendship- Rahim, Hemang, Ash, Sudhir, Vikram, Jas, Suma, Umesh, Sunny, Mayank, Ganatra, Agam, Bala, Rima, Preethi, Mohan, Manisha ... I may or may not have spent much time with you'll lately, but I reminisce & relish our special moments & wonderful conversations: be they about space, fashion, markets, the Himalayas, healing, lost civilizations, the pyramids, the spirit world, relationships, a green, recycled economy, living rocks, heavy metal & psychedelic rock, a new education paradigm, political reforms, corporate cultures, digital marketing, even poker & how to beat the house! There was Zen in each of these...

To some wonderful seniors, colleagues & friends from Citi: Sanjiv, Pia, Nigel, Vipin, Lisa, Asim, Naeem, Sriram, Anish, Arun, Mak, Varun, Sunil...

To my team members, current & former- Varun, Abhijeet, Frank, Pai, Resham, Swami, Tina, Camille, Tins, Susie, Rica, and all others, who have worked with passion & commitment with me- thank you!

To the special women of Citi Philippines- Bea, Alma: thank you for faith & help; and my other friends- Rio, Myra, Mel, Mag, Lotus, Martha, Nette, Bam et al- the list continues... you are living examples of the feminine energies mentioned here, balancing both family & work, ambition & caring, with the utmost effortlessness that can only come to true women- those connected with their feminine energies...

Suma: You were right- I needed to experience this to get a different perspective- the *real* perspective- on women in the workplace; one that is not ruthless, insecure & selfish, but genuine, caring, balanced & confident…My book spoke about it. *Here I saw it…it's amazing…*

My associates, often friends: Rajiv Popley, Nilesh Gupta, Margaret, Jenny, Dylan, Herve, Nimish, Mahesh, Reem…

The wonderful friends I have met in the Philippines- Minna, Analei, Tisha, Amena, Dr. Mala, Pinka, Falguni- I have felt magic with you, and your elevated energies…it was all guided…nothing was a chance…

A special mention of two very beloved friends & kindred souls- Minna & Tisha... Something really got unlocked after meeting you… thank you for being there- I know our connection is special…

Thanks to my family-Malik & Seetha for all our lovely times; and of, course, that very special boy- my nephew, friend & potential co-author: Rumi- you truly are Rumi's poetry in motion…a blessing in our life…I look forward to writing a children's book with you, buddy!

My parents, who have shown me both the paths- of devotion & intellect; and in whose prayer fields I trust more than anything else in this world. I am deeply indebted to you, mom-dad! It is only because of you that I am what I am…and with your prayer shield, I feel protected like nothing else…

And finally- to my best friend, constant companion through ups & downs, and a special, understanding, forgiving soul- my wonderful wife, Archana...

Archie- this project, like most things in my life, would be incomplete without you, your friendship & your support. I know I am a bundle of volatile energy, radical thoughts & forever in motion- very difficult to handle, much less to live with- so a deeply heartfelt thank you for always standing by me, as my anchor & balancing force. Our friendship is very, very special…

Love
Malik

ABOUT THE AUTHOR

Malik defies stereotypes, much like the characters in this book- a dreamer, a thinker, a believer, a visionary, an ordinary man rooted in life's day to day realities, a pragmatic individual, a corporate executive, a critical analyst, a music aficionado, especially of the uplifting genre, a deeply spiritual man, a rebel... he is all of this, yet not slotted into any single one...gliding, sliding & fitting into the relevant role with effortless ease...

There is nothing solemn about him. He is as much as ease discussing the energy/spirit world as the world of economics & management; he relishes discussions & debates about economic crises & reform of capitalism as much as immersing himself into Floyd & Metallica. He has an easy sense of humor, the innocent ways of a baby, the intensity of a fighter, the philosophical disposition of a thinker, and the lyrical beauty of a poet...

Zorba the Buddha, he would like to model himself upon...